URBAN POLICY MAKING

SAGE YEARBOOKS IN POLITICS AND PUBLIC POLICY

Sponsored by the

Policy Studies Organization

Series Editor:

Stuart S. Nagel, *University of Illinois, Urbana*

International Advisory Board

Albert Cherns, *University of Technology, England*
John P. Crecine, *University of Massachusetts*
Kenneth M. Dolbeare, *University of Massachusetts*
Yehezkel Dror, *Hebrew University, Israel*
Joel Fleishman, *Duke University*
Matthew Holden, Jr., *University of Wisconsin*
Charles O. Jones, *University of Pittsburgh*
Harold Lasswell, *Yale University*
Leif Lewin, *University of Uppsala, Sweden*
Klaus Lompe, *Technical University of Braunschweig, Germany*
Julius Margolis, *University of Pennsylvania*
Henry Mayer, *University of Sydney, Australia*
Joyce Mitchell, *University of Oregon*
Jack Peltason, *American Council on Education*
Eugen Pusic, *University of Zagreb, Yugoslavia*
Austin Ranney, *University of California, Berkeley*
Peter Szanton, *Rand Corporation*
Enrique Tejera-Paris, *Venezuela Senate*

Books in this series:

1. What Government Does (1975)
   MATTHEW HOLDEN, Jr. and DENNIS L. DRESANG, *Editors*

2. Public Policy Evaluation (1975)
   KENNETH M. DOLBEARE, *Editor*

3. Public Policy Making in a Federal System (1976)
   CHARLES O. JONES and ROBERT D. THOMAS, *Editors*

4. Comparing Public Policies: New Concepts and Methods (1978)
   DOUGLAS E. ASHFORD, *Editor*

5. The Policy Cycle (1978)
   JUDITH V. MAY and AARON B. WILDAVSKY, *Editors*

6. Public Policy and Public Choice (1979)
   DOUGLAS W. RAE and THEODORE J. EISMEIER, *Editors*

7. Urban Policy Making
   DALE ROGERS MARSHALL, *Editor*

Volume 7. Sage Yearbooks in Politics and Public Policy

URBAN
POLICY MAKING

DALE ROGERS MARSHALL
Editor

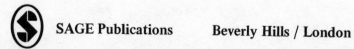SAGE Publications   Beverly Hills / London

For information address:

SAGE PUBLICATIONS, INC.
275 South Beverly Drive
Beverly Hills, California 90212

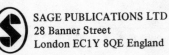

SAGE PUBLICATIONS LTD
28 Banner Street
London EC1Y 8QE England

Printed in the United States of America

Library of Congress Cataloging in Publication Data

Main entry under title:

Urban policy making.

  (Sage yearbooks in politics and public policy ; v. 7)
  Bibliography: p.
  1. Urban policy--United States--Addresses, essays, lectures. I. Marshall, Dale Rogers.
HT167.U753   301.36'0973   79-19162
ISBN 0-8039-1367-2
ISBN 0-8039-1368-0 pbk.

FIRST PRINTING

CONTENTS

PART IV: Distribution of Benefits

SERIES EDITOR'S INTRODUCTION

This is the seventh volume in the series of Yearbooks in Politics and Public Policy published by Sage Publications in cooperation with the Policy Studies Organization. All volumes in the series have covered a general approach to the nature, causes, or effects of alternative governmental policies. They have, for example, dealt with what government does, public policy evaluation, federal-state relations, cross-national policy analysis, the policy process from agenda setting to termination, and rational choice applied to policy analysis. This general orientation can be contrasted with one that might focus on specific policy problems such as criminal justice, economic regulation, education, environment, health, housing, energy, poverty, transportation, or foreign policy. The series thus brings out that one can combine broadly theoretical scholarship with the highly practical aspects of public policy analysis.

That general orientation also appears in the present volume on *Urban Policy Making* under the editorship of Dale Rogers Marshall. The volume emphasizes broadness because urban policy issues deal with nearly all the specific policy problems mentioned above. The volume also emphasizes broadness in that it is not organized by specific policy problems, but rather in terms of issues that cut across those problems, such as (1) in the urban context, what determines why one policy is adopted or implemented rather than another; (2) the role of minority racial or ethnic groups in shaping urban policies; (3) the cross-cutting issue of fiscal crisis which has placed new constraints on urban policy making; and (4) the metaproblem of how services designed to reduce problems are distributed across neighborhoods and groups in the urban context.

It is useful to know what determines urban policies or policies in general, not only because such causal knowledge is a fundamental part of political science but also because that knowledge can help in evaluating the political and administrative feasibility of alternative public policies. Many policies have been proposed for resolving various urban social problems such as pollution and substandard housing, but sometimes without an adequate concern for the political determinants. For example, a pollution tax on urban businesses in theory might get them to reduce their pollution if the tax is proportionate to the amount of polluting they do. Such a tax would also tend to add to each firm's profit-and-loss perspective the costs that are now being borne externally by the public in absorbing the health and other costs of air, water, noise, and solid waste pollution, as well as by the general taxpayer in paying remedial costs that could be prevented. The likelihood of adopting such a tax, however, is rather low, because it places the burden so directly on politically powerful firms rather than diluting the burden more widely. Political scientists are also concerned with the determinants of successful implementation, as well as successful adoption. In that regard, the Nixon program of home ownership for the poor may have failed, because such a program lacks administrative feasibility if it is left to private-sector real estate operators to administer rather than government employees. The private administration led to large-scale overassessments, misrepresentation of costs, and bribery to obtain favorable government payments.

Blacks and Hispanics are playing an increasing role in urban policy making as a result of white suburbanization, black migration from the South, and Hispanic migration from Latin America. Minorities, such as the Irish, Italians, Jews, and Poles, dominated northern innercity politics since about 1900 rather than white Anglo-Saxon Protestants. Minority politics is thus not new in the urban context. What is new about the increasing role of blacks and Hispanics is that their political advancement is occurring during a period of urban decline rather than growth. The new minorities are thus faced with lessened resources for dealing with more severe policy problems. Thus, when a black gets elected mayor of a big city or the black representation substantially increases on the city council, less money tends to get appropriated for schools, housing, welfare, and other programs in which blacks have a strong interest, simply because there is less money available, much of it having moved to the suburbs.

Although the urban fiscal crisis is related to the move of a lot of taxable income and property to the suburbs, much of it is due to national economic factors. Those factors represent a combination of recession and unemployment in the early 1970s which hurt purchasing power and the national economy, and then severe inflation in the later 1970s which may have hurt it even more, especially since the excessive unemployment did not diminish. That kind of economic crunch has turned the taxpayers and their elected representatives away from a willingness to appropriate national and state funds for social programs, including funds that would otherwise go to the cities. This fiscal crisis does not seem to be a short-term quirk in the economy, but possibly an indication of chronic excessive unemployment and inflation, due to inflexibilities in a less competitive economy that no longer adjusts well to supply-and-demand forces. One of the few sets of people that may be benefiting from this fiscal crisis is the policy analysts who are increasingly being put to work trying to find ways of getting more governmental services out of a decreasing dollar, or of using fewer dollars while satisfying a minimum service level.

A particularly tough problem for policy analysts is trying to determine what might be an optimum way of allocating a limited urban budget across both activities and neighborhoods. The distribution problem generally refers to neighborhoods, and it can be illustrated by talking about how many police to assign to each neighborhood. There are many distribution criteria that make sense. One could distribute on the basis of population, which is often done, but that might not reflect the fact that the less-populous neighborhood may have more crime. Allocating police on the basis of both population and crime, however, may not be politically meaningful because it does not consider the political power of various neighborhoods. It may also not be economically efficient because it does not consider that a dollar spent in one neighborhood may have a greater incremental crime-reduction effect than a dollar spent in another neighborhood. What also complicates the situation is that we do not have very good information on the marginal rate of return of dollars spent for various activities in various neighborhoods, even if we wanted to be economically efficient. It is hoped that books such as this will stimulate more research on urban politics, economics, and other perspectives toward urban policy making.

Although the Sage-PSO Yearbooks in Politics and Public Policy have covered a number of general approaches to policy analysis, there are many important approaches that still need covering. The next volume will be coedited by Helen Ingram and Dean Mann on *Why Policies Succeed or Fail.* It will bring the series into the 1980s—doubtless along with new variations on old policy problems and new approaches for dealing with them.

Stuart S. Nagel
Urbana, Illinois

VOLUME EDITOR'S INTRODUCTION

The study of urban politics generally, and of urban policy making in particular, has been characterized by high levels of activity and excitement in the last two decades. The major upheavals taking place in the nation and its cities during those years focused political and intellectual energies on urban problems. However, as we look to the 1980s, issues such as fiscal scarcity, "the death of growth," "propulism," and tax/spending limitations are pushing city issues such as race, housing, and employment further down on the national agenda. Urban analysts are asking themselves what is the future of the urban field and of urban policy analysis? They are no longer the fad, no longer favored by the foundations. What, then, are the prospects in the coming years?

The panels in the urban and rural politics section of the 1978 meeting of the American Political Science Association were organized to facilitate an assessment of trends in urban research. With one exception,[1] the chapters in this volume were selected from the papers presented at those panels. All the contributions illustrate major research directions and findings in the study of urban policy making and provide excellent reviews of the literature in each of these areas.

The decision to focus on urban policy research reflects the fact that it has become an important approach within the urban field, generating influential studies and controversies. More than 10 years ago James Q.

AUTHOR'S NOTE: *Special appreciation is due to the people who chaired the panels in the urban and rural politics section of the 1978 American Political Science Association meeting: Stephen David, Fordham University; Marian Palley, University of Delaware; Michael Preston, University of Illinois; Francine Rabinovitz, University of Southern California; Donna Shalala, Assistant Secretary, U.S. Department of Housing and Urban Development; Alvin Sokolow, University of California, Davis; Douglas Yates, Yale University; Betty Zisk, Boston University. They organized interesting panels and helped select essays for this volume. Comments made at the panels were very valuable in writing this introduction. Elinor Ostrom, Program Chair for the 1978 meeting, had the wisdom and initiative to create the urban and rural politics section. And peripatetic Stuart Nagel of the Policy Studies Organization made it possible to transform the endeavor into a book.*

Wilson (1968) edited a volume called *City Politics and Public Policy* which provided encouragement and some coherence to urban policy research. Wilson called for increased "research on local government that makes public policy a central concern" (p. 3), defining policy research as an effort to explain "why one goal rather than another is served by government, and the consequences of serving that goal, or serving it in a particular way" (p. 3). Wilson pointed out that this kind of research flows from a tradition as old as Aristotle and combines both the empirical and normative aspects of the political science discipline. The amount of subsequent research activity suggests that the time is right to evaluate the work that has been done, to push for further theoretical development, and to assess the possible impact of changing conditions on the urban policy field.

EMERGENCE OF THE
URBAN POLICY FOCUS

The interest in urban policy, like the interest in the urban politics field in general, reflects both developments in the cities and trends within political science. Even though academics are inevitably criticized for being isolated, intellectual discourse is both influenced by societal trends and an influence on them. When city issues such as race and poverty became important in the 1960s, many academics oriented their research in those directions. People flocked to the study of urban problems; urban studies programs, journals, and professional associations were created; new leaders emerged on the urban scene because that was "where the action was."

Developments in the urban field have already been well described (Jacob and Lipsky, 1968; Hawley and Lipsky, 1976; Masotti and Lineberry, 1976), but three main approaches will be briefly delineated here. The first was characterized by a focus on the formal structures and institutions of government. The central question was how should governments be organized to maximize effectiveness and efficiency? Lawrence Herson's (1957) important essay described this formalistic study of local politics as a "lost world" within political science. The academic as well as the political debates centered on the merit of reformed government structures such as nonpartisan elections, at-large elections, and city managers. The major political cleavage in cities was between the supporters of these reforms and the opponents who favored machines. The reformers assumed that the best way to end machine-related corruption was to eliminate the formal structures on which party machines appeared to be based.

Although the dichotomy between machine and reform still underlies some of the analysis in the urban field, it was gradually supplemented by a new dichotomy between elite and pluralist views of community power. The focus on community power in the 1950s and 1960s was the second major approach to urban politics and was primarily responsible for increasing the stature of the urban field (Jacob and Lipsky, 1968). The central question was how widely dispersed is political power in cities? The debates centered on whether governments were democratic: whether the leaders were controlled by citizens or vice versa. Just as the issue of corruption was a central concern in the structural approach, democracy was the concern in the community power approach. Studies of who governs were based on the assumption that formal political structures were not nearly as important in explaining political systems as informal processes, especially the distribution of power. This approach coincided with the growth of empirical analysis but still contained important normative elements. Some analysts saw power as narrowly dispersed and stable. They identified an elite power structure outside the local government (Hunter, 1953), so changes in government structures or officials were not seen as important. Other analysts saw power as more widely dispersed and variable. They identified a pluralist power structure including government officials in which different players influence different issues and government officials respond to demands (Dahl, 1961).[2]

In the 1960s, disciplinary and political developments led to a third approach, the focus on urban policy. This can be seen as an aspect of both policy analysis and urban analysis. Although policy can be defined in different ways, it essentially means "whatever governments choose to do or not to do" (Dye, 1972: 1), in other words, governmental decisions or actions or failures to act. Policy can be viewed either as a dependent variable, as the result of prior causes, or as an independent variable which causes subsequent results, outcomes, or impacts. Policy analysts are interested in explaining why governments do what they do and why the actions or lack of actions have certain results. Urban policy analysis is used in two senses. It can mean the study of what local governments do or it can refer to the study of actions taken by all levels of government which have impact on urban areas.[3]

Many of the practitioners of earlier approaches might argue that they, too, were interested in policy, that the focus is not new. And in a sense they are right, but they emphasized a different part of the causal chain composed of system inputs, a conversion process, and policy outputs and outcomes. They assumed that the conversion process shaped policies so that if one understood structures or distribution of power, one would understand policies. What they assumed became a central question for urban policy analysts. They asked what are the main factors shaping policy? Or what difference does it make who governs? This question reflected impatience with the failure of past approaches to focus on policy problems, a scientific response to demands for relevance (Dye, 1972). It was an effort to look directly at the presumed proximate cause of urban problems, namely, policy.

One problem the urban policy approach shares with the larger urban field is a lack of attention to theoretical concerns (Hawley and Lipsky, 1976). The literature is characterized by metaphors rather than theories and has been aptly described as being "adrift on an atheoretical sea" (Masotti and Lineberry, 1976: 4). Concern with developing more adequate theory pervades the field of urban politics. Yet there are elements of theories, statements of causal relationships, implicit in much of the urban policy literature. The next section classifies the urban policy literature in an effort to make the theories more explicit, so findings from studies in this volume and future work can be cumulated into more comprehensive theories.

THEORIES OF URBAN POLICY

Urban policy theories or approaches are classified in diverse ways. Some classify them according to the independent variable central to the explanation (Kirlin and Erie, 1972; Hofferbert, 1972). Others classify the theories according to the type of policy being explained, varying from functionally defined policy categories, such as education, police, housing, and so on (Palley and Palley, 1977; see also, Montgomery and Marshall, forthcoming), to more abstract policy categories, such as the nature of the governmental intervention (Lowi, 1964, 1972) or the type of benefits (Ostrom and Ostrom, 1978). The classification used here is based on the conceptual framework—the kind of question asked, the assumptions made, and the modes of analysis and explanation. The assumption is that these constraints shape the theories, shape what we see and how we explain it, and are important in determining the strengths and weaknesses of the theories. Obviously, many studies are difficult to classify because they include elements from several different frameworks. And indeed the urban policy literature shows a trend toward convergence as analysts synthesize aspects from various frameworks to compensate for their limitations. Although this makes classification increasingly difficult, it suggests progress toward cumulation and more comprehensive theories of urban policy.

Three main types of urban policy theories are distinguished here: policy input/output, policy process, and policy change. Then, a typology of urban policy is proposed which builds on Lester Salamon's (1977) classification.

POLICY INPUT AND OUTPUT

Policy input/output analysis is the most widely recognized approach to policy. Kirlin and Erie (1972) call it the resource model; Hofferbert (1972) calls it comparative input/output analysis, Peterson's chapter in this volume calls it the taxation/expenditure tradition; David and Kantor's chapter calls it the environmental approach.

These studies explore the relationship of socioeconomic and political inputs to policy outputs, usually budgetary allocations. Based on cross-sectional aggregate data from a large sample of cities, they typically use correlation or regression statistical techniques to assess the amount of variance in policy outputs which can be accounted for by the independent variables. The studies focus on the issue of the relative importance of socioeconomic versus political variables.

Hofferbert's (1972) excellent review of this approach indicates its historical links to economic analysis and the close relationship between state and local policy studies. Dawson and Robinson's (1963) analysis of state policy challenged the importance of the political variables which political scientists had traditionally assumed were important. Thomas Dye (1966) expanded that work, concluding that political variables such as party and governmental structure (using party control, party competition, apportionment, and voter turnout measures) did not have an independent effect on policy. He concluded that socioeconomic variables were the major factor in shaping state policy. These state studies were subsequently repeated in many urban studies which examined the relative influence of socioeconomic and political variables on city policies (see, for example, Aiken and Alford, 1970; Clark, 1968a, 1968b, 1973; Lineberry and Fowler, 1967; Wolfinger and Field, 1966). Review of this literature shows some agreement that socioeconomic conditions have an important independent effect on policy but that political characteristics, usually measured by formal structural characteristics, may also have an independent effect (Hawkins, 1971). The literature balances earlier studies that examined governmental structures or power distributions in isolation from the larger context without examining the ways in which the context shaped the politics.

Nevertheless the input/output approach has been charged with neglecting theory development and simply plucking indicators out of data books, running "barefoot through the data" (Peterson, 1978: Appendix A). As Hofferbert pointed out, the multiple regression technique is "effective in orienting us toward categories of data worthy of explanation. . . . But it does not go very far in the actual business of accounting for variance in policy" (1972: 43). It has indicated the broad parameters or conditions associated with outputs but has not identified the causal processes or linkages by which those conditions are translated into governmental action or provided explanations for the deviant cases. The implicit theory in the literature emphasizing the explanatory power of socioeconomic conditions is that political processes adapt policy to the environment without exerting any independent effect because they are optimizing mechanisms. Thus, political decision making is equated with the rational economic model of individual and corporate behavior (Larkey, 1979). The input/output literature has also typically assumed that political variables if they are important function like socioeconomic variables as independent determinants of policy and have applied tests for political effects which inappropriately bias the results (Godwin and Shepard, 1976). Godwin and Shepard have argued that political variables are not independent determinants but mediating factors which link socioeconomic conditions and policy, so the tests which have been used to determine their policy effects are inappropriate. They suggest that the question which should be asked is how much translation error is introduced by different kinds of political linkages.

These kinds of critiques have contributed to increasing sophistication in the input/output literature as analysts develop more elaborate measures, justifications of measures, and analyses in order to increase the levels of statistically explained variance. More attention is given to utilizing comparable units of analysis (Peterson, 1978) and disaggregating types of policies (Fry and Winters, 1970; Sullivan, 1972). And policy outputs besides expenditures are examined, such as the adoption of program innovations (Downs, 1976) and performance levels (Ostrom and Ostrom, 1978).

The Peterson and the Welch and Karnig studies in this volume are two good examples of the more focused theory-testing input/output designs currently being utilized in urban policy research. Peterson explains types of local revenues and expenditures as resulting from rational decisions made by city governments. Welch and Karnig examine the amount of variance in expenditures explained by the presence of black mayors and councilmembers. Both these studies are in marked contrast to some of the "fishing expeditions" which characterized earlier input/output studies. Input/output analyses will continue to be refined but their major contributions may have peaked. Other analysts want a finer-grained understanding of how diverse environmental contexts or conditions and political processes shape various kinds of policies at different points in time. The suspicion is growing that "you can't get there from here"; that simply doing more and more sophisticated input/output analyses will not provide theories with enough specificity. Input/output analysis is essentially static and has not been able to handle the complex, interactive nature of social systems in which a great many conditions have a major impact on the way variables operate and on the relationship among the variables being examined. Variables are associated in different ways not only in various policy areas but also under diverse conditions (Jacob and Lipsky, 1968). Indicators of socioeconomic conditions such as level of education can also be seen as measures of past public policies (Hofferbert, 1972). Input/output theories have not been able to specify these conditions except in the most general way or to explain changes in policy over time (Kirlin and Erie, 1972; David and Kantor in this volume).

The input/output analysts would say that their theories, although admittedly at a high level of generality, are useful shortcuts for making predictions even though some of the intervening mechanisms are not specified (Larkey, 1979). Proponents of the process and change approaches to be discussed next would say that useful theories depend on better theories of organizational behavior.

POLICY PROCESS

Policy process analysis is also concerned with the determinants of urban policy, but it focuses on how political processes and participants shape policy and how policy shapes political processes and the larger society.[4] Because many diverse studies can be classified in this category, generalizations are difficult. Yet most of these studies, such as the pluralist studies of community power, are based on the decision-making tradition within organization theory and incorporate models of organizational behavior. Using data from case studies or comparative case studies, research on the policy process may examine the way issues are handled at the policy formulation or implementation stages or the consequences of governmental performance for the distribution of benefits (see the Eisinger, Silbiger, and Rich chapters in this volume).

Process studies focus on the issue of the relative rationality of the political process and/or the relative power of the players in the process.

There are three main alternative theories of the process. One theory suggests that urban policy is the result of rational, value-maximizing decisions by city organizations (Peterson, this volume). A second theory suggests that urban policy is primarily the result of bureaucratic routines and discretion (Larkey, 1979; Levy et al., 1974; Pressman and Wildavsky, 1973). A third theory explains urban policy as the result of bargaining among competing players in the political decision-making game (Pressman, 1975; Ingram, 1977; Wirt, 1974; Yates, this volume). Any of these types of theories may also include theories about the impact of various participants on policy making including one or more of the following:

(1) elected officials—mayors, councils, school boards (Yates, 1977; Eulau and Prewitt, 1973; Kirby et al., 1973)
(2) appointed officials—city managers or administrative officers, department heads, bureaucrats (Loveridge, 1971; Lowi, 1969)
(3) political parties and interest groups—business, labor, civic and neighborhood associations, racial and ethnic groups, media, and so on (Orren, 1976; Silbiger, this volume; Lipsky, 1970; Mollenkopf, 1973; Zisk, 1973; Jones, 1976)
(4) electorate (Hawley, 1973)
(5) other cities and higher levels of government (Yates, this volume; Caraley, this volume).

Process theories typically examine a much wider array of political variables than input/output studies (Greenstone and Peterson, 1973; Downs, 1976), but like the aggregate studies, these theories often explain city policy making at least partly on the basis of political structures, particularly reformed and unreformed (Greenstone and Peterson, 1973) or centralized and decentralized structures (Crenson, 1971), and on environmental characteristics such as size, wealth, political culture, and region of the country.

Note that policy process studies include but are not limited to the narrow, technical, applied policy analysis associated with some schools of public policy. They are not as interested in explaining how policy is made as in advising policy makers about the cost and benefits of alternative policies. Like the early urban reformers who looked for the best governmental structure, applied policy analysts are looking for the best policies, and prescription is seen as more important than explanation.

Although there is no generally agreed on process theory which will explain why different policies are followed in apparently similar cities or why similar policies are found in different cities, the main contours of urban policy-making processes have become clearer after two decades of studies. Conflicting process theories which have arisen from observation of different issues, cities, and time periods have also alerted analysts to the importance of the interaction between contexts and variables in explaining the impact of those variables on policies (Greenstone and Peterson, 1973). Criticisms of process theories are largely the reverse of the criticisms directed at input/output theories, namely, they are not generalizable, they are too specific, and they do not explain enough. Process theories are limited by the observations out of which they arose and use measures which are difficult if not impossible to replicate in practice if not in theory in spite of claims to the contrary. Process theories are also criticized for being inherently fragmented and impossible to cumulate into more comprehensive theory. Another charge often made is that they fail to give enough weight to the constraints imposed by socioeconomic conditions and/or formal governmental structure on the one hand and by private interests on the other (Alford, 1975; Katznelson, 1976a, 1976b) which bias policy making in subtle ways often unnoticed by process analysts.

Both process theories and input/output theories are subject to the criticism that they are essentially static theories which do not specify the conditions under which policy changes. An important article by Lester Salamon (1977) suggesting a classification scheme for urban policies and cities contributes to the cumulation of policy theories and the development of a theory of political change. It will be discussed in the next section on policy change theories.

POLICY CHANGE

Analysis of policy change is the least developed of the three approaches to urban policy, but there is growing interest in explanations of the conditions leading to changes in urban policies. This has come about partly because dramatic changes in the fiscal and demographic characteristics of cities have resulted in shifts in processes and policies not anticipated by more static theories and have intensified interest in specifying the conditions under which certain types of relationships will occur (David and Kantor, this volume). Even after developing a process theory of policy, one may not be able to explain changes in policy because the limiting conditions are not well understood and the unit of analysis or time frame may be too narrow to reveal important larger trends and cycles.

Three major studies of changes in urban politics are useful precursors of Lester Salamon's (1977) typology which links politics with policy. Robert Dahl (1961) says that rulers change as a result of shifts in the socioeconomic characteristics of society and in the issues generated by those shifts.

The trend is from oligarchy to pluralism due to a change from cumulative to dispersed inequalities in the larger society. Dahl argues that the Patrician City was replaced by the Industrialist City when the rise of industry separated wealth from social position and political office went to the wealthy. Then the Working Class City arose when the influx of immigrants enabled political office to go to those who could get their vote. The trend, according to Dahl, is toward the rise of New Men,[5] bureaucrats and experts and politicians who know how to use them. This reform style politics is said to result from increases in social mobility which lessen the importance of class and ethnicity and from new issues centering on the provision of collective rather than divisible benefits. Banfield and Wilson's (1963) *City Politics* provides similar explanations for these trends. They emphasize a change from predominantly lower class private regarding political styles to predominantly middle-class public regarding styles of reform politics (Wilson and Banfield, 1964, 1971). Agger and Goldrich (1972), comparing political changes in four cities over approximately 10 years, also identify a trend toward a reform style associated with community conservationist ideologies which are oriented toward rule by professionals and the provision of amenities to meet the needs of the collectivity.

Lester Salamon (1977) modified earlier schemes to encompass the current concern with urban policy. The typology he proposes facilitates the synthesis of many urban process studies and also contributes to a theory of policy change because each category can also be viewed as a state of policy development or evolution. A city or policy arena in a city can fit into different categories at different points in time.[6] The two dimensions of his classification are the set of interests at work and the substance of policy, namely, the role government plays in relation to the interests. Applying his framework he distinguishes three types of policy arenas or urban polities: the private city, the bureaucratic city, and the democratic (policy planning) city. In the first, city government adapts itself to the uncoordinated and particularistic demands of private economic interests and government plays a passive, adaptive role. In the bureaucratic city or policy arena, the role of government is also passive but the policy is adapted to the maintenance needs and standard operating procedures of the bureaucracies. Only in the third category, the democratic (policy planning) case, does the government take an active role in shaping policy to promote greater equality and reduce the negative effects of private development. Salamon suggests that these classifications may coincide with different stages in a city's history, but he stresses the difficulty of moving to the democratic (policy planning) category. He says this change only occurs when there is "a weak and divided business community, an activated citizenry, and a political leader with the will and the capacity to mobilize a pro-redistributive electoral coalition sufficient to neutralize the bureaucracy and promote activist policies" (1979: 426). Salamon's typology is very useful for understanding urban policy and policy change because it identifies two key components: the interests to which policy responds and the kind of actions government takes in response to those interests. Its de-emphasis of formal reform and machine structures seems appropriate because the distinctions between the two are not as clear as they once were (Yates, this volume). Machines have a different style now and no longer are able to deliver the votes automatically; similarly, some reformed cities are becoming more politicized (Browning et al., 1979).

Yet additions to the typology can increase its applicability to diverse urban policies and patterns of policy change.[7] The revised typology presented in Figure 1 is an effort to suggest augmentations of Salamon's scheme. It completes the empty cells for each of the sets of interests which he identified. Cell d uses Agger et al.'s (1964) term *Progressive Conservative* for the case when government plays an active role in promoting business interests. Both elected officials and their coalitions and bureaucrats may favor policies such as downtown renewal which are supported

Figure 1   Revision of Salamon's Typology of Urban Policy[1]

		Set of Interests to which Government Responds		
		Business	**Bureaucrats** (Middle Class)	**Redistributive** (Lower Class)
Role of Government in Relation to Interests	Passive	Private[2] a	Bureaucratic b	LIBERAL PRAGMATIST c
	Active	PROGRESSIVE[3] CONSERVATIVE d	COMMUNITY CONSERVATIVE e	Democratic (Policy-Planning) f

1. Salamon (1977)
2. Salamon's labels are *underlined*.
3. Additional labels are in CAPS.

by progressive business groups and may exercise major initiative to promote these policies. Salamon refers to this case when he talks about the
sophisticated private city or the warmed over version of the private city
when officials are co-opted to serve business interests, but he does not give
it a separate label. When this occurs, the situation is distinct enough from
the private city to deserve a separate classification. Cell e in the revised
typology uses Agger et al.'s term *Community Conservative* for the case
when government plays an active role on behalf of broader bureaucratic
interests. Some bureaucrats favor active governmental leadership to promote professional norms such as "long-range planning in the public interest by nonpolitical administrators" (Agger et al., 1964: 25). These norms
are not identical with redistributive interests, so a distinction needs to be
made between the Community Conservative and the Democratic (policy
planning case.) The Community Conservative category roughly coincides
with the reformist category used in the earlier urban politics typologies,
especially because bureaucratic interests both as manifested in cell b and
cell e seem to be one form of middle-class interests. The third addition to
Salamon's typology, cell c, uses Greenstone and Peterson's (1973) term,
Liberal Pragmatist, to refer to the case when redistributive or lower class
interests are responded to passively by government. Salamon's typology
only has a place for active response to redistributive interests, but a passive
response is also possible as indicated by the classic case of machine politics
and private regarding policies which distribute individualized benefits to
lower class supporters.

This revised typology allows more differentiation among types of
policy arenas and urban polities and thus the identification of more
patterns of policy change. Like Salamon's original typology, the revision
includes bureaucratic interests in the policy system but it elaborates the
forms these interests take. It also underscores the possibility of bureaucrats favoring active governmental policies in response to business,
bureaucratic, or redistributive interests. The revision also attempts to
differentiate more of the roles and orientations of elected officials. It can
accommodate cases when political leaders and their electoral coalitions
actively promote either business, bureaucratic, or redistributive interests
(cells d, e, and f). The revised typology is consistent with various combinations of political and bureaucratic initiative in each cell. For example,
Salamon (1977) suggests that Democratic (policy planning) only occurs
when political leaders neutralize the bureaucracy, but that is too narrow a
view. Sometimes bureaucrats are the ones who prod elected officials in this
direction rather than vice versa. The revised typology also coincides well
with the categories used by Dahl, by Banfield and Wilson, and by Agger et

al. For example, Dahl's Industrialist City fits in the Private cell, the Ex Plebe City in the Liberal Pragmatist cell, and the New Men City fits in either the Progressive Conservative or Community Conservative cell.

Perhaps the most troublesome aspect of the typology is that changing economic conditions may be modifying the meaning of active and passive governmental roles. An era of fiscal scarcity is leading many people who traditionally supported active governmental roles in urban policy to rethink those beliefs (see the Caraley and Masotti articles in this volume). Some would call it irresponsible retrenchment; others see it as an admirable effort to adjust to changing economic conditions and to the limited capacities of large-scale bureaucracies. In any case, the readjustments may mean that the active/passive dimension of the typology will need to be modified to reflect the most important dimensions of policy substance under the new conditions.

Yet the typology captures some of the diversity which has staggered urban analysts in the last two decades. They, like the feds, may have started out thinking that cities, if not all alike, could at least be categorized using simple dichotomies. But two decades of policy research, program evaluation, and implementation analysis have resulted in the rediscovery of urban complexity. And to add insult to injury, the economic, demographic, and intergovernmental conditions are changing so rapidly that they seem to defy efforts even to describe the accompanying changes in policy. Yet this typology and the David and Kantor chapter in this volume are attempts to identify key pieces in the puzzle so that partial explanations can gradually be cumulated into more general theories of urban policy change.

CURRENT RESEARCH ON URBAN POLICY

The contributions to this volume represent important types of research now being done on urban policy, including studies of policy input/output, process, and change. They also highlight significant features of urban policy making, such as the growing importance of fiscal scarcity, changes in the politicization of minorities and the formation of potentially competing coalitions supporting tax and spending limitations, and shifts in the federal role in cities. These trends create critical tensions which may influence both policy making and the consequences of policy. They underscore the need for theories which treat urban policy in broader contexts encompassing historical, structural, and vertical components. The studies included in this volume take steps in the direction of more comprehensive theories by examining how changes over time in national and local conditions and in cities' positions in the federal system influence the complex patterned interactions among players in the urban policy process. The studies also illustrate the trend toward the convergence of approaches as analysts learn from the growing body of research. Input/output studies move in the direction of disaggregation and specification in order to get closer to the underlying processes; process studies take into account the socioeconomic and formal political structural variables in order to understand the constraints within which policy processes operate.

The first section of the volume on determinants of urban policy includes two studies which focus on two of the levels of government making urban policy—the local and the national levels. These policy process studies characterize the decision-making process at each level and the relative influence of the various players and conditions, setting the stage for the chapters in subsequent sections which consider different components in more detail.

Yates's chapter elaborates on his earlier argument (Yates, 1977) that fragmented political and administrative structures result in extreme pluralism in the city policy-making process. This street-fighting pluralism, a penny arcade is Yates's metaphor, is a free-for-all with unstructured, multilateral, unstable conflict among diverse contestants. Thus, according to Yates, cities are more ungovernable than states or the nation. Yates's chapter in this volume examines the relationship between one of the players, the mayor, and the other main players in the eight-ring circus: neighborhood groups and other local interests, citizens as taxpayers, other local governments, urban bureaucracies, higher level governments, public employee unions, press, and business. He argues that policy change is likely to occur because the emergence of a new issue on the urban agenda, fiscal scarcity, enhances the mayor's ability to influence the policy process. Scarcity shapes the power resources and expectations of the groups and the mayor is in the best position to build new coalitions and strategies because the mayor is the only player with extensive links to all the other players. Yates describes a new balance of power resulting from a decrease in pressure from neighborhood groups (as groups learn about the limitations of protest and of public bureaucracies) and a flow of power toward the private sector, a decrease in the coalition of service demanders and providers and a rise in a coalition giving priority to financial management, control of taxes and spending, and economic development. Earlier issues of race and urban decay have been replaced, says Yates, so the policy-making process itself will change.

In broadest outline Yates's account of policy change seems to fit the cycles suggested by Piven and Cloward (1971), a period of disruption and expansion of programs to quiet discontent in the 1960s is followed by a period of program reduction once the disruption has been eliminated. But Yates like Banfield (1968) might interpret this trend as a necessary response to economic limitations in the system, whereas Piven and Cloward (and other proponents of what Masotti and Lineberry, 1976, call the critical approach to urban politics, which unfortunately is not represented in this volume) might interpret it as an indicator of unwillingness to do the redistribution which is still possible and necessary.

Caraley's research examines the national policy process which is so important in formulating urban policy. It serves to emphasize the trend toward the federalization of urban programs (Masotti and Lineberry, 1976) that has meant that cities must be seen in a federal context, as part of a vertical system involving many levels of government. Note that Yates's list of key participants in city policy making includes higher levels of government. Although scholars disagree over the relative importance of national and local levels in shaping policy making at the local level (Reagan, 1972; Elazar, 1966), no one argues that the national level is unimportant.

Caraley's study of the factors shaping the development of national urban aid programs analyzes congressional voting in the first, or 1977, session of the 95th Congress on eight aid programs with major impacts on large cities: public works, jobs, public service jobs, countercyclical assistance, community development block grants, subsidized housing, food stamps, legal services for the poor, and welfare. Congress voted favorably on all these pro-urban programs except welfare reform. Whereas Yates only gives brief mention to political parties, Caraley finds that the party identification of the legislators was more important in determining how they voted than their constituency (urban/suburban/rural), section, or region. Thus, regardless of the characteristics of their districts, Democrats are more likely to be pro-urban and Republicans are more likely to be anti-urban. Caraley argues that the heavily Democratic and pro-urban Congress would have supported a much stronger urban policy than the one proposed by President Carter in March 1978. In Caraley's view both Presidential and legislative support are necessary in order to pass strong urban aid policies and in the absence of Presidential leadership in 1978 such policies did not materialize. Caraley argues that if Carter's program was based on the assumption that Congress would not support a stronger urban program, it was a false premise.

Whereas Yates is relatively optimistic about the future governability of cities in conditions of fiscal scarcity, Caraley suggests that a valuable opportunity was missed and that fiscal, demographic, and delivery system considerations will make it increasingly difficult to provide the necessary aid to large cities. He is critical of what he sees as the increasing reliance on formula rather than categorical grants because they make it more difficult to target aid for large cities.[8] Federal officials have elaborated on the decision process in the executive branch which led to Carter's urban policy, contrasting Lyndon Johnson's use of outside task forces with Carter's reliance on a very open process involving participation by the agencies. Urban policy making in Washington has been likened not to a jungle but to a crap game.

The second section of this book consists of two chapters on minorities. Minority activities and issues have been an important component of urban politics and policy in the last two decades. In fact, some people incorrectly use the term *urban* to refer exclusively to racial and ethnic concerns. The Welch and Karnig study views black elected officials as an independent variable and asks how much influence they have on city expenditures. The Eisinger study considers black elected officials as the dependent variable and asks whether a past policy—the war on poverty—influenced these officials.

Welch and Karnig's input/output analysis, using data on expenditure changes in 139 cities, finds that cities with black mayors have larger increases in social welfare expenditures and intergovernmental grants than cities without black mayors. However, black representation on city councils was not consistently associated with expenditure changes. Welch and Karnig are explicit about the limitations of input/output analysis and call for closer attention to the processes which explain the general patterns.

Studies by the Policy Implementation Project (see Note 7) pursue some of the lines they suggest, namely, an examination of shifts in targeting of a given type of expenditure within cities and of the relation between minority officials and minority employment (Browning et al., 1978a, 1978b). The research also develops a theory of political and policy change, focusing on city government responsiveness to minorities, which explains changes in terms of: the political mobilization and incorporation of minorities; the ideologies and interests of coalitions and populations; the replacement of resistant dominant coalitions by new coalitions that include minorities; and the implementation of federal programs. This examination of the process of ethnic succession elaborates on the factors leading to minority representation and the impact of representation on policy.

Eisinger's study examines the long-term consequences of the war on poverty for black leadership using a survey of 210 black elected officials.

He finds that nearly a quarter of those elected since the Economic Opportunity Act of 1964 had substantial involvement with the war on poverty prior to their elections. They are more politically ambitious, more likely to hold state rather than local office, and more likely to come from big cities. The war on poverty also provided leadership training and support. The federal program, according to Eisinger, was successful in increasing the leadership cadre of black elected officials, offering an alternative to political parties as a vehicle for political advancement.

This positive assessment of the war on poverty contrasts with Charles Hamilton's (1979) argument that in New York City the war on poverty and other federal grant program depoliticized the black electorate. In Hamilton's view, black program organizing in the bureaucratic arena substituted for precinct organizing in the electoral arena resulting in decreased black voting and the failure to win electoral victories. Pressman's (1975) study of Oakland, California, also suggested that it might be difficult to translate success in the federal program arena into the electoral arena. But all these authors agree that electoral victories are important for improving policy for minorities. And that heatedly debated position does seem to reflect accurately the assumptions underlying the emphasis minorities have given to electoral strategies in the 1970s.

The third section of the book consists of three chapters on fiscal questions which reflect the increasing interest of political scientists in these issues as they become more visible and controversial. A good deal of self-castigation goes on within the discipline about the inability to anticipate these trends. We were caught off guard first by racial and now by fiscal unrest.

Peterson's input/output analysis of the determinants of local tax and expenditure policies starts with a unitary theory of local policy making. This theory posits that local revenue and expenditures are different from national fiscal policy because local governments must maximize their economic well-being relative to other units of local government by attracting capital and labor. Operating within this constraint, cities rationally design taxation and expenditure policy to enhance their competitive positive. Using aggregate data, Peterson demonstrates that cities rely on taxes based on the benefits-received principle, e.g., user charges, rather than on the ability-to-pay principle, e.g., income tax. Similarly, cities choose expenditures in which the beneficiaries are also the taxpayers (such as police and fire), rather than expenditures which redistribute benefits (such as welfare and health). Peterson's multiple regression analysis of levels of spending in three types of policies (redistributive, developmental, and allocational) finds they are determined by different economic characteristics of the cities. Peterson concludes that redistributive tax and expenditure policies are largely absent at the local level, not because of bias in the internal policy process or distribution of power but because the competition among cities makes such policies impractical. Thus Peterson, like Yates, sees city policy as influenced by other cities and higher levels of government and as distinct from national policy. Peterson's chapter highlights the controversy between proponents of the unitary and bargaining models of policy making. It is interesting that political scientists are throwing political variables out just when economists are discovering their value; the two groups are like ships passing in the night.

David and Kantor's research looks at the impact of changing economic and political conditions on the formulation of city budgets. This longitudinal study proposes a theory of policy change. Instead of asking why the New York City fiscal crisis occurred (Newfield and Du Brul, 1978), the authors put the crisis in perspective by examining New York City's budgets since 1945. They criticize segmental theories of policy for ignoring interrelationships among environments, processes, and outputs and for failing to explain how changes occur in policies and policy making. They identify three different systems of budgetary policy making which have existed sequentially in New York City: incremental (characterized by stable roles, acceptance of revenue constraints, and incremental expenditures); pluralist (unstable roles, rejection of revenue constraints, and nonincremental expenditures); and elite (expenditures designed to optimize the revenue base and the competitive position of the city). The transition from one type of policy making to the next, in their theory, results from shifts in both the economic and political conditions. They argue that minorities and public employee unions that were beneficiaries of the pluralist budgetary phase have lost ground to the financial and business leaders who dominate the centralized budget phase. This chapter suggests the need for more research into variations in the way different cities respond to declining fiscal conditions. How much will the responses be shaped by socioeconomic conditions and how much by political conditions, particularly disagreements among participants about how to invigorate the economy and who should bear the cost?

Louis Masotti's essay does not explain past policy but rather recommends future policy which he thinks is necessary if urban areas are to survive under conditions of fiscal scarcity. His policy prescriptions are: decentralization, deinstitutionalization, and deregulation.[9] He argues that mediating structures, appropriate technology, neighborhoodism, and self-help groups all promote valuable capacity building, enablement, and empowerment. He acknowledges that there may be difficulties in relating these small-scale efforts to large-scale bureaucratic institutions, but suggests that urban policy should shift in the direction of creating incentives for the private sector to do things in the public interest. He also examines potential political, social, and economic consequences of the policies he proposes, such as the rise of a new coalition including liberals, neoconservatives, and conservatives; an increase in the use of referenda; and disproportionate hardships for the poor who have been the most dependent on the expanding public bureaucracies.

This essay underscores the controversy about the trend to fiscal conservatism. Public officials partially welcome tax and spending limitations, the clones of California's Proposition 13, because they give the officials enough backbone to say no to the demands from interest groups and may increase their power relative to bureaucracies, but at the same time there is fear that necessary programs will be lost and low-resource groups will suffer most.

The final section of the book consists of two studies of the consequences of policy for the distribution of benefits. They illustrate the way policy analysts have applied Lasswell's question about "who gets what?" to the study of policy outputs (the services government provides) and outcomes (the effects these services have; Masotti and Lineberry, 1976).

Richard Rich's essay reviews the burgeoning literature on the distribution of urban services including police, fire, libraries, streets, health, and solid waste collection. He traces its lineage to a concern about equality of service distribution and reviews the findings about distribution patterns for given services within a jurisdiction, comparing results using objective indicators and citizen perceptions. He also summarizes the explanations given for the observed patterns which typically emphasize the organization of the delivery system rather than political variables. Rich goes on to assess the literature, suggesting gaps which need to be filled by future research. He emphasizes the need (1) to compare service levels across jurisdictions in a metropolitan area rather than looking solely at intrajurisdictional distributions, (2) to examine the outcomes of services and not just outputs, (3) to analyze the role of neighborhoods in service provision, and (4) to focus on questions of equity as well as equality. Like other contributors to this volume, he criticizes the tendency to view a given aspect of cities, such as service distribution, in isolation from urban and national politics. He also calls for more attention to the relative levels of allocations for different programs within a city, pointing out that certain mixes of program expenditures benefit lower classes, but middle classes often attempt to reduce government provision of services which they obtain from private sources, such as medical services, to decrease their taxes. Note this challenge to the characterization of the middle class as public regarding (Wilson and Banfield, 1964, 1971).

Another component of the urban services literature, not dealt with directly in Rich's chapter, gives particular attention to levels of performance.[10] It is an outgrowth of the traditional concern with improving organizational effectiveness and efficiency. For example, the work of the Ostroms examines the factors in the urban service delivery process which influence levels of performance, emphasizing the importance of organization size. Impressive micro level data have been collected on service delivery in diverse jurisdictions often including a whole metropolitan area (Antunes and Ostrom, 1979; Parks et al., 1978). This approach continues the interest in metropolitan reform characteristic of the structural focus in urban politics, but the new public choice theoretical framework produces contrasting generalizations and prescriptions, emphasizing multinucleated metropolitan governance rather than comprehensive hierarchical structures (Ostrom, 1973; Ostrom and Bish, 1973).

The chapter by Sara Silbiger, like the one by Rich, addresses the question of distribution of benefits, but it is a case study of the policy process, looking at both the causes of contractual education policy in New York City and its consequences. The case focuses on a public employee union, the United Federation of Teachers, and the competitive advantages which result from collective bargaining. Silbiger argues that the resources of the union and the weaknesses of the board of education in the decisional process result in union victories. The distributive consequences of the contracts are complicated. One hypothesis is that the largely white provider groups are the main beneficiaries at the expense of the clients who are disproportionately the poor and the minorities. Using one measure, the views of nonteacher educational interests, Silbiger finds support for the view that teachers win at the expense of students. Using another measure, spatial distribution of education resources, she finds contradictory evidence which shows that the contract directs extra resources to the schools with the heaviest concentration of poor and minority children so these schools receive higher per-pupil expenditures. This chapter serves to emphasize the importance of public employee unions mentioned by Yates and by David and Kantor, but more research is needed on whether fiscal scarcity will decrease the competitive advantage of the unions and shift the distribution of benefits.

PROSPECTS FOR RESEARCH ON
URBAN POLICY MAKING

If urban policy research was a response to calls for relevance, what happens when relevance is no longer relevant? What happens when the issues which led to the sense of urgency are replaced by other issues? This review of the theories of urban policy and current research suggests that there is life in the urban policy field yet. The research and movement toward more comprehensive theories in the last two decades show signs of continuing. The new issues such as fiscal scarcity have major ramifications for city policy and provide a continuing sense of urgency. (The cynical among us might suggest that fiscal crises are a godsend for urban policy analysts, that there is "money in fiscal scarcity.") This new crisis in a long line of periodic urban dislocations has infused the field with renewed activity and interesting intellectual problems such as explaining variations in city responses to the crisis and their implications for issues of race, housing, employment, and the like. One wonders whether the new concerns will supplement or substitute for the earlier concerns. If we forget the past rather than learn from it, the next generation of urban analysts may be "surprised" by a new wave of racial unrest and have to rediscover the race-related city issues. In any case, the current crisis challenges old theories and requires new syntheses which better explain the dynamics of the full range of urban policy making and its consequences under changing conditions.

Perhaps the biggest change in the study of urban policy is in the expectations of the analysts. Just as policy makers and community activists have been chastened by their limited ability to improve urban policy, so too have analysts had to accept the limitations of research. As they become more experienced (and older), they realize that the kinds of theories some dreamed were possible will be much more difficult and slower to develop and that better theories may not have much of an impact on improving urban policies and solving problems. From the current vantage point those earlier expectations seem inflated and naive, signs of the field's ahistorical adolescence. Those who stay in the urban field now expect less but still see value in attempting to develop more comprehensive theories which at least pose issues about urban policy making not typically raised by other participants with higher stakes in the process. A blanket denial of our contribution to the dialogue would be just as misguided as the inflated expectations of the past.

The most basic reason for studying urban policy remains unchanged.

The analysis of urban policy provides important insights into national political systems which cannot be obtained from a focus solely on the central government. Note that Wilson (1968) does not justify the study of urban policy in terms of timely issues but rather as a contribution to the study of government. Similarly, Banfield and Wilson (1963: 2; 345-346) argue that cities are a unit of analysis with close links both "upward" to the whole governmental system and "downward" to individuals. Cities are also accessible mirrors of trends in postindustrial societies and provide valuable opportunities for comparative research. Some analysts emphasize the differences between city policy making and national policy making (Yates, this volume; Peterson, this volume; Kirby et al., 1973); others stress the comparability (Jacob and Lipsky, 1968). Yet most would agree that both the similarities and differences make comparisons between the levels instructive.

For all these reasons the prospects for research on urban policy making are good. There has undeniably been an element of faddism in the past which may well continue. But the basic tasks remain important, work over the past two decades has improved our theories, and the current studies enhance the possibility of cumulation and the development of more comprehensive theories.

One wishes that the outlook for cities and the people who live in them was as bright. Yet an examination of trends in urban policy making suggests that an era of retrenchment will undo some of the gains that only now, too late, are being acknowledged. Things may not have gotten as much better in the last two decades as people hoped, but we now may see that they can get worse, not because of the disruption Banfield (1968) feared but because of government's increased inability to act, however clumsily, to correct the inequities in society.

NOTES

1. The study by Richard Rich was not presented at the meeting but was selected from among several unsolicited papers.

2. For commentary on the community power literature, see Hawley and Wirt (1974) and also Wolfinger (1971) and Frey (1971).

3. No effort is made here to develop a precise definition of urban. The term is used loosely to refer to cities of varying sizes. Cities over 50,000 whether central cities, suburbs, or free-standing cities are the clearest examples of urban areas. Small cities under 50,000 are also considered urban. In addition the Bureau of the Census classifies all places of 2,500 or more inhabitants as urban.

4. In this volume, Peterson calls this approach the bargaining model; David and Kantor distinguish two types of process theories, decisional and output. Jacob and Lipsky (1968) discuss a similar approach in their section on synoptic indicators of the political process.

5. It is hoped that if Dahl were revising his typology today, he would feel compelled to use a term not linked to gender, as the 1970s witnessed a marked increase in the number of women politicians, bureaucrats, and experts.

6. Jacob and Lipsky (1968) review some of the other city classification schemes such as size of city, governmental structure, socioeconomic states, and political culture.

7. These observations on Salamon's typology grow out of research being done by the Policy Implementation Project supported by the National Science Foundation; the Institute of Governmental Affairs, University of California, Davis; the Institute of Governmental Studies, University of California, Berkeley; and San Francisco State University. The principal investigators are Rufus P. Browning and David Tabb of San Francisco State and Dale Rogers Marshall, University of California, Davis.

8. For a concise review of New Federalism and formula grants see Carl Van Horn (1979). DeLeon and LeGates (1978) use the term *cybernetic federalism* to describe formula grants. See also the voluminous literature on federal program implementation and evaluation (Pressman and Wildavsky, 1973; Sabatier and Mazmanian, forthcoming; and publications by the Urban Institute).

9. An excellent discussion of community control and decentralization is presented in Fainstein and Fainstein (1976).

10. See the work on urban indicators by the Urban Institute and Rossi et al. (1974).

REFERENCES

AGGER, R. and D. GOLDRICH (1972) The Rulers and the Ruled. Belmont, CA: Wadsworth.
——— and B. SWANSON (1964) The Rulers and the Ruled: Political Power and Impotence in American Communities. New York: John Wiley.
AIKEN, M. and R. ALFORD (1970) "Community structure and innovation: the case of public housing." American Political Science Review, 64 (September): 840-864.
ALFORD, R. (1975) Health care politics: ideological and interest group barriers to reform. Chicago: University of Chicago Press.
ANTUNES, G. and E. OSTROM (1979) "Situational, personal, and behavioral determinants of citizen satisfaction in specific encounters with police: an initial analysis." Prepared for presentation at the Western Political Science Association Annual Meeting.
BAHL, R. [ed.] (1978) The Fiscal Outlook for Cities. Syracuse, NY: Syracuse University Press.
BANFIELD, E. (1968) Unheavenly City. Boston: Little, Brown.
——— and J. WILSON (1963) City Politics. Cambridge, MA: Harvard University Press.

BROWNING, R., D. MARSHALL, and D. TABB (1979) "Minorities and urban electoral change: a longitudinal study." Urban Affairs Quarterly 15, 2.

——— (1978a) "Implementation and political change: sources of local variations in federal social programs." Prepared for the Policy Implementation Workshop, Pomona College. *Policy Studies Journal* symposium, forthcoming in P. Sabatier and D. Mazmanian, Effective Policy Implementation.

——— (1978b) "Responsiveness to minorities: a theory of political change in cities." Prepared for delivery at the Annual Meeting of the American Political Science Association.

CLARK, T. (1973) Community power and policy outputs. Beverly Hills: Sage.

——— [ed.] (1968a) Community Structure and Decision-Making: Comparative Analyses. San Francisco: Chandler.

——— (1968b) "Community structure, decision making, budget expenditure and urban renewal in 51 American communities." American Sociological Review 33 (August): 576-593.

CRENSON, M. (1971) "The unpolitics of air pollution: a study of nondecision-making in the cities." Baltimore: Johns Hopkins University Press.

DAHL, R. (1961) Who governs: Democracy and Power in an American City. New Haven: Yale University Press.

DAWSON, R. and J. ROBINSON (1963) "Inter-party competition, economic variables, and welfare policies in the American states." Journal of Politics 23: 265-289.

DeLEON, R. and R. LeGATES (1978) "Beyond cybernetic federalism in community development." Urban Law Annual 15: 17-52.

DOWNS, G. (1976) Bureaucracy, Innovation, and Public Policy. Lexington, MA: Lexington Books.

DYE, T. (1972) Understanding Public Policy. Englewood Cliffs, NJ: Prentice Hall.

——— (1966) Politics, Economics, and the Public: Policy Outcomes in the American States. Chicago: Rand McNally.

ELAZAR, D. (1966) American Federalism: a View from the States. New York: Thomas Y. Crowell.

EULAU, H. and K. PREWITT (1973) Labyrinths of Democracy: Adaptations, Linkages, Representation, and Policies in Urban Politics. Indianapolis: Bobbs-Merrill.

FAINSTEIN, N. and S. FAINSTEIN (1976) "The future of community control." American Political Science Review 70: 905-923.

FREY, F. (1971) "Comment: on issues and nonissues in the study of power." American Political Science Review 65, 4: 1081-1104.

FRY, B. and R. WINTERS (1970) "The politics of redistribution." American Political Science Review 64 (June): 508-522.

GODWIN, K. and W. SHEPARD (1976) "Political processes and public expenditures: a re-examination based on theories of representative government." American Political Science Review 70 (December): 1127-1135.

GREENSTONE, J. and P. PETERSON (1973) Race and Authority in Urban Politics: Community Participation and the War on Poverty. New York: Russell Sage Foundation.

HAMILTON, C. (1979) "The patron-recipient relationship and minority politics in New York City." *Political Science Quarterly* 95: 211-228.

HAWKINS, B. (1971) Politics and Urban Policies. Indianapolis: Bobbs-Merrill.

HAWLEY, W. (1973) Nonpartisan Elections and the Case for Party Politics. New York: John Wiley.

——— and M. LIPSKY (1976) "Introduction: the study of city politics," in W. Hawley et al., Theoretical Perspectives on Urban Politics. Englewood Cliffs, NJ: Prentice-Hall.

——— and F. WIRT [eds.] (1974) The Search for Community Power. Englewood Cliffs, NJ: Prentice-Hall.

HERSON, L. (1957) "The lost world of municipal government." American Political Science Review 51 (June): 330-345.

HOFFERBERT, R. (1972) "State and community policy studies: a review of comparative input-output analyses." Political Science Annual, Vol. 3. Indianapolis: Bobbs-Merrill.

HUNTER, F. (1953) Community Power Structure. Chapel Hill: University of North Carolina Press.

INGRAM, H. (1977) "Policy implementation through bargaining: the case of federal grants-in-aid." Public Policy 25 (Fall): 499-562.

JACOB, H. and M. LIPSKY (1968) "Outputs, structure, and power: an assessment of changes in the study of state and local politics." Journal of Politics 30: 510-538.

JONES, T. "The press and the new urban politics," in L. Masotti and R. Lineberry (eds.) The New Urban Politics. Cambridge, MA: Ballinger.

KATZNELSON, I. (1976a) "Class capacity and social cohesion in American cities," in L. Masotti and R. Lineberry (eds.) The New Urban Politics. Cambridge, MA: Ballinger.

——— (1976b) "The crisis of the capitalist city: urban politics and social control," in W. Hawley et al., Theoretical Perspectives on Urban Politics. Englewood Cliffs, NJ: Prentice-Hall.

KIRBY, D., T. HARRIS, R. CRAIN, and C. ROSSELL (1973) Political Strategies in Northern School Desegregation. Lexington, MA: Lexington Books.

KIRLIN, J. and S. ERIE (1972) "The study of city governance and public policy making: a critical appraisal." Public Administration Review 32 (March/April): 173-184.

LARKEY, P. (1979) Evaluating Public Programs: The Impact of General Revenue Sharing on Municipal Government. Princeton: Princeton University Press.

LEVY, F., A. MELTSNER and A. WILDAVSKY (1974) Urban Outcomes: Schools, Streets, Libraries. Berkeley: University of California Press.

LINEBERRY, R. and E. FOWLER (1967) "Reformism and public policies in American cities." American Political Science Review 61: 701-716.

LIPSKY, M. (1970) Protest in City Politics: Rent Strikes, Housing and the Power of the Poor. Chicago: Rand McNally.

LOVERIDGE, R. (1971) City Managers in Legislative Politics. Indianapolis: Bobbs-Merrill.

LOWI, T. (1972) "Four systems of policy, politics and choice." Public Administration Review 32 (July): 298-310.

——— (1969) The End of Liberalism: Ideology, Policy, and the Crisis of Public Authority. New York: W. W. Norton.

——— (1964) "American business, public policy, case studies, and political theory." World Politics 16 (July): 677-715.

MASOTTI, L. and R. LINEBERRY (1976) The New Urban Politics. Cambridge, MA: Ballinger.

MOLLENKOPF, J. (1973) "Community organization and city politics." Ph.D. dissertation, Harvard University.

MONTGOMERY, R. and D. R. MARSHALL (forthcoming) "Housing policy." Policy Studies Journal

NEWFIELD, J. and P. DU BRUL (1978) The Abuse of Power: The Permanent Government and the Fall of New York. New York: Penguin.

ORREN, K. (1976) "Corporate power and the slums: is big business a paper tiger?" in W. Hawley et al., Theoretical Perspectives on Urban Politics. Englewood Cliffs, NJ: Prentice-Hall.

OSTROM, V. (1973) The Intellectual Crisis in American Public Administration. University: University of Alabama Press.

——— and R. BISH (1973) Understanding Urban Government: Metropolitan Reform Reconsidered. Washington, DC: American Enterprise Institute.

——— and E. OSTROM (1978) "Public goods and public choices," pp. 7-79 in E. Savas (ed.) Alternatives for Delivering Public Services: Toward Improved Performance. Boulder, CO: Westview Press.

PALLEY, M. and H. PALLEY (1977) Urban America and Public Policies. Lexington, MA: D. C. Heath.

PARKS, R., G. WHITAKER, and E. OSTROM (1978) Patterns on Metropolitan Policing. Cambridge, MA: Ballinger.

PETERSON, P. (1978) "The politics of taxation and expenditure: a unitary approach." Prepared for the Annual Meeting of the American Political Science Association.

PIVEN, F. and R. CLOWARD (1971) Regulating the Poor. New York: Pantheon.

PRESSMAN, J. (1975) Federal Programs and City Politics. Berkeley: University of California Press.

——— and A. WILDAVSKY (1973) Implementation. Berkeley: University of California Press.

REAGAN, M. (1972) The New Federalism. New York: Oxford University Press.

ROSSI, P., R. BERK, and B. EIDSON (1974) The Roots of Urban Discontent. New York: John Wiley.

SABATIER, P. and D. MAZMANIAN (forthcoming) Effective Policy Implementation. Lexington, MA: Lexington Books.

SALAMON, L. (1977) "Urban politics, urban policy, case studies, and political theory." Public Administration Review 37, 4: 418-428.

SULLIVAN, J. (1972) "A note on redistributive politics." American Political Science Review 66 (December): 1301-1305.

VAN HORN, C. (1979) "Evaluating the new federalism: national goals and local implementors." Public Administration Review 30, 1: 17-22.

WILSON, J. [ed.] (1968) City Politics and Public Policy. New York: John Wiley.

——— and E. BANFIELD (1971) "Political ethos revisited." American Political Science Review 65, 4: 1048-1062.

——— (1964) "Public regardingness as a value premise in voting behavior." American Political Science Review 58 (December): 876-887.

WIRT, F. (1974) Power in the City: Decision Making in San Francisco. Berkeley: University of California Press.

WOLFINGER, R. (1971) "Nondecisions and the study of local politics." American Political Science Review 65, 4: 1063-1081.

――― and J. FIELD (1966) "Political ethos and the structure of city government." American Political Science Review 60: 306-326.

YATES, D. (1977) The Ungovernable City: The Politics of Urban Problems and Policy Making. Cambridge, MA: MIT Press.

ZISK, B. (1973) Local Interest Politics: a One-Way Street. Indianapolis: Bobbs-Merrill.

Dale Rogers Marshall
Davis, California

PART I

DETERMINANTS OF POLICY

1

THE MAYOR'S EIGHT-RING CIRCUS:
The Shape of Urban Politics in
Its Evolving Policy Arenas

DOUGLAS YATES

Yale University

Having recently completed a study of urban government (Yates, 1977), in which I argued that the large American city is becoming increasingly ungovernable, I have come to feel that a number of important stones have been left unturned. My original argument about the "ungovernable city" is briefly summarized below. But first I want to indicate the character of the defects that I wish to meet if not repair in this chapter. First, having emphasized the fragmentation of urban government and the multiplicity of players on the urban stage, I believe that it is not quite enough to point to the complexity and diversity of conflict. The next step is to specify the political and policy relationships that exist between the main players. And this is what I hope to do in looking at the major's eight-ring circus: his/her relationship with community groups, urban bureaucrats, taxpayers and citizens (in another guise), higher level governments, business, other local governments, the press, and public employee unions.

Second, I believe that any persuasive account of urban government must obviously pay great attention to the politics of fiscal scarcity—an

Author's Note: *A version of this article was published in* New York Affairs *(Volume 5, Number 3, Spring 1979). It is republished here with permission.*

issue that has come to replace the politics of race and even urban decay which have dominated urban governance in the last two decades. As we will see below, fiscal scarcity critically affects the power resources and policy expectations of various groups in the urban political circus.

Third, and most important, it is not quite enough to spell out—whether accurately or not—the difficulties of urban governance. Diagnosing a problem is a useful task, but in medicine as in other professions it is necessary to have something to say next. In particular, I believe that the city's fiscal problems, along with the advent of the New Federalism, have somewhat eased the stalemate that has resulted among different community, bureaucratic, and higher level governments and have given the mayor some new maneuvering room.

After California's Proposition 13 and New York City's, Cleveland's, and Detroit's fiscal crises, it is quite clear that the cities are in deep trouble. The compelling question is: What is a mayor to do? What political and policy strategies exist (if any) which might make a dent in the accumulation of urban problems and at the same time increase the mayor's capacity to govern (and attract public support). On this last point, I am struck by the relative optimism of recent leading students of urban government. For Wallace Sayre and Herbert Kaufman (1965), New York City was a fairly well-run city featuring a healthy politics of pluralism. For Edward Banfield (1961), in his Chicago writings, the city was also viewed as a relatively stable bargaining citizen with a functional balance of interest-group pressure and central coordination. And for Robert Dahl (1961), the city (of New Haven) was a striking example of democracy working through the participation of different political groups operating in different policy arenas and with a mayor managing an executive-centered coalition to provide coordination and leadership. In more recent writings, the prospects for urban political leadership and governance have appeared anything but dim. Theodore Lowi (1967) believed he saw the beginning of a "new machine" in the coalition of a mayor allied with his/her own public service unions. And various paeans to Richard Daley's Chicago have suggested that the old-time urban religion might still be able to deliver the goods—and services.

Even more pessimistic accounts of urban government have not always called into question the political- and problem-solving capacity of urban leadership. Edward Banfield's *Unheavenly City* (1968) placed the blame for urban problems heavily on the disorganized poor. Other writers have identified assorted bureaucrats and higher level governments (especially the feds) as villains in the urban troubles.

It seems to me that these analyses, although clearly important and persuasive in many respects, circumvent the central question that exists for anyone in the practice of urban government; that is, can the folks in city hall hope to govern and, if so, how and with what kind of political coalition and policy program? It seems to me that the overwhelming fact of urban government today is that there is no consensus at all on how a mayor might pull together his/her politics and policies to provide a viable regime.

More precisely, on the political side, what coalitions (if any) might a mayor form in place of the New Deal coalition (or white ethnic coalitions), civil service or reform coalitions, or liberal-minority coalitions—designed to improve the conditions of the poor, such as John Lindsay forged in his second New York mayoral campaign in 1969. The difficulty of identifying possible coalitions is underscored by the fact that we no longer always know how to label different political battalions and often wonder whether particular political groups are marching together in anything approaching closed rank. One reflection of this difficulty is that the traditional distinction between reformers and regulars no longer seems to cut as deeply as it once did. Machine "politics" may endure, as Raymond Wolfinger (1974) has usefully shown, but that does not mean that city "machines" are still able to function efficiently as candidate-selecting and vote-delivering organizations. More broadly, political appeals to neighborhoods, minority groups, homeowners, the elderly, public service unions, women, and liberals (e.g., Wilson's, 1962, "amateur democrats") lack clarity. Increasingly, there are fine-grained political divisions within the categories of neighborhoods, reform groups, minority groups, liberals, ethnic groups, and so forth. In short, the calculus of political support that any mayor must undertake has become more complicated and uncertain. And this has to do, I believe, with the decline of the more stable urban bargaining system depicted by Dahl, Banfield, Sayre, and Kaufman—a system that promised a steady accommodation of group demands, often in different arenas, and which therefore did not require different groups to enter into head-to-head combat or for that matter call into question whether a particular group definition of political interest satisfied subgroups within the traditional group classification.

Put a slightly different way, I believe that as long as the public sector, and especially the service "pie," was expanding as it did dramatically in the last two decades, city hall could juggle, with some success, the service demands of different neighborhoods, minorities, and ethnic groups. But with the steady increase of racial tensions and later the onset of the fiscal crisis and the end of Great Society investment in urban problems, the myth of the ever-expanding service pie was exploded. That meant, in turn, that urban politics fell back on its inherent tendency of "street-fighting pluralism," in which myriad permutations and combinations of age, race, neighborhood, and need produce enormous demands on city hall arising from the city's basic units: the building, the block, and the small neighborhood group. In this sense, the urban polity was increasingly fragmented, and the mayor's problem of building a political coalition became accordingly more difficult. That is, it is a successful mayor's job to build a political community and the more fragmented the elements of the urban polity, the more demanding the mayoral task.

On the policy side, today's big-city mayor is caught somewhere between the 1960s' approach of increasing services and expenditures in order to solve urban problems and the late 1970s' ethos that would reduce services and increase fiscal control in order to keep city budgets in balance. The current mayor has no dearth of policy initiatives and strategies from which to choose. The mayor is urged to centralize and decentralize, adopt tough fiscal control mechanisms, professionalize bureaucracies, increase citizen participation, turn to the state for greater aid and authority, implement the New Federalism, and wait for the feds to come up with a national urban policy. Many if not all of these strategies have merit but their interrelationship in a coherent policy package and their implications for generating political support are not clear.

I have emphasized the choice-making role of the mayor because I believe mayors inevitably provide whatever style and strategy may exist in city government, or at least they are the *focal* point for issues of style and strategy. If the mayor does not lead and present a coherent strategy in urban government, who will? Surely not the myriad of groups and neighborhoods that comprise the urban politic.

In recent years, several styles and strategies have been particularly apparent in city government.

THE MAYOR:
STYLE AND STRATEGY

The most venerable style is that of the city boss, running a machine oiled with patronage and responding to the needs of an immigrant population willing to trade votes for service considerations. Richard Daley was perhaps the last great example of the type—unless one counts Erastus Corning and his political museum in Albany.

So also has the entrepreneurial style of Richard Lee of New Haven and Ivan Allen of Atlanta withered in the face of the New Federalism and the general decline of boldness and optimism in federal urban problem-solving strategies. Lee and Allen and Dilworth in Philadelphia made their reputations by attracting large amounts of federal money, enabling them to build a variety of shiny redevelopment projects in their communities. These were the mayors who were able to use the federal grant-in-aid system as a source of tangible public benefits and thus, too, as a way of widening political support. Although the federal grant system may have been an "ordeal by paper" for many cities, for the entrepreneurial mayor it constituted an enduring "urban" bank dispensing large amounts of political and financial capital for those who knew how to write grant proposals.

Another recurrent style of mayoral leadership which was well-known to citizens of New York City during the LaGuardia and Lindsay administrations is that of crusaders against urban problems who use a rhetorical, moralizing style to dramatize the needs of their cities to state legislatures or the national government. A fourth type of mayor is that of the cautious broker who attempts to keep his urban political constituencies together and will rarely venture beyond the logic of reconciling those coalitions (Yates, 1977).

Clearly, the bosses and the entrepreneurs built their political records on positions of strength. The bosses had their machine organizations, as long as they survived, and the entrepreneurs had their federal money and their professional grant writers, such as Edward Logue of New Haven (Wolfinger, 1974).

On the other hand, the crusaders and the brokers had and have a tougher row to hoe. The crusader needs a special gift of rhetoric, and the broker must have the balancing skills of a political gymnast. For the future, I have argued that we are likely to see more crusaders and brokers around city hall because the political and financial resources of big city mayors are not as impressive as they once were.

There is yet another style of mayoral leadership that has emerged rapidly in recent years: the style of the tough "manager" who says he/she will keep the city's budget intact without decimating essential urban services. It is obvious why the managerial style and strategy should be attractive at this moment in American urban history. Whereas the managerial appeal is easy to assert and politically convenient to make, it is not at all clear what meaning the idea of the mayor as "manager" contains. In the simplest sense, the managerial mayor is one who makes his/her handling of property taxes and budget expenditures a primary policy emphasis. That much is easily understandable and is certainly smart politics *and* policy in most of our large cities. Indeed, as many recent accounts show, city hall administrations have been able to control deficits and even produce significant budget surpluses. Many mayors have also been able to modernize antique financial and accounting control systems. But having put a lid on spending, the managerial mayor is still left with the fundamental issues that face city government in this decade. Simply put, if the city is going to have to live with a smaller (or at least not rapidly expanding) service pie, what philosophy of the city or strategy of governance should guide that painful process of readjustment? How should city government define or redefine its role? What should the city *be* in the 1980s? Those are the questions. And these issues cannot be satisfactorily answered by indefinite mayoral hand waving about improved management and control techniques. One can only "cut out the fat" for so long before one hits bones, sinews, and vital functions. Rather, the above questions call for the negotiation of a new "social contract" between the mayor and his/her main political constituencies and equally for a policy package that could both address urban problems *and* provide a general strategy that many different constituencies could find acceptable.

I believe that the mayor is and must increasingly be the key player in urban government because the mayor is in the best position to build new political coalitions and design new policy strategies to meet the constraints of fiscal scarcity. This is, in part, because the mayor is one of the only urban political actors with electoral or administrative connections with all the other players. Further, the mayor is held accountable by most of these groups for the city's conditions—regardless of whether the mayor controls all the levers and players. It follows that the mayor is the natural nerve center for the urban policy process. Put more positively, if anyone can link the interests of neighborhoods, business groups, city bureaucracies, and higher level government, it is the man or woman in city hall. That is what I had in mind in speaking of the "mayor's eight-ring circus" and by offering the thought—to be examined in more depth below—that there may now be political and policy strategies available to the mayor that would give greater coherence to the city's eight-ring circus. These will not be magical strategies, because the politics of the eight-ring circus are inherently hard to orchestrate and because urban problems are inherently hard to manage. To see why this is so, let us look briefly at the main political, social, and administrative characteristics of city government and see why, in aggregate, these characteristics would tend to make for an ungovernable city.

THE DIMENSIONS OF
URBAN FRAGMENTATION

Fragmentation is, in my view, the main source of the urban problem, seen as a problem of government. Fragmentation surely has many dimensions in cities, but it begins with and grows out of the city's distinctive task or function: the delivering of ordinary services to urban residents. That is, urban services are direct, visible, locality-specific, and often depend on a subtle service relationship between citizens and public employees. A central point is that city services such as police, fire, sanitation, and education are highly divisible and delivered to citizens with a wide variety of needs and demands. Being divisible means that services can be and are delivered in very different ways to different individuals, blocks, neighborhoods, or racial groups. It is not merely a question of "more or less" service (though that is a part of it), it is also a question of how carefully and effectively services are tailored to particular local demands. That is the "responsiveness" problem in urban government, and it arises not only from the divisibility of services but also from the fact that individuals, blocks, and neighborhoods identify their problems and order their service priorities in very different ways. These characteristics of service delivery inevitably push city government into highly variable patterns of service delivery, and, of course, this can be a virtue when differences in service packages reflect efforts to be responsive to local demands. But from an administrative point of view, this highly variegated structure of service supply and demand also produces systematic fragmentation in the ordering and control of service delivery.

Moreover the political expression and organization of service demands greatly reinforce the underlying fragmentation of the service structure. Service demands are channeled through myriad neighborhood and other interest groups and are then lodged at the door of the mayor and his/her service bureaucracies. In many if not most cases, neighborhood and other groups also fight among themselves for improved service. Understood in this way, city government is a mosaic of street-level disputes between neighborhood groups, between neighborhood groups and service bureaucracies, between different service bureaucracies, and between each of these and the mayor in City Hall.

Given the number of different neighborhood groups (and other interest groups), the number of service bureaucracies, and the number of different issues involved, the diversity, range, and uncertainty of potential and actual conflicts are enormous. I think this free-for-all over who gets (and controls) what in urban services can therefore be accurately depicted as "street-fighting pluralism" (Yates, 1977).

Add to this picture another kind of fragmentation—which is a social division on fragmentation between the servers and the served. Because urban services, as in police and fire, are so often *personal services,* their successful delivery depends to an unusual degree on the street-level relationship between citizens, what Lipsky (1976) has so usefully termed street-level bureaucrats. If the service relationship lacks trust, the city's basic task is impaired. If citizens and public employees are indeed estranged or alienated, responsive service delivery would seem nearly impossible. This leads to the problem of social fragmentation in service delivery, for when service providers are white and middle-class and service recipients are poor and nonwhite, the basis for trust is already very shaky. And this, I believe, has increasingly become a pervasive problem in accomplishing the service task in most large American cities. But even if this social fragmentation did not exist, the underlying fragmentation in the service delivery process would be aggravated by many other characteristics of the urban polity.

Imagine a perfectly responsive and racially sensitive police officer. He/she still poses a problem of administration fragmentation in another way, because the discretion inherent in the street-level job makes control of what the city is doing in the streets highly difficult. This point has been widely discussed (Wilson, 1968) and I will not belabor it here. But it does mean that the administrative ties that bind the street with central service bureaucracies are apt to be loose and unstable.

In addition, as city government has added more and more services for its citizens, it has proliferated new service bureaucracies which are themselves fragmented. And as higher level governments have added more and more administrative duties to cities, there is a further proliferation of fragmented bureaucratic structures. Add to this the fact city hall has had to deal, in both old and new federalisms, with a highly fragmented administrative structure in state and national governments, and we begin to get a full picture of the number of political and administrative fragments that float around city hall.

In sum, the urban fragmentation begins with the street fight between blocks and neighborhoods for services and is aggravated by bureaucratic fighting between city service bureaucracies and between city, state, and national bureaucracies. The mayor is caught squarely in the middle of this eight-ring circus, and many of the demands and conflicts come to rest at the steps of city hall. As a consequence, in this simple model of a turbulent city, the mayor is constantly forced to react to pressures coming from all sides and to bureaucratic conflicts on all sides and above. That is apt to make the mayor reactive and crisis-oriented and to cause an erratic pattern of response to problems. From the point of view of the city as a whole, these patterns create an unstable and uncertain system of policy making.

What is the mayor caught in the middle to do? Let us first look briefly again at the basic structural problems, then to the mayor's main political and policy problems, and then look to see what relationships exist between the two as a guide to future strategies of urban governance.

From the mayor's point of view, presiding over the kind of service-delivery system described above, there are several dominant structural problems—not all of which are consistent or compatible. First, the city is too decentralized to provide strong public control over services at the street level. That is because of the intricacy of local service demands and bargains and because of the inherent discretion of street-level bureaucrats. A related problem is that, given this looseness of control, the problem of financial management, though obviously critical, becomes a very difficult one. It is never quite certain what the production function is in urban services: What investment of resources will yield what effect in service delivery with what resulting change in client satisfaction? So unless budget cutting per se is the point of the enterprise (and it sometimes will be and should be), the question of what to do to achieve greater performance and control at the street level remains a compelling one for any mayor.

On the other hand, the city is often too centralized to permit the kind of hand-tailored service delivery to satisfy proponents of "responsiveness" to neighborhood needs. This is because central bureaucracies have often succeeded in their controlling and regulating functions to impede tailored neighborhood service strategies without at the same time achieving the kind of systematic control over street-level bureaucrats that they would desire. As a consequence, the mayor is constantly beset with demands to be more responsive to local needs, but the mayor is not quite sure how to achieve this purpose in the face of the bureaucratic power of his/her own central service bureaucracies.

A third structural problem is that wave after wave of federal innovations and interventions, beginning with the New Deal and moving through the Great Society and the New Federalism, have substantially overburdened the operating ability and capacity of the mayor's administrative machinery. For 20 years, the mayor has been asked to do more and more, as an operating agent, by higher level governments when, in truth, he/she had his/her hands full in the first place.

At this point, we might conclude that "coping" would be the highest form of art for a big-city mayor. But, as noted above, I believe there have been changes in the urban political order, in large part due to fiscal problems, that suggest new and perhaps more manageable relationships between the city's politics and public policies.

Let us look at the mayor's political relationships first—that is, the mayor's ability to govern his/her volatile eight-ring circus.

THE MAYOR AND POLITICAL CONSTITUENCIES

NEIGHBORHOOD GROUPS AND OTHER LOCAL INTERESTS

At the peak of what Daniel Bell and Virginia Held (1969) called the "community revolution," there was an explosion in the number of groups purporting to represent some part of some neighborhood on some aspect of urban policy. Many of these were stimulated by the Great Society's War on Poverty and especially the community action program. They came in many shapes and sizes and often operated out of small storefronts. They included health centers and neighborhood multiservice centers, tenants' councils, drug prevention groups, lead poisoning groups, food cooperatives, housing task forces, block associations, and some called simply "neighborhood associations." In response to this mobilization in poor neighborhoods, middle-income white groups usually developed a parallel array of organizations, often to defend against the perceived activism and influence of nonwhite groups. On issues such as busing, scattered-site housing, street crime, and blockbusting, many such groups would troop to city hall to argue their cases against each other and to make their conflicting demands on the mayor. This was also, of course, the great era of protests and demonstrations, and most city halls consequently became a revolving door for protest groups and had a permanent police detail at work to keep the procession of community groups literally and figuratively "in line." As Bell and Held put it:

> Forty years ago, a Tammany political boss could give an order to a mayor. Today no such simple action is possible. On each political issue—decentralization or community control, the mix of low income and middle income housing, the proportion of blacks in the city colleges, the locating of a cross-Manhattan or cross-Brooklyn expressway, etc.—there are dozens of active, vocal, and conflicting organized opinions. The difficulty in governing New York—and many other cities as well—is not the "lack of voice" of individuals in city affairs, or the "eclipse of local community," but the babel of

voices and the multiplication of claimants in the widened political arena. In this new participating democracy the need is for the creation of new political mechanisms that will allow for the establishment of priorities in the city, and for some effective bargaining and trade-offs between groups; without that the city may end in shambles [1969: 142].

Faced with this cross-fire of demands and complaints, what strategy does a mayor pursue? The natural tendency is to accommodate as many interests as possible—to use the available distribution of benefits to build political support. Consider the political economy of political support for a big-city mayor. On any given day, the mayor is likely to make decisions in which far fewer clients are satisfied than are displeased. Particularly on issues where there is a street fight with multiple contestants, as is so often the case, it is inevitable that the ratio of satisfied (or rewarded) clients to unrewarded ones will be low. In the end, this is the mayor's bottom-line calculus of political support because the mayor is fundamentally in the business of distributing and withholding service benefits. The mayor's fear, of course, is that over time the denominator of unsatisfied groups will grow so large in relationship to his/her local allies that the mayor will have lost a critical mass of political support. This is all the more so if one adds the factor that responding positively to a community group once does not settle the city hall-neighborhood relationship for all time. "What have you done for us lately" is the timeless question in urban politics, and local groups can easily move from the numerator of satisfied clients to the denominator of unsatisfied ones. Given these service pressures and this political calculus of support, the mayor's natural strategy is likely to be one of maximizing the number of service benefits that he/she dispenses to neighborhood groups. And, with an expanding service pie, it is therefore easy to see why the politics of pluralism in the cities in the 1960s led to an ever increasing level of service delivery to the mayor's numerous neighborhood constituencies. Yet even in an expanding urban public sector, the something-for-everyone strategy had its clear difficulties and limitations. For one thing, it simply was not possible to reward *all* neighborhood demands all the time—even with expanding budgets there were not enough benefits to go around. Moreover, many of the service and policy demands were conflicting if not contradictory. That is, one cannot satisfy probusing and antibusing proponents, pro-scatter site housing and anti-scatter site housing groups at the same time. More important, there were two inherent political and policy flaws in the strategy of distributing service benefits as widely as possible. First, in political terms, when city hall has honored a great many demands, especially in low-income areas, the political penalty attached to denying a service demand becomes all the greater. "If you're doing so much for all these other groups, why can't you even fix our potholes," was a refrain heard widely in the late 1960s and early 1970s. And the logic of the complaint reveals a great deal about the rising vehemence of white middle-income complaints against city halls, perceived to be giving away the store to those "other people" in low-income neighborhoods.

Second, in policy terms it is hard to see how a mayor can build a stable agenda of problems (or strategy of attention) given the number of disparate demands flooding into city hall. The natural tendency of a mayor encountering this kind of street-fighting pluralism is to become increasingly reactive, to rush from fire to fire, in short, to be caught up in a persistent pattern of crisis-hopping. in particular, the mayor is apt to respond first to the largest fire or apparent crisis as there is no other explicit guide to agenda-setting in the logic of crisis-hopping. The trouble with this reactivism is that it rewards aggressive crisismongering by community groups and encourages those groups that have not been pressing their demands as vociferously as others to escalate their rhetoric and the urgency of their cause. And this only reinforces and exacerbates the street-fighting pattern in city politics. (For example, as I discovered in New York City Hall in 1966, the best way for a community group to get a bureaucratic response to an ordinary service problem was to make an emergency call to city hall and announce that a riot was just about to break out in the neighborhood.[1])

All in all, the something-for-everyone strategy of service distribution was not one that could go on forever. The ratchet effect on spending and the crisis atmosphere that was engendered took a severe toll both on the budget and the people holding the fort in city hall.

Today, I believe that there is good reason to suspect that the relationship between the mayor and his/her neighborhood constituencies is changing and in a way that reduces the level of street-fighting pluralism. In the first place, problems of fiscal scarcity makes it obvious that mayors cannot continue to dispense service benefits in the style to which community groups may have become accustomed. Second, neighborhood groups have clearly learned the limitations of protest activity—or wearied of it—especially in a context in which rival groups escalate their own appeals to stay even with new levels of political assertion (Lipsky, 1970). Third, and perhaps most important, neighborhood groups have now had time to test the validity and limitations of their original critique of city hall—namely, that services were deficient because city bureaucracy was unresponsive, rigid, and insensitive. This is the argument for community made on the *negative* grounds that city government was not performing its essential tasks adequately. More precisely, the negative argument says that city hall should be made to respect neighborhood entities and be more responsive in the hope that a neighborhood-oriented approach would improve the functioning of city bureaucracies, increase citizen satisfaction with services, and at the same time strengthen neighborhoods as the basic building block of the urban political system. In the last decade, city halls in fact launched many new initiatives and programs to increase the responsiveness of government to neighborhood demands. Little city halls, ombudsmen, citizen advisory boards, and strategies of administrative decentralization are only a few of the attempts made to increase responsiveness and trust at the street level. For anyone viewing these experiments in responsiveness and trust-building, at least two lessons can safely be drawn. First, many of the experiments worked well (Yin and Yates, 1970) and served both to increase trust and reduce the intensity of the urban street fight. Second, many neighborhood leaders learned that more responsive behavior on the part of city hall was not sufficient to solve community problems as quickly and decisively as they had hoped. For many of the neighborhood's problems turned out to be more complex and intractable than those with a devil theory about city hall's performance had originally believed. This is particularly true for those neighborhood leaders who went beyond a negative critique of city hall's performance in neighborhood to a stronger positive argument about the potential of communities to solve their own problems if only they were left alone and given the power and resources to govern themselves. Though strong community control strategies were rarely implemented, neighborhood leaders in community school boards quickly found that the intraneighborhood conflicts and administrative hassles with the bureaucracies did not go away just because the locus of political responsibility was moved to the neighborhood. This, again, in my view, is an example of a significant learning process in the past few years in which overly simple conceptions of the city hall-neighborhood relationship have been tested and changed in the face of shared experience.

CITIZENS AS TAXPAYERS

Having just discussed the role of citizens in urban politics as members of community groups, it may seem odd to view them as another urban constituency called taxpayers. But given California's Proposition 13 and other local tax revolt movements, it seems obvious that the citizen as taxpayer is a growing force in urban policy making. The reason for this apparent schizophrenia between citizens as community group members and taxpayers lies in the fundamental disjunction between the policy arenas of service delivery (expenditures) and taxes (revenue policy). It is no surprise that many urban residents desire both better services and lower taxes. This had long been so and can be rationalized on the basis that somebody else should suffer service cuts or pay higher taxes. I believe that the new element in urban policy today is the increasing awareness that any one group cannot escape so easily from the tax-service tradeoff and that the future of the city for all its residents is jeopardized by severe fiscal imbalances.

Whether deservedly or not, New York City's struggle against bank-ruptcy has become the leading urban morality play of the decade. So the mayor now has a new increasingly powerful coalition of citizens whose policy issue is the "bottom line" of taxes and deficits and who are therefore highly alert to city hall's successes and failures in financial management. Again this constituency is not at all independent of the demand side push for services by neighborhood groups. Many people play the game both ways, but the important point is that the taxpayer constitu-ency acts *as* if it were an independent force and that, in itself, has changed the structure of demands and expectations of city government.

OTHER LOCAL GOVERNMENTS

The mayor's relationship with rival suburbs and cities in his/her en-vironment is the dog that does not bark in urban politics. Proponents of metropolitan government and regionalism have been heralding the arrival of new megacity political structures, but, in the main, progress toward government based on the concept of a metropolitan community has been feeble to say the least. The reasons for the suburb's aversion to greater coordination with the city are strong and durable, as Willis Hawley (1976) and others have persuasively shown. The advances that cities have made in resource sharing with their neighbors have come not as a result of inter-community agreements but as a result of new federal and state formulas, court decisions supporting a greater equalization of resources, and national policies, such as A-95 review which requires at least a minimum level of metropolitan cooperation and joint review of public projects. So, from the perspective of city hall, the constituency of other local governments remains an obstacle to the creation of any new political order rather than the source of new influence and maneuvering room for mayors.

URBAN BUREAUCRACIES

Historically, the mayor's greatest administrative problem may well be that of gaining any kind of executive control of his/her own service bureaucracies. Some of the structural reasons for this loose control have been noted above. It is also worth repeating the historical point that this fragmentation of administrative responsibility was a direct result and intention of the urban reform movement's attack on big-city machines. Creating independent boards and commissions and giving school and even police boards their own separate governance structure was a way of breaking up the consolidation of power (and abuse of power) that reformers discerned in machine government. The consequence for an aggressive mayor was that a large part of the mayor's policy domain was controlled by people the mayor, in turn, had little ability to control. The "good government" tradition also produced the ethos in many cities that it was bad form for a mayor to intervene very much if at all in the work of service institutions such as police and education. Political influence was assumed to be tainted, at least when juxtaposed with the ideal of service bureaucracies run by nonpolitical supposed professionals. Indeed a main source of the independence of service bureaucracies has resulted from the idea of professionalism and supposed neutral competence in service delivery. As Theodore Lowi has argued:

> The legacy of Reform is the bureaucratic city-state. Destruction of the party foundation of the mayoralty cleaned up many cities but also destroyed the capacity for sustained central, popularity-based action. This capacity, with all its faults, was replaced by the power of professionalized agencies. But this has meant creation of new bases of power. Bureaucratic agencies are not neutral: they are only independent.
>
> Modernization and Reform in New York and other cities has meant replacement of Old Machines with New Machines. The bureaucracies—that is, the professionally organized, autonomous career agencies—are the New Machines.
>
> The New Machines are machines because they are relatively irresponsible structures of power. That is, each agency shapes important public policies, yet the leadership of each is relatively self-perpetuating and not really subject to the controls of any higher authority [1967: 86].

In the last decade, I believe that the relationship between mayors and their service bureaucracies has evolved substantially, but I do not believe that the strands of evolution are at all symmetrical and consistent. One strand of evolution is that in the crisis years of the 1960s, mayors increasingly involved themselves in the offering of their service bureaucracies in order to avert racial conflicts and to answer the accusations that city hall simply was not responsive to the needs of its citizens. This strongly countered the tradition that a mayor should rarely if ever talk to his/her police commissioner (Kahn, 1978).

At the same time, the proliferation of federal programs in the last decade increased the fragmentation of executive control. But once again, these are several crosscurrents. First, many mayors invented agencies, particularly in the policy arenas of urban renewal and community action, they designed as close adjuncts of the mayor's office and over which they could execute considerable control. It turns out that for the next mayor, these in-house agencies were not as easy to control, but they were often effective instruments of entrepreneurial policy for the mayors that built them in the first place (Murphy, 1971).[2]

Second, the decline in federal intervention in recent years has lead to a contraction in the number of agencies that were once being built around the mayor at a helter-skelter pace.

Third, one consequence of general revenue-sharing is to give greater managerial control over urban policy to the mayor, and this has forced the bureaucracies to look to the mayor for resource allocation decisions more than in the past.

All this has to be weighed against the persistent ability of service bureaucracies to forge independent relationships with both street-level clients and, more especially, with state and federal officials who monitor and evaluate urban programs. This intergovernmental bureaucratic connection is a critical source of power for urban bureaucrats and provides urban bureaucracies with a certain amount of autonomy from city hall as long as grantsmanship and professional networks have any force in urban government. On balance, these strands of evolution would suggest that mayors have gained slightly in their struggle to exercise executive control over urban administration. But the critical variable in this equation almost certainly rests with state and federal governments and with the character of their relationships with local service bureaucrats.

HIGHER LEVEL GOVERNMENTS

Ten years ago it was far easier to analyze the role and impact of the federal government in urban affairs. The grants-in-aid process provided a powerful resource for the entrepreneurial mayor, as we have seen above. Also, as noted, Washington's innovations in the policy arena of antipoverty programs produced a great proliferation and fragmentation of social welfare bureaucracies. All the while, the federal-urban relationship stimulated a strong professional connection between specialists in Washington and the cities which led in the direction of a vertical fragmentation of authority in which the specialists in welfare, education, or renewal became a relatively self-contained administrative structure for their particular policy domain. Terry Sanford (1967) described this system vividly as "picket-fence federalism" to underscore the importance of these vertically connected and increasingly independent policy subgovernments. The consequences for the mayor was that his/her own service bureaucracies had a leverage over grants, revenues, evaluations, and reports and were entrenched in a series of national and state professional networks in a way that tended to insulate many policy issues from the scrutiny and control of city hall. According to Richard Nathan (1975), Richard Nixon sought to break the stranglehold that he believed the various professional subgovernments held over social policy by pressing for New Federalism strategies which would supposedly give greater control over resources (namely, general revenue-sharing monies) to the mayors.

The effects of New Federalism are as yet not perfectly understood—in part because the experience with revenue-sharing is both new and varied. Nevertheless, there is now enough knowledge and analysis of the New Federalism to say that its effects are ambiguous—especially for the mayor. On the one hand, there is little doubt that general revenue-sharing has given mayors a stronger grip over policy making in that arena. At the same time, revenue-sharing still represents only a small percentage of all federal grants, and therefore the realm of categorical grants in which the intergovernmental policy subgovernments can operate and dominate remains large. In addition, the feds have not exactly adhered to the hands-off administrative policy which many advocates of New Federalism envisioned. Rather, federal bureaucracies have engaged in an intricate game of policy making by guideline and regulation—such that the rules of New Federalism are constantly shifting. This kind of erratic and uncertain policy making subverts the imagined discretion and greater authority of the mayor because it makes the local service bureaucrats indispensable once again as the decoders of federal guidelines and the proprietors of needed professional networks of communication about what cities can and cannot do with revenue-sharing monies (Kettl, 1978).

A cautious conclusion about the effect of New Federalism to date would be that the strategy has given mayors slightly more discretion and authority but has by no means broken the back of the federal-urban policy subgovernments. Even this conclusion has to be qualified because, in one important respect, the mayor's position has, in fact, been made more difficult by revenue-sharing programs. That is, in the heyday of the entrepreneur such as Richard Lee, the mayor could pick his target of opportunity in the federal grant storehouse of available funds, write a winning grant, and "bring home the bacon" as if he/she and his/her city were the winners of some esoteric contest. More precisely, the mayor could develop a set of priorities in his/her grantsman strategies and then take clear political credit for whatever federal resources the mayor could garner. If the mayor opted for a renewal program, he/she could not be attacked by day-care center advocates because it was clear the mayor's grant victory was for renewal not day-care. Revenue-sharing, however, puts a large realm of policy decisions up for grabs and in giving mayors a certain amount of new resources also exposes them to demands from all sides. The mayor is now responsible in the policy arena of revenue-sharing for making difficult tradeoffs between different kinds of service demands, and the mayor no longer has much ability to hide behind the specifications of federal grants in explaining why he/she can do x with federal money but not y. This means that the dramatic victories available to mayors under the old grantsmanship system are harder to come by, and at the same time there are more groups that feel rightfully entitled to a share of the new revenue-sharing money (that the mayor can take no credit for attracting in the first place).

PUBLIC EMPLOYEE UNIONS

The 1960s undoubtedly represented the high-water mark of the power and growth of public employee unions. As urban services expanded, so did the need for street-level bureaucrats—in policy, fire, education, and wel- fare—to deliver them. More important, as Wellington and Winter (1971) have persuasively argued, the discipline that attaches inherently to demands for salary increases in the private sector does not apply in the same way in the public sector. Wellington and Winter point up the classic tradeoff between salary increases and layoffs in the private sector. If a company cannot afford to pay x workers an increased amount, they can solve their problem by reducing their work force. But, in the public sector, in an environment of expanding services, the tradeoff exists faintly if at all. Unions therefore could try to have it both ways and very often did. If they were frustrated at the bargaining table, they could strike, and recent urban history has demonstrated, if nothing else, how feeble antistrike laws are in preventing walkouts by public unions. The problems for the 1960s mayor in dealing with his/her unions were, in fact, even worse than this. For if the unions went on strike and basic services were interrupted, citizen pressure was quickly exerted on the mayor to get the city running again. This citizen pressure may have only provided an unwitting con- stituency for union demands, but it surely made it all the harder for a mayor to resist union demands while the garbage piled up and the buses or subways sat idle.

Add to this the factor that public service employees and their families and their friends constitute a significant fraction of the urban electorate (Lowi, 1967) and it is easy to see why mayors have had such difficulty controlling public union demands. Finally, add in the factor that a mayor is, in the end, held responsible for the delivery of ordinary services, and a mayor who cannot manage to even pick up the garbage or field a police force does not greatly endear him/herself to the service-demanding constituencies. The onset of fiscal scarcity has by now changed the prior relationship between the mayor and his public employee unions in a significant way. That is, cities are now being forced to layoff municipal employees (or at least achieve smaller staffs through attrition), and that greatly firms up the tradeoff between salary demands and levels of employment. In addition, the rapid growth of the urban public sector could hardly have kept growing at the rapid rates experienced in the 1960s. As one analyst has commented (Stanfield, 1976), the "slowdown" in public sector growth has many causes: public school enrollment has declined; municipal, county, and state salaries have caught up with the private sector, and the enormous expansion of federal aid over the past two decades has peaked now and is leveling off. This slowdown reinforces the realization among union officials that they can no longer expect to preside over everexpanding and, in that sense, more powerful unions. Along with the impact of fiscal scarcity, this largely changes the comparative political advantage that public unions have come to enjoy. This is not to say by any means that public unions have lost all their political power, but it is no longer the case that unions have mayors at their mercy as they seemed to five years ago. In addition, fiscal scarcity has made the citizen as taxpayer more aware of which groups are causing more expenditures and possibly deficits; and my suspicion is that this awareness makes it considerably harder for unions to pressure city hall by resorting to strikes and withholding public services. In short, public unions have lost or blunted some of their political weapons and mayors have gained some weapons—namely the threat of budget-balancing layoffs. And this means that in this urban policy arena, mayors are in a substantially stronger position than they were several years ago.

THE PRESS

The urban press corps plays a special role in urban politics because it has a great deal to do with what is placed on the mayor's agenda and in determining what are or *appear* to be the critical problems in urban government. As Lipsky (1970) has shown, in the 1960s the print and television media provided an important resource for protesting community groups in that they gave these groups coverage and this provided a broad hearing and perhaps even legitimacy to the complaints of the various community groups. Also, at the high point of the so-called urban crisis, the press played a crucial part in shaping the crisis-hopping response of mayors by presenting the occupants of city hall with one horror story or disaster after another and then asking the mayor on film or radio what he/she was going to do about it. Given this potential for embarrassment, it is not surprising that mayors often felt they had no choice but to direct their crisis management to the problems that were put to them and in this way dramatized by the press.

In the aftermath of the protest era, the role of the press in urban politics has substantially changed—but again not in a one-dimensional fashion. On the one hand, many local newspapers and television stations have recently engaged in a burst of obsessive fascination with crimes and fires—reminiscent of a more primitive nineteenth-century police gazette tradition of journalism. A new twist on the gazette tradition is the attraction to fires on the evening news—presumably because arson and fires contain action and are visually exciting, certainly more visually interesting than a community school board meeting. Still, there is something almost pathetic about this approach to action news, and the mayor hardly benefits from the perception that some portion of the city is burning down every night—with all the physical destruction and human suffering that fires entail. In this sense, I believe that the press, for its own reasons, is reinforcing the doomsday prophecies that cities are collapsing—literally in flames.

On the other hand, the press has also paid meticulous attention of late to the fiscal problems of city governments, and this kind of coverage provides the mayor with a powerful source of education and concern directed to the city's problems of financial management. The mayor may not always look good in this type of coverage, but it is plain that the fiscal issue has been broadcast loud and clear throughout urban communities. The obvious losers in this evolution of press attention are the community groups who could once command considerable threat by demonstrating in their neighborhoods or marching on city hall. The consequence, I believe, is a lessening of political of pressure from and power in the neighborhoods and an increase in the pressure to do something about budgets and taxes. (What the mayor is supposed to do about suspicious fires is beyond me. Perhaps Fiorello LaGuardia had the right idea for the 1970s media when in the 1930s he rode fire engines to dramatize his concern with the everyday problems of his constituencies.)

BUSINESS

There is no more controversial topic in urban political analysis than the role and power of business in the governance of cities. This, of course, was the subject of one of the liveliest scholarly debates in political science in the last 20 years—the community power debate (Polsby, 1964). I certainly do not intend to delve into that debate in any detail here. All I wish to do is present several of the main models of the relationship between the public and the private sectors and see how these models now square with present urban patterns, affected as they are by the pervasive concern with fiscal problems.

For Floyd Hunter (1953) in his Atlanta study, the role of business was both easily discernible and dominant. Business per se may not have run everything; there were some other social sources of "clout." But looking at power relations among various groups in the city, there is no doubt that Hunter assigns business in Atlanta a position of dominance in the city's power structure.

In his northern counterargument, Robert Dahl (1961) has difficulty finding the footprints of businessmen in city hall. Rather, the policy arenas he examines are occupied by professional politicians and bureaucrats, citizen groups, and other largely public actors. Even in the policy arena of urban renewal, business is noticeably silent or absent. The mayor is the prime mover, and the other major players are the feds and the local planning bureaucracy. Richard Lee is described there and elsewhere as having to drag businessmen kicking and screaming into any public involvement with his renewal programs. Incidentally, this squares with Mayor Robert Wagner's recollection of the difficulties he had engaging business interest in urban affairs in the 1950s and early 1960s in New York City.

This is not to say that, in this view, business is invisible. It is to say that business is viewed as tending to its own affairs and trying to avoid entanglement with the public sector. I would call this the "two spheres" conception model of the public-private relationship and liken it to the imagined relationship between the church and state in this country and in certain other Western democracies.

One reason to take the two spheres model seriously is that in the 1960s there was a severe disjunction between the beliefs and purposes of public and private managers. That is, in the generally antibusiness climate of the 1960s, urban officials, engaged in a war on poverty, often viewed businessmen as the enemy: mercenary, conservative opponents of activist urban programs and a large part of the problem themselves. On the other hand, many businessmen felt that their concern for the prudent management of public programs was ignored and that there was little if any appreciation in city hall of the importance of business activity to the city's political economy.

In his Chicago writings, Edward Banfield (1961) offers yet a third model of the public-private relationship which I will term the model of "proprietary interest." In Banfield's version, in those areas in which business interests were directly and tangibly affected, such as planning for a downtown renewal project and a convention center, business interests were strongly represented. But in other decisions which did not involve economic development or real estate packages, the voice of business was not particularly evident. On this model of public-private relationships, business will act strongly to protect its proprietary interest in the arenas of economic and downtown development, tax policy, and budget deficits.

Whatever merits these three models of business-government interaction may have had in the past, I have no ability here to adjudicate confidently among the competing claims. Sometimes, one is tempted to say that the main difference between Hunter and Dahl is the difference between the old South and the immigrant North, but then one encounters a case such as Pittsburgh in which the power of business has been widely and often positively noted. The important point, I think, is that the rise of fiscal problems as a central urban issue has substantially changed the relationship between business and city hall in politics.

In terms of the three models described above, I would suspect that the two spheres model in which both public and private sectors operate in separate world is in decline. The importance of jobs and tax revenue is by now sufficiently important to city hall to cause an activist, hospitable attitude in city hall determined to keep its industries from leaving town; and businessmen, in turn, now know their calls to the mayor will be answered. Equally, the increased salience of the issue of jobs and taxes gives business increased leverage in the framework of the proprietary interest model. On this account, we would expect business and government to pay increased attention to strategies of economic development, and indeed we see this evolution occurring in most large American cities.

In terms of the third model, that of business dominance, we may be seeing some evolution in that direction but, in my view, not for the reasons that Hunter envisioned. I believe that cities will increasingly look to business management techniques for new approaches to their financial and administrative problems (Rogers, 1978). Equally, to the extent that cities incur serious budgetary deficits, the power of the municipal board experts and accountants will increase tremendously (if New York City is any guide). Finally, to the extent that cities are experiencing hard times financially, cities will increase their sensitivity to problems of business confidence and related issues of what government can do for (and can do to keep) business within city limits.

All of this represents a considerable flow of power toward the private sector, at least in comparison to the 1960s. But it does not entail a vision of city government run directly or indirectly by businessmen with the concern of the private sector given highest priority. Rather, I am talking about a pattern of conciliation and "boostering" in city hall that gives the private sector far more influence than it held at the height of street-fighting pluralism with its strong neighborhood service delivery orientation.

THE MAYOR'S "FRIENDS AND ENEMIES": THREE URBAN POLITICAL COALITIONS

So far I have argued that the mayor's difficulty in governing the city stems in the first place from the fragmentation and street-fighting pluralism of urban politics, and that these patterns are themselves shaped by the city's basic task of delivering daily services to diverse individuals, blocks, and neighborhoods. The next step in the analysis was to see if we go beyond the general picture of multidimensional conflict and specify the mayor's relationships with his major constituencies. This analysis suggests that the mayor is indeed dealing with very different policy arenas and that his/her governance problems and degree of management and policy control vary greatly from one policy arena to another. Also in considering the evolution of the different arenas, I have noted—though only in a tentative way—that there are signs, especially in the neighborhood policy arena, that the street fights over services have somewhat moderated and that there are signs in other arenas (especially in terms of urban bureaucrats and public unions) that the mayor's position is stronger now then it was 10 years ago.

I believe we can usefully carry this analysis of the mayor's governance problem one step further by considering what linkages if any may exist between the different players and arenas and what effect these relationships may have on urban policy making. My argument is that there are indeed three discernible political coalitions in the mayor's eight-ring circus and that these coalitions have had a dramatic impact on the demand for and supply of urban services in the city. One coalition is in the business of demanding ever more services; a second is in the business of controlling the delivery of services; and the third is in the business of advocating strong financial controls over spending along with reduced taxes. Two of these coalitions are inadvertent in the sense that the players do not consciously work together; the third coalition is intentional and professional in its organization. Let me now be somewhat more precise about the political and policy characteristics of the three coalitions.

The first coalition, the "service-demanding" coalition, consists of neighborhood groups, urban bureaucrats, public unions, and until recently the press. Now it is perfectly true that these groups fight intensely among themselves, but they are united in their common assault on city hall for more services. The neighborhoods demand more services because that is their initial conception of what responsiveness in government means. The urban bureaucracies demand more services because various professional cadres seek to extend their domanins in service delivery; and public unions fight for more services because more services means more jobs. The important point is that this service-demanding coalition represented in the 1960s an overwhelming massing of political pressure and, although many mayors were willing victims in adopting a something-for-everyone strategy, they were surely faced with a formidable coalition demanding higher levels of services.

If the mayor has faced a dominating coalition on the *service*-demand side for services, so also has the mayor encountered a dominating coalition on the supply side. That coalition was explicitly forged between city, state, and federal bureaucrats in the exercise of "professional" control over the regulations, guidelines, and other decisions that govern the local allocation of services.

The upshot of this analysis is that not only did the mayor face an overwhelming coalition for more services on the demand side but he/she also faced a domineering coalition of service professionals on the supply side at all levels of government.

The third political coalition in city government is more recent in its emergence and salience but no less powerful for being so. It combines business, citizens as taxpayers, and the press (in a new orientation) sharing a dominant concern for financial management, control of taxes and spending, and economic development.

If we look at the workings of these coalitions 5 or 10 years ago, we find the mayor in an isolated if not captured position. The service-demanding coalition worked to drive up service and spending levels and the coalition of professional bureaucrats operated to control the substance and detail of service delivery in a way that was largely independent of the control and authority of city hall. The simple point is that, on this account, the mayor was faced with coalitions that blocked strong central control by the mayor in the most fundamental arena of urban policy. The rise of the financial management coalition provides an opposition to these forces, and it is with this new balance of power between the three coalitions that we can begin to think of a new urban policy package and a set of coalitions that would both address the city's main policy problems and provide support for a mayor with a new strategy of governance.

A THREE-PART STRATEGY
OF GOVERNANCE

THE CONNECTION BETWEEN POLICY AND POLITICAL SUPPORT

In considering how a mayor might develop a new political order and a regime capable of governing and attracting political support, let us remember first the three central policy problems that a mayor faces in his/her effort to govern the ungovernable city.

The first structural and policy problem is that city government is too centralized to respond as subtly and sensitively as it might to local demands. This calls for a neighborhood policy in which decentralized policy making is given greater emphasis.

The second structural problem is that of inadequate centralization in the sense that city hall has had only weak control of its budgets and service-delivery strategies.

The third structural problem is that of overload, resulting from the tendency of higher level governments to repeatedly dump operating responsibilities on city hall. Here the need is for a mayor to remove some of this pressure and overload so as to make cities more manageable and governable.

THE LOGIC OF A NEW STRATEGY OF GOVERNANCE

Having considered these policy problems and the background of political influence and conflict in cities, what can a mayor do to develop a viable regime both in terms of policy initiatives and political support?

On the policy side, my argument is that mayors should stress neighborhood decision making, emphasize stronger financial management in city hall, and at the same time attempt to get higher level governments to assume more of the operating burden in service delivery.

Imagine, then, a mayor's policy program which stresses strategies of neighborhood government, stronger management and financial control at the center, and seeks to turn various service functions over to higher level governments. I believe—and it can only be a surmise—that this is sound urban policy, but it also has interesting political implications—in the sense of attracting the political support necessary to govern effectively in the urban polity.

The negative version of this argument is that a strategy of this sort would prevent a mayor from being captured by the service-demanding and professional-control coalitions because it would be offset by the financial-management coalition. Viewed more positively, the combination of neighborhood, financial management, and transfer (to higher level government) strategies is even more appealing in both political and policy terms.

In the first place, if neighborhoods and these local bureaucrats could be brought into a stronger partnership, this would both reduce street-fighting pluralism and increase, in my view, the responsiveness of street-level service delivery. It would also tend to break up the implicit coalition of neighborhoods, bureaucracies, and public unions. For a neighborhood strategy does not entail in any obvious way an increase in the number of policemen, teachers, or social workers. The neighborhoods' strategy will often be one of using existing resources in different ways and developing new administrative mechanisms to increase trust and responsiveness (Yin and Yates, 1970). In any case, the mounting of a decentralized neighborhood strategy may well increase community support for a mayor and reduce street-fighting pluralism in the sense that neighborhoods would play a stronger role in setting their own service priorities and resolving their conflicts, and therefore the panoply of disputes between and within neighborhoods would not automatically be directed to city hall.

The strategy of improved financial management and policy coordination in city hall would meet obvious needs in urban government and at the same time rally the support of the financial-control constituency.

Finally, the strategy of urging higher level governments to assume greater direct responsibility for some urban functioning (either through direct state control or federal "banking"—income transfers—would presumably reduce the current overload on city hall produced by the steady increase in its duties as the operating agent of the American intergovernmental system. Also, to the extent that higher level governments assume independent financial and/or administrative responsibility for more urban programs, the professional coalition between federal and local bureaucrats would be weakened if not broken, and the mayor would have a greater chance to be the master-manager of services in his/her own house.

In sum, I believe that the three-part strategy I have sketched above has six significant advantages, in *both* political and policy terms. First, the strategies do speak to the most pressing current policy problems in urban government. Second, also in policy terms, the neighborhood, financial, and intergovernmental strategies are not incompatible. Indeed, they are consistent in one crucial sense (which is the third policy advantage); that is, taken together, the strategies do seek to reduce the demands and pressures on city hall and to reduce the level of street-fighting pluralism in the city. And to the extent that they should, in fact, achieve these objectives, the mayors would find themselves in a far less reactive posture and might be able to perform more effectively as the central coordinators, evaluators, and agenda setters in city government. Fourth, in political terms, the three strategies do work to reduce the once-dominating grip of the service-demanding coalition and the professional service-control coalition, and that should greatly increase the mayor's ability to act as a chief executive in the service delivery arena. Fifth, the strategies offer the mayor at least the prospect of political support for his/her policies—namely, community support for a neighborhood policy and business and taxpayer support for the strategy of stronger financial management. Sixth, the two coalitions which might increasingly support a mayor on this strategy themselves represent a health balance of power between a concern for better services and a concern for budget and tax control.

Finally, I should cheerfully confess that to make this strategy persuasive, I would have to say far more, in detail, about the particular strategies involved. And I should make very clear what implications these strategies have for the basic conception of the city's tasks and aspirations in the future. Put very simply, the three strategies constitute a formula for a more manageable, less ambitious urban regime and one that might better hold together politically and also deliver its services more effectively. This is not a dimple endorsement of the less-is-more credo, but it does focus city hall's attention on the delivery of basic services. Also, it emphasizes political and administrative means for improving the governance of cities, not financial ones. That is, the strategy is based squarely on the premise that there is a great deal that a mayor can do in developing decentralized neighborhood strategies for improved service delivery and in increasing financial control and service coordination at the center in city hall (without spending a lot of money). The tougher problem is how to get higher level governments to relieve the current administrative burden on cities. President Carter has, of course, enunciated a new national urban policy, but that is a different story.

NOTES

1. In this case, the problem involved nothing more than the location of a street play; but, as one of the only people available in city hall on Friday afternoon, I was nevertheless dispatched to the scene of the supposed impending riot.

2. Ironically, when the current New Haven mayor, Frank Logue, took office, one of the first problems he faced was that of trying to assert mayoral control over a now quite independent Community Progress, Inc., which was opposed to the mayor and his policies.

REFERENCES

BANFIELD, E. (1968) The Unheavenly City. Boston: Little, Brown.
——— (1961) Political Influence. New York: Free Press.
BELL, D. and V. HELD (1969) "The community revolution." Public Interest 16: 142-177.
DAHL, R. A. (1961) Who Governs? New Haven: Yale University Press.
HAWLEY, W. (1976) "On understanding metropolitan political integration," pp. 100-145 in W. Hawley et al. (eds.) Theoretical Perspectives on Urban Politics. Englewood Cliffs, NJ: Prentice-Hall.
HUNTER, F. (1953) Community Power Structure. Chapel Hill: University of North Carolina Press.
KAHN, R. C. (1978) "Political change and police accountability politics." Presented at the Annual Meeting of the Midwest Political Science Association, April.
KETTL, D. (1978) "Managing community development in the new federalism." Ph.D. dissertation, Yale University. (unpublished)
LIPSKY, M. (1976) "Toward a theory of street-level bureaucracy," pp. 196-213 in W. Hawley et al. (eds.) Theoretical Perspectives on Urban Politics. Englewood Cliffs, NJ: Prentice-Hall.
——— (1970) Protest in City Politics. Chicago: Rand McNally.
LOWI, T. (1967) "Machine politics—old and new." Public Interest 9: 83-92.
MURPHY, R. (1971) Political Entrepreneurs and Urban Poverty. Lexington, MA: D. C. Heath.
NATHAN, R. (1975) The Plot That failed: Nixon and the Administrative Presidency. New York: John Wiley.
POLSBY, N. (1964) Community Power and Political Theory. New Haven, CT: Yale University Press.
ROGERS, D. (1978) Can business Management Save the Cities? New York: Free Press.
SANFORD, T. (1967) Storm Over the States. New York: McGraw-Hill.
SAYRE, W. and H. Kaufman (1965) Governing New York City. New York: Russell Sage Foundation.
STANFIELD, R. (1976) "State and local governments struggle to make ends meet." National Journal (September 18): 1318.

WELLINGTON, H. and R. WINTER (1971) Unions and the Cities. Washington, DC: Brookings Institution.

WILSON, J. Q. (1968) Varieties of Police Behavior. Cambridge, MA: Harvard University Press.

––– (1962) The Amateur Democrat. Chicago: University of Chicago Press.

WOLFINGER, R. (1974) The Politics of Progress. Englewood Cliffs, NJ: Prentice-Hall.

YATES, D. (1977) The Ungovernable City. Cambridge: MIT Press.

YIN, R. and D. YATES (1970) Street-Level Governments. Lexington, MA: D. C. Heath.

2

CARTER, CONGRESS, AND THE CITIES

DEMETRIOS CARALEY

Barnard College
Columbia University

The explanation often given for the modest nature of the Carter administration's urban aid policy announced in March of 1978 was that a more aggressive and expensive one would have been unsupportable politically in Congress. Then HEW Secretary Joseph Califano reportedly argued to President Carter while the administration's urban policy statement was being formulated that because most members of Congress did not come from large cities, a policy that favored those cities would "[fly] in the face of political reality" and meet with congressional rejection (Rosenbaum, 1978: 15).

The Califano argument and, in so far as it was based on it, the Carter urban policy reflected a minor and a major fallacy: The minor fallacy was that members of Congress are compelled to vote their constituencies' characteristics—such as whether those constituencies are predominantly urban (that is, central city) or suburban or rural—and that presumably only those members from urban, or large-city, constituencies can support

Author's Note: *I thank Ralph Nunes and Susan Olds for assistance in the research on which this chapter is based; Mary Ann Epstein for editorial assistance; the Barnard College Faculty Research Fund for a grant to help defray the costs of research assistance; and Columbia University's new Center for the Social Sciences for computing facilities and the services of consultants.*

strong urban programs. The major fallacy was that the 95th Congress was not a pro-urban Congress and that it would refuse to support important urban initiatives.

With respect to the minor fallacy, numerous political science studies over the years have shown that the party affiliation of a member of Congress has almost always been more predictive of the nature of his or her vote than the nature of that member's constituency (see, e.g., Clausen, 1973; Mayhew, 1966; Shannon, 1968; Truman, 1959; Turner, 1970). Specifically with respect to congressional voting on urban aid programs, I (Caraley, 1976) have shown that from 1945 to 1975 Democratic members of Congress supported urban aid programs strongly, regardless of the urban, suburban, or rural character of their constituencies, and Republican members did not, again regardless of the type of constituency they were representing.

Concerning the major fallacy, even an impressionistic awareness of the 95th Congress's voting on various urban-oriented aid programs in 1977 should have indicated that this Congress was potentially a pro-urban Congress. For when faced with numerous pro-urban or anti-urban choices in floor votes, majorities in the House and Senate almost always voted the pro-urban position.

This essay reports findings from a systematic analysis of congressional voting on urban aid proposals during the first, or 1977, session of the 95th Congress. The analysis tries to account for differences in urban support provided by members of the House and Senate in terms of their party affiliations, the urban character of their constituencies, and the sectional and regional location of their districts or states. After this analysis, there is discussion of the key fiscal, "delivery-system," and political considerations that I believe will shape the prospects for urban aid in the years ahead. This essay should be considered an interim report on a broader, ongoing study of congressional behavior on urban issues.

CONGRESSIONAL DIFFERENCES
IN URBAN SUPPORT

Although in 1977 the Carter administration never did announce any "urban program" or "urban policy" as such, it did submit proposals to Congress for the continuation and expansion of eight aid programs that had a significant impact on large cities: public works jobs, public services jobs, countercyclical assistance, community development block grants, subsidized housing, food stamps, legal services for the poor, and welfare. The administration also asked for the adoption of a new program for training and employment of young workers aged 16 to 23. This set of 1977 proposals could be considered as President Carter's first-stage, or implicit, urban policy as opposed to the explicit urban policy he announced in the spring of 1978. Congress acted favorably on all the 1977 proposals except the one for welfare reform. That proposal was submitted late in the session in August, called for a complete overhaul of how to spend approximately $30 billion a year, and, in any event, its quick adoption was never pressed. As part of an "economic stimulus" package Congress did approve were: a doubling of the public works jobs grants to local and state governments for fiscal 1977, from $2 to $4 billion, plus another $2 billion for fiscal 1978 that could be committed immediately; an additional $7.99 billion for grants to local governments to raise the number of CETA public service jobs from 310,000 to 600,000 in fiscal 1977 and to 725,000 in fiscal 1978; an extension of the countercyclical assistance program of grants to local and state governments with an additional $632.5 million in grants for fiscal 1977 and up to $2.25 billion for fiscal 1978; and a $1 billion spending level for fiscal 1977 for the new youth employment and training program.

Congress also approved in 1977 a three-year extension of the Housing and Community Development Act of 1974 (HCDA), increased the authorization level for formula-generated community development block grants to local governments to $11.25 billion for the three years, added an alternate entitlement formula that worked to the advantage of the older cities of the Northeast and Midwest, and added a $400 million a year authorization for nonformula, discretionary "action grants" reserved exclusively for "distressed cities." Finally, Congress in 1977 authorized an additional $378 million in fiscal 1977 for housing assistance payments to low-income persons, extended the period for which housing assistance contracts could be made from 20 to 30 years, and increased the authorization for public housing operating subsidies by $19.6 million; extended the food stamp program for four years and eliminated the requirement that recipients pay cash for part of the value of their stamps; and extended for three years the authorization for the legal services corporation to fund neighborhood legal services for the poor and raised the funding level previously authorized.

METHODOLOGY

In the process of approving the set of programs just described, 35 recorded votes were taken in the House and 24 in the Senate. This included votes both on final passage and adoption of conference reports and on amendments at intermediate stages of floor consideration. It is these 59 votes that form the basic data base for the analysis in this section of the essay.[1] The position of each representative and senator was recorded as were constituency characteristics and the section and region of the country in which the representative's or senator's district or state was located. "Urban support scores" were then generated for each representative and senator based on the percentage of votes on which he/she took the pro-urban position. This pro-urban position was considered to be (1) on the question of having or not having an urban program, to have the program; (2) on the question of having higher or lower funding or having longer term or shorter term authorization, to have the higher funding or the longer term authorization; and (3) on the question of different allocation or eligibility formulas, to have the formula that would tend more to "target" funds to so-called hardship cities (those larger and older cities primarily in the East and Midwest with the most serious social and economic problems) rather than to "spread" those funds among local governments more generally and to make it more, rather than less, easy to qualify as a recipient of individual benefits, such as food stamps. Once these individual urban support scores were established, average urban support scores were developed for members from different parties, types of constituency, sections, and regions. The average support scores were then compared and also subjected to formal analysis of variance in order to find the relative impact of party, constituency, section, and region. In addition to generating and comparing urban support scores, each recorded vote was cross-tabulated by party, section, and region. The percentage of support for the pro-urban position on that vote was thus established for each party, section, and region in general and for different sections and regions within each party.

THE PRO-URBAN 1977 SESSION

Evidence for the assertion that the 95th Congress was in 1977 a pro-urban Congress is that on 30 of 35 (or 86%) of the votes in the House and on 21 of 24 (or 88%) of the votes in the Senate, the pro-urban position prevailed. The contribution to these pro-urban victories varied sharply, however, according to party. In the House, majorities of the Democrats who voted supported the pro-urban position on 33 of 35 (or 94%) of the votes, whereas majorities of the Republicans supported the pro-urban position on 10 votes, or 29% of the time. Similarly in the Senate, majorities of voting Democrats were in favor of the pro-urban position on 23 of 24 (or 96%) of the votes, whereas the Republicans gave such majority support on only 10 (or 42%) of the opportunities afforded to them (see Figure 1).

Figure 1 Percentage of Votes with Majorities in
Support of Prourban Position, 1977

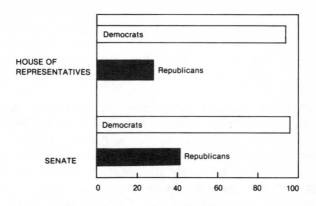

Two more indicators of the much greater support for urban programs given by the Democrats than by the Republicans are the average percentage from each party who supported the pro-urban position over all the votes and the average "urban support scores" for the members of each party.

	House	*Senate*
Average percentage supporting pro-urban position on floor votes		
Democrats	82	80
Republicans	39	52
Average urban support scores (in percentage)		
Democrats	80	77
Republicans	44	54

Thus all indicators make clear that in 1977 the Democrats continued to be the pro-urban, and the Republicans the anti-urban, party in Congress.

PARTY VERSUS CONSTITUENCY

The following breakdown should make clear that the difference in urban support provided by the Democrats and Republicans was not a

simple reflection of the members of each party representing different
kinds of constituencies.[2]

House (68%)	Urban	Suburban	Rural	Chamber
Democrats	86% (84)	83% (85)	70% (73)	80% (291)
Republicans	40% (19)	46% (53)	40% (48)	44% (144)

As can be seen, for every kind of constituency the score for the Democrats
is about twice as high as for the Republicans. Moreover, the difference in
the scores between the most urban (that is, the central city) and least
urban (that is, the rural) constituencies was only about one-third to
one-half the difference between the Democrats and Republicans from the
same kind of constituency. One further way to appreciate the predomi-
nant impact of party is to note that the score for *rural* Democrats
(including rural *southern* Democrats) was almost twice as high as for *urban*
Republicans.

When House urban support scores for central city representatives are
further broken down by size of the central city, we have the following
array.

Central City Districts (78%)

City size	Democrats	Republicans
50,000-99,999	85% (4)	56% (1)
100,000-249,999	81% (3)	35% (3)
250,000-499,999	81% (22)	40% (5)
500,000-999,999	82% (19)	39% (5)
1,000,000 and over	92% (36)	30% (3)

The scores show that for Republican House members, size of city was, if
anything, negatively correlated with urban support, and that for the
Democrats those members representing cities of 1 million in population or
larger had somewhat higher scores than those who represented smaller
cities. The dramatic differences were thus not between representatives
from different size cities but once again between parties: For cities of any
population size, Democrats had two to three times higher urban support
scores than did Republicans. Furthermore, Democrats even from the
smallest central cities of 50,000 to 99,999 had support scores almost three
times as high as Republicans from the largest central cities of over 1
million.

In the Senate, too, a breakdown of individual urban support scores by party and type of constituency shows that the more pro-urban position of Democratic senators was not a function of their coming from "more urban" states.[3]

Senate (68%)

	More uban states (largest city 250,000 or over)	Less urban state (largest city under 250,000)	All states
Democrats	76% (34)	77% (28)	77% (62)
Republicans	66% (18)	43% (20	54% (38)

First, Democratic senators had essentially the same score regardless of the size of their state's largest city and, second, this score was higher than that of the Republican senators from either category of states. Thus, in a pattern similar to that found in the House, even Democratic senators from the "less urban" states had a higher score than Republican senators from the "more urban" states. Among the Republicans, however, senators from the more urban states did have an average urban support score 23 points higher than those from the less urban states—a very substantial point spread, as large as that between all Democratic and all Republican senators.[4]

SECTION VERSUS PARTY: AN EMERGING SNOWBELT-SUNBELT SPLIT?

The 1977 urban support scores also allowed analysis of whether a new sectional politics, splitting a purportedly bipartisan, pro-urban "snowbelt" against a bipartisan, anti-urban "sunbelt" is superimposing itself on and overriding the traditional voting cleavages in Congress. If such a snowbelt versus sunbelt sectional cleavage were to become dominant, combined majorities of Democrats and Republicans from the East and Midwest would presumably be opposing combined majorities of Democrats and Republicans from the South and West.[5] And they would be doing so more consistently than Democrats would be opposing Republicans or than Republicans and southern Democrats would be opposing northern Democrats—these being the traditional party and "conservative coalition" voting splits. Considerable discussion of the possible emergence of sectionalism took place in 1977 both on the floor of Congress and in the media, especially after a dramatic House urban vote pitted an almost completely unified snowbelt coalition of eastern and midwestern representatives against a less completely unified but still highly cohesive sunbelt coalition of westerners and southerners.

A breakdown of the scores of House and Senate members according to the snowbelt or sunbelt location of their districts and states but without regard to party shows that in both chambers, the snowbelt did give higher support to urban programs than did the sunbelt.

	House	Senate
All Snowbelt	74% (238)	81% (48)
All Sunbelt	61% (197)	56% (52)

This in itself, however, proves only that the snowbelt and the sunbelt differed significantly on urban voting, especially in the Senate, but not that they had become more salient as voting groups than the parties. One test of this last point is whether the difference between the average support scores of the two sectional groupings was larger than between the parties. The following is a breakdown of the scores according to party.

	House	Senate
Democrats	80% (291)	77% (62)
Republicans	44% (144)	54% (38)

It turns out that in the House, the difference between all Democrats and all Republicans (a point spread of 36) was almost three times as large as between the snowbelt and sunbelt sectional groupings (a point spread of 13). In the Senate, on the other hand, the difference between all snowbelt and all sunbelt senators was slightly *larger* than between all Democrats and all Republican senators (a point spread of 25 versus 23).[6]

A second test of the relative impact of party and section is whether the snowbelt coalition had replaced the Democratic membership as the most pro-urban grouping in Congress and whether the sunbelt coalition had replaced the Republicans as the least pro-urban. Once again the results between the two chambers differed. In the House the Democrats had a higher urban support score than the snowbelters (80% versus 74%) and the Republicans had a lower score than the sunbelt coalition (44% versus 61%). In the Senate, whereas the snowbelt senators did have a slightly higher score than the Democrats (81% versus 77%), the Republicans still had a lower score than the sunbelt senators (54% versus 56%).

A third test of relative impact was to compare the average cleavage (that is, the percentage voting pro-urban in one grouping minus the percentage voting pro-urban in the other grouping) between the Democratic and Republican party memberships and between the snowbelt and sunbelt coalitions on the floor votes. As measured over the 35 House and 24 Senate votes, the average cleavages were as follows.

	House	Senate
Average party cleavage	38%	24%
Average sectional cleavage	15%	26%

For a third time the chambers differed, with the part cleavage being two-and-one-half times the sectional cleavage in the House, but the sectional cleavage being slightly larger than the party one in the Senate.

The fourth test of the relative impact of party and section was to analyze the kinds of cleavages revealed by floor votes in terms of what majorities were voting together and in opposition. In the House, 10 of the 35 votes were bipartisan, meaning that majorities of Democrats and majorities of Republicans took the same position. Twenty-five of the votes were "party votes," in which majorities of the Democratic membership as a whole opposed majorities of the Republicans. Of these 25 party votes, 16 were party votes "strictly defined" in the sense that separate majorities of both the northern and the southern Democrats voted together against Republican majorities. The other 9 party votes were "loose" ones in which, although majorities of all Democrats were voting against majorities of all Republicans, majorities of the southern Democrats were voting with the Republicans and against the northern Democrats.

When one categorizes these same votes in sectional terms, one finds only five House votes on which majorities of all snowbelt representatives opposed majorities of all sunbelt representatives. On four of these five votes, however, neither majorities of all western Democratic representatives nor even majorities of western representatives as a whole sided with the rest of the sunbelt to take the anti-urban position. Only a single House vote out of 35 was a "strict" snowbelt versus sunbelt sectional split in which majorities of each of the sunbelt components, the southern Democrats, southern Republicans, western Republicans, *and* western Democrats, opposed majorities from each of the snowbelt's four party-regional components. That vote, in which the differential sectional impact was explicit, was to delete a new alternate formula for the distribution of community development grants from the bill extending the Housing and Community Development Act of 1974 for three years. The original formula enacted in 1974 was based on the size of a city's population, its amount of overcrowded housing, and its percentage of poor (the last factor counted twice). By 1977 it became widely recognized that this formula favored the newer and still-growing cities of the western and southern sunbelt at the expense of the older cities of the East and Midwest whose populations were declining and whose fiscal problems were the most acute.

The new, alternate formula was based on the amount of older, pre-1940 housing (weighted 50%), poverty (weighted 30%), and population growth lag (weighted 20%). Population growth lag was defined as the degree to which a city's population growth between 1960 and 1973 was less than the average population growth for all central cities of metropolitan areas. The amendment to strike this formula which would benefit the snowbelt failed in a vote of 149 to 261; in the 12 eastern states the vote was 110 to 1 and in the 12 midwestern states, 108 to 7 against the motion to strike; in the 26 southern and western states the vote was 141 to 43 in favor of deleting the alternate formula.

In the Senate, 10 of the 24 party votes were bipartisan, while 14 were party votes. Of these 14 party votes, 7 were party votes strictly defined where majorities of both northern and southern Democrats voted together against majorities of Republicans; the other 7 were loose party votes in which majorities of the southern Democrats voted with majorities of Republicans in a conservative coalition. In sectional terms, majorities of snowbelt senators opposed majorities of sunbelt senators on 9 occasions. But only on 4 of those 9 loose sectional votes did majorities of all western senators join majorities of all southern senators. Furthermore, only on a single vote was there a strict sectional split with the majority of the western Democrats joining with the rest of the sunbelt in an antiurban position. This strict sectional vote came on an amendment to eliminate application of the new Housing and Community Development Act alternate formula to cities under 50,000 in population.

This analysis of the cleavages on floor votes makes the impact of sectionalism appear somewhat weaker than did the analysis of urban support scores, but it does still confirm the greater importance of sectionalism in the Senate than in the House.

	House	Senate
Total Party Votes	72% (25)	58% (14)
Strict Party Votes	46% (16)	29% (7)
Loose Party Votes	26% (9)	29% (7)
Total Sectional Votes	14% (5)	38% (9)
Strict Sectional Votes	3% (1)	4% (1)
Loose Sectional Votes	11% (4)	34% (8)

Thus in the House, as can be seen, there were five times more party votes than sectional votes, over three times more strict party votes than loose sectional votes, and 16 times more strict party votes than strict sectional ones. In the Senate, section showed greater impact than in the House, as was the case in the analysis of urban support scores; there were only one-and-one-half times more Senate party votes than sectional votes, but still seven times more strict party votes than the strict sectional one.

As measured by these four tests, then, party remained clearly more important than snowbelt versus sunbelt sectionalism in the House. In the Senate, however, when measured by analysis of urban support scores and comparison of average party and sectional cleavages, as in the first three tests, the snowbelt versus sunbelt cleavage comes out to be at least as important as the party one. Indeed, some differences in point spread suggest that sectionalism might have been slightly more important than party. When the relative impact of party and section was measured by analysis of floor votes, party remained clearly more important than section not only in the House but even in the Senate; for what the anti-urban, sunbelt majorities in the loose sectional splits reflected in almost every instance was overwhelming anti-urban majorities among the southern Democrats, the southern Republicans, and the western Republicans. It was these majorities that, even when coupled with pro-urban majorities among the smaller total number of western Democrats, turned the count of the sunbelt as a whole into an anti-urban one. Thus the anti-urban sunbelt majorities did not indicate that western Democrats had switched from their traditional Democratic, pro-urban position to an anti-urban position because of their sunbelt sectional location. These loose sectional votes were little more than traditional conservative coalition versus northern Democrats cleavages in which the seeming solidarity of the sunbelt was only an artifact of there being a larger number of conservative coalition members than of northern Democrats in the sunbelt.

The general implications of these findings are that there was some reality to a snowbelt versus sunbelt sectionalism on urban voting in 1977, though it far from overshadowed traditional party cleavages and was less powerful in the House than in the Senate. In the House, at best only five of the eight party-regional elements needed for a strict snowbelt versus sunbelt realignment were in place. The eastern and midwestern Democrats were, as snowbelters presumably should be, more pro-urban than the chamber as a whole, whereas the southern and western Republicans and the southern Democrats were, as sunbelters, more anti-urban. The eastern and especially the midwestern Republican House members were, however, still voting more as anti-urban Republicans than as pro-urban snowbelters, and the western Democrats were still voting more as pro-urban Democrats than as anti-urban members of the sunbelt. It should also be recognized that although the southern Democrats in the House were voting less pro-urban than the chamber as a whole, they were nevertheless more pro-urban than the snowbelt's eastern and midwestern Republicans and also voted with the northern Democrats and against the Republicans on 16 of 25 (or 64%) of the party votes, thus raising the question of whether even the southern Democrats should be considered already in place as part of a House anti-urban, sectional coalition.

In the Senate, six of the necessary eight elements for a snowbelt versus sunbelt coalition were firmly in place in 1977, largely reflecting the fact that southern Democrats were more deviantly anti-urban and eastern Republicans much more deviantly pro-urban in the Senate than in the House. Thus the eastern and midwestern Democrats and the eastern Republicans were, as snowbelters presumably should be, more pro-urban than the chamber as whole. And the southern and western Republicans and the southern Democrats were, as sunbelters, more anti-urban, with the southern Democrats in the Senate, unlike in the House, voting as often with the Republicans as with the northern Democrats in party votes. The western Democrats and the midwestern Republicans were still out of place, each grouping being closer to its party than to its sectional cohorts, though even this was less so in the Senate than in the House.

PARTY VERSUS REGION

A further analysis of urban support scores, by party and region, reveals strong regional differences in urban voting—regional differences that appear to be the underlying building blocks for the snowbelt versus sunbelt sectionalism that has emerged. A breakdown of scores according to the nation's four broad regions shows the following.

	House	Senate
East	82% (117)	85% (24)
South	56% (121)	53% (26)
Midwest	66% (121)	77% (24)
West	68% (76)	59% (26)

Thus in both the House and the Senate there were sharp differences between the easterners and the southerners, with the easterners having the highest levels of urban support and the southerners, the lowest. The midwesterners fell between those two regions in urban support, switching in relative position from the House to the Senate.

When one examines the impact of region and party combined, one finds that in both the House and Senate the urban support scores of Democrats exceeded that of Republicans in every region, by an average of 36 points in the House and 24 points in the Senate. Indeed, in the House the least pro-urban Democrats—the southerners—had an average urban support score that was higher than the most pro-urban Republicans—the easterners. But in the Senate, the least pro-urban Democrats—again the Southerners— had a score that was exceeded by the most pro-urban Republicans—the easterners—and almost matched by the next most pro-urban Republicans— the midwesterners.

	House		*Senate*	
	Democrats	Republicans	Democrats	Republicans
Easterners	91% (82)	60% (35)	88% (14)	81% (10)
Southerners	64% (91)	32% (30)	60% (19)	33% (7)
Midwesterners	85% (67)	42% (54)	86% (16)	59% (3)
Westerners	81% (51)	42% (25)	76% (13)	42% (13)

A further breakdown of urban support scores by party and region reveals three highly significant intraparty patterns. First, both in the House and Senate southern Democrats were significantly less pro-urban than the other, or "northern" Democrats, and this held true regardless of the character of their constituencies.

	House		*Senate*		
	Urban	Suburban	Rural	More urban	Less urban
Northern Democrats	90% (66)	88% (70)	80% (35)	83% (21)	84% (20)
Southern Democrats	71% (18)	63% (15)	60% (38)	64% (13)	53% (6)

Indeed, in the House the average urban support score of southern Democrats from urban constituencies was less than the average score of northern Democrats from *rural* constituencies. In the Senate, too, southern Democrats from both more and less urban states had lower urban support scores than either category of northern Democrats.

Second, just as the southern Democrats proved to be less pro-urban than the rest of the Democrats, the eastern Republicans were much *more* pro-urban than the remainder of the Republicans.

	House			*Senate*	
	Urban	Suburban	Rural	More urban	Less urban
Eastern Republicans	81% (1)	57% (17)	55% (9)	87% (6)	73% (4)
Noneastern Republicans	38% (18)	40% (36)	37% (39)	56% (13)	35% (14)

In every category of constituency, the eastern House Republicans were more pro-urban than the noneastern Republicans and in a pattern similar to the one between northern and southern Democrats, the average urban support score of eastern Republicans from *rural* constituencies was higher than the average score of noneastern Republicans from *urban* constituencies. Similarly in the Senate, eastern Republicans from either the more or less urban states had much higher scores than noneastern Republicans from both categories. And on urban floor votes when a majority of Democrats was opposing a majority of Republicans, *a majority of eastern Republicans voted with the Democrats 11 of the 25 times (or 44%) in the House and 14 of the 14 times (or 100%) in the Senate.*

Third, the southern Democrats' deviance from their party colleagues toward a more anti-urban position was stronger and the eastern Republicans' deviance toward a more pro-urban position, much stronger in the Senate than in the House. Specifically, although the urban support score of the southern Democrats in the House was slightly closer to the Republicans than to the northern Democrats, in the Senate it was four times closer.

	House	*Senate*
Northern Democrats	86%	84%
Southern Democrats	64%	60%
Republicans	44%	54%

Similarly, the eastern Republicans in the House had an average urban support score about midpoint between the Democrats and the noneastern Republicans, but *in the Senate the eastern Republicans were somewhat more pro-urban than the Democratic senators as a whole* and were indeed only slightly less pro-urban than all northern Democratic senators.

	House	*Senate*
Noneastern Republicans	39%	44%
Eastern Republicans	60%	81%
Democrats	80%	77%
Northern Democrats	86%	84%

The very strong impact of region on congressional urban voting in 1977 essentially reflects the extremity regardless of party of the easterners' pro-urban and the southerners' anti-urban stance, especially in the Senate. In the House, the difference in urban support levels between the Democrats and Republicans was nevertheless still larger than that between all eastern and all southern representatives—though only by about a third. And the least pro-urban Democratic regional group, the southerners, were still slightly more supportive of urban programs than the most pro-urban Republican regional group, the easterners. Thus by these two tests, party was more important than region in the House in accounting for differences in urban support. In the Senate, however, the difference in urban support between all eastern and all southern senators was almost one-and-one-half times that between all Democrats and all Republicans. Furthermore, among the Republicans one regional group—the easterners—exceeded by a large margin the support levels of one Democratic regional group—the southerners—and exceeded by a small margin the support level of still another Democratic regional group—the westerners. Finally, another Republican regional group in the Senate—the midwesterners—almost matched the urban support level of the southern Democrats. On the basis of these measures, then, one must conclude that in the Senate in 1977 regional location was in some respects more important than party affiliation in urban voting.[7]

COMPARATIVE SUMMARY: PARTY VERSUS CONSTITUENCY VERSUS SECTION VERSUS REGION

Summarizing for the 1977 session of the 95th Congress the impact on urban support of party, constituency, section, and region, I draw for the House the following conclusions.

First, that Democrats were more pro-urban than Republicans; urban representatives were more pro-urban than suburban ones who were in turn more pro-urban than the rural ones (though these interconstituency differences were accounted for completely by the Democrats); and eastern and western representatives were more pro-urban than midwestern and southern ones.

Second, that in terms of broad, combined party and regional groups, the northern Democrats were the most pro-urban group and the noneastern Republicans, the least, with the southern Democrats and eastern Republicans being just about midway between the two and being equally deviant from their respective parties.

Third, that in terms of narrower groupings, the most pro-urban group was the urban northern Democrats and the least, the rural noneastern

Republicans, with the differences between these two in urban support levels being very large (90% versus 37%).

Fourth, that in terms of the comparative size of interparty, interconstituency, intersectional, and interregional differences, the largest one was the interparty difference between Democrats and Republicans (36 points); the next largest, the interregional one between easterners and southerners (26 points) and the interregional ones within the Democratic party between northern and southern representatives (22 points) and within the Republican party between eastern and noneastern representatives (21 points); and the smallest differences were the interconstituency differences between urban, suburban, and rural members (a maximum point spread of 18) and the sunbelt versus snowbelt intersectional one (13 points).

Summarizing the impact of party, constituency, section, and region in the Senate, I draw the conclusions below.

First, that the Democrats were more pro-urban than the Republicans; the senators from states with cities 250,000 in population or larger were more pro-urban than senators from states without such cities (though this difference was completely accounted for by the Republican senators); and senators from the East and Midwest were more pro-urban than senators from the West and South.

Second, that in terms of broad, combined party and regional groups, the northern Democrats were the most pro-urban senators and the noneastern Republicans, the least; the southern Democrats were as in the House about midway between the two, *but the eastern Republicans, unlike in the House, were 12 times closer to the northern Democrats than to the noneastern Republicans* and about one-and-one-half times more deviant from their party than the southern Democrats were from theirs (point spreads of 27 versus 17).

Third, that in terms of more narrowly defined, combined party and regional groupings, the eastern Democrats were the most pro-urban senators and the southern Republicans, the least, with the urban support score of the former being almost three times that of the latter (88% versus 33%).

Fourth, that in terms of the comparative size of the interparty, interconstituency, intersectional, and interregional differences, the largest difference in the Senate was not the interparty one between Democrats and Republicans (23 points). Larger than that were the interregional difference within the Republican party between easterners and noneasterners (37 points), the interregional one between eastern and southern senators (32 points), the intersectional difference between snowbelt and sunbelt senators (25 points), and the interregional one within the Democratic party between northern and southern senators (24 points). The smallest difference was between senators from the more or less urban states (10 points).

Finally, two important overall differences emerge from a comparison of urban voting between the House and the Senate. First, in the House, party was clearly more significant than region in urban voting regardless of what kind of test was used and both party and region were more important than section or constituency. In the Senate, on the other hand, depending on what tests were used, region was as important or more important than party in accounting for urban support, with party and region each being more important than urban character of the state. Though in terms of point spread, section also appears to be as important as party in the Senate, this is largely an artifact of the extreme deviance of one regional group within each party—the eastern Republicans and the southern Democrats. Second, while the Republicans were less pro-urban than the Democrats both in the House and Senate, they were closer to the Democrats and more supportive of urban programs in the Senate than in the House (urban support scores of 54% versus 44% and interparty point spreads of 23 versus 36).

POLITICAL LESSONS

The major political lesson from the analysis in this section should be clear: it was not the number of central city or large city constituencies or the number of more urban states in Congress, but the number of Democratic members that was crucial to passing urban programs. Indeed, over the past four decades, Congress has been seriously responsive to the needs of urban areas only in those few years of the Roosevelt and Johnson administrations (1933-1937, 1965-1966) when a Democratic president was serving with a Congress that had large Democratic majorities. The large Democratic majorities were needed so that there would be enough Democrats to constitute floor majorities for urban programs even in the face of substantial southern Democratic defections.

The roughly two-to-one Democratic majorities of the 95th Congress were large enough to constitute strong potential support in 1978 for important urban initiatives, and these Democratic majorities were serving with a Democratic President in the White House. But in order to galvanize those potential pro-urban majorities into actual ones, strong leadership was necessary from a forceful, energetic, and skillful President who was willing to dramatize the special problems of hardship cities and was not reluctant to spend money on efforts to deal with them.[8] It is a tragedy for the governments and people of America's large cities that the potential pro-urban majorities that did exist in the 95th Congress were so wasted in 1978.

There is no reason to believe, incidentally, that continued high levels of support for urban programs from Democratic members of Congress regardless of the urban character of their districts or states can be taken for granted. If Democrats who do not represent urban districts or more urban states hear too often Califano-type arguments to the effect that they cannot afford politically to support urban programs, these nonurban or less-urban Democrats may well begin to believe such arguments and make Califano's prediction a self-fulfilling one.

THE FUTURE OF URBAN AID PROGRAMS

The prospects for an increase in urban aid in the years ahead depend on fiscal considerations, on the kind of delivery-system used for such aid, and most importantly on the distribution in Congress of party and sectional strength.

FISCAL CONSIDERATIONS

The most crucial fiscal consideration influencing the prospects for increased urban aid will be the state of the national economy. As long as the economy remains as recessionary and with as high a level of unemployment as in fiscal 1977 and 1978, there will be no budget margins or fiscal dividends (that is, increases in revenues in excess of those needed to meet the cost of existing program commitments) that can be supposedly painlessly diverted to new or expanded urban programs. New funding would thus have to come at the expense of nonurban programs or by increasing the federal deficit. Also, even if the deficit began to drop with any sharp strengthening of the economy, significant increases in spending for urban aid programs would interfere with the Carter administration's campaign commitment to balance the budget by fiscal 1981 and to limit the proportion of the gross national product for government spending to 21%.

Moreover, under the new congressional budgetary process, Congress can no longer easily disregard a President's concern for a balanced budget and appropriate large additional funds for urban or other programs that it may favor. Before the enactment of the Congressional Budget and Impoundment Control Act of 1974, Congress could simply add appropriations and not be particularly concerned about the resulting size of any deficit. Now Congress must enact preliminary and final budget resolutions for each fiscal year which show total projected spending and how it is allocated by broad program area, total anticipated revenues, and the gap—deficit or surplus—between expenditures and revenues. Consequently, in order to increase spending for urban programs over and above that proposed by the President, Congress must make a reduction in spending somewhere else, provide for more revenue, or explicitly declare a larger deficit. If it does the last, Congress joins the President in bearing responsibility for the possible inflationary consequences.

Of course, if the economy again reaches a prosperous, full-employment level, some measure of supposedly free budget margins or fiscal dividends may reappear. The Brookings Institution analysis of the fiscal 1978 budget and of the Carter administration's economic and budgetary commitments projected a $10 billion to $26 billion budget margin for new initiatives by 1981 (see Pechman, 1977). But even if the assumptions on which this projection was based—the most important being achieving a full-employment economy and an inflation rate not exceeding 5%—held true, which is extremely doubtful, there certainly would be competing claims from the military, new energy research and development programs, national health insurance, and a variety of other programs for any margin of uncommitted revenues. Undoubtedly there would also be demands for further tax reductions as inflation continued to force people to pay taxes at steadily higher effective rates.

DELIVERY SYSTEM CONSIDERATIONS

The funds needed for substantially improved urban aid are extensive not only because of the large needs of hardship cities but also because, since the Nixon-Ford administration, the trend in the delivery system for urban aid has been away from categorical project grants and toward a reliance on formula grants with broad eligibility.[9] This trends has made it very expensive to deliver a particular amount of dollars to the older, hardship cities. For under formula grants, a very large number of local governments is eligible or "entitled" to a share of the funds appropriated for a program. (General revenue sharing makes all of them eligible.) Thus to increase aid to a few dozen large, hardship cities requires sufficient funding to "spread" to hundreds or thousands of other jurisdictions the additional dollars to which the formula automatically entitles them.

By contrast, funding authorized under the pre-Nixon categorical project grants did not have to be so widely spread but could be targeted primarily to the smaller number of jurisdictions that demonstrated the greatest need. Project grants also gave advantages to the superior "grantsmanship" abilities of many large cities, which had (1) sizable, experienced staffs to prepare grant applications; (2) extensive contacts in the urban-oriented Washington departments; and (3) a track record of successfully implementing projects in the past.

Of course, additional funds could be targeted to the hardship cities without increasing total spending by changing entitlement formulas to weight more heavily the adverse factors found disproportionately in those cities or by returning to project grants. But it will be much more difficult for Congress to narrow the eligibility for formula grants or to shift from formula grants to project grants than it was to shift from project grants to formula grants. This is because narrowing eligibility would reduce the number of constituencies to which benefits would flow, whereas the shift from project to formula grants expanded it. Admittedly, members of Congress were in the past willing to authorize and appropriate funds for urban project grants on the basis of need, even though they knew that their own constituencies or states would get little direct aid. But once the constituencies of large numbers of members already benefit as a matter of legal entitlement, members of Congress will typically refuse to vote for a proposal to reduce their constituencies' share or eliminate it. A "hold harmless" provision for all existing beneficiaries (that is, a guarantee not to get fewer dollars in the future than they were getting in the past) thus becomes a key prerequisite for changing the formula or for adding project grants so as to direct more funds to hardship cities.

One ploy for targeting more money to hardship cities that may have a chance of succeeding is to maintain or even slightly increase funds for the existing formula beneficiaries so that no one loses dollars—that is, to hold everyone "harmless" in current dollars—but also to add funds for new discretionary categorical project grants. The Carter administration took this tack by proposing in the extension of HCDA not only a slight increase for the regular block grants but also the setting aside of an additional $400 million for action grants to economically distressed cities. But even with the sweetener of increased funding for the regular block grants, the $400 million for action grants proved especially vulnerable. First, by an overwhelming 2 to 1 vote in the House and by voice vote in the Senate, 25% of the $400 million was reserved for suburban and rural cities below 50,000 in population; second, when the Senate Banking, Housing, and Urban Affairs Committee decided to add still another alternate formula for regular HCDA block grants, it provided that the extra funds needed for recipients choosing to take their grants under it would come out of the $400 million for action grants, rather than out of the shares of those staying on the old or first alternate formula. The committee estimated that after these withdrawals, only $288 million would be left for action grants in fiscal 1978, $202 million in fiscal 1979, and $125 million in fiscal 1980.

CONSIDERATIONS OF PARTY AND SECTIONAL STRENGTH

The most important political consideration for the prospects of increased urban aid is whether future Congresses will again have the heavy Democratic majorities of the 95th Congress and whether the typical Democratic representative and senator will remain as pro-urban as in the past. The very great importance of the size of the Democratic majorities in the 95th Congress must be stressed: In the House during most of 1977,[10] there were 291 Democrats, of whom 200 were from outside the South and 91 were southerners, and there were 144 Republicans. This meant that the number of northern Democrats alone was not much smaller than the number of Republicans and southern Democrats combined—the maximum potential voting strength of the anti-urban, conservative coalition (see Figure 2A). This distribution of seats also meant that whenever the northern Democrats all voted alike and picked up even a 20% minority of the southern Democrats or a 15% minority of Republicans, the northern Democratic, typically pro-urban position would prevail. Roughly the same situation obtained in the Senate.

Yet for the Democrats to control as large a number of seats in Congress as they did in 1977 was highly atypical: It happened before in recent history only between 1933 and 1938 in the Roosevelt administration, between 1965 and 1966 in the Johnson administration, and in the 94th Congress (1975-1976) when, however, President Ford's power to veto frequently raised to two-thirds the majorities required to pass pro-urban programs. A much more typical distribution of seats in Congress since World War II was represented in the 87th Congress, which was elected with President Kennedy in 1960 and was in session in 1961 and 1962. During most of the 87th Congress, there were 263 Democrats and 174 Republicans in the House of Representatives, making it appear that the House was safely in the control of the pro-urban Democratic party. And the Democrats did in fact have nominal control, being able to organize the House and elect members of their party as Speaker and as chairmen of the various committees. However, the appearance of control was deceptive, as only 159 Democrats were nonsouthern and 104 were southern. The result was that the total number of 174 Republicans plus 104 southern Democrats greatly outnumbered the 159 northern Democrats. Working control of the House was thus usually in the hands of the Republican-southern Democratic, anti-urban conservative coalition, and almost no pro-urban legislation was passed (see Figure 2B).

Because the power of incumbents to get reelected is great (see, e.g., Burnham, 1975), there may not be any sharp drop in the number of Democrats elected in the next few Congresses. But as the stigma of Watergate and the Nixon administration fades (and as the Carter administration or Democratic members of Congress produce important scandals of their own), the number of Democrats in Congress will probably decrease and move somewhat closer to the post-World War II norm, thus weakening the voting strength of the pro-urban forces.

There is, of course, an even more fundamental threat to pro-urban strength: In the economics and politics of scarcity that appear to be imposing themselves on American society, however large the number of Democrats in Congress, they may not be as ready to support spending programs as much as they did in the more affluent past.

The second fundamental political consideration is that in the past two decades a twofold population trend has weakened the political strength of the urban East and Midwest. Within metropolitan areas, large cities, and especially the older cities of the East and Midwest, have been losing population to their suburbs. Within the nation, the east and Midwest have been losing population to the South and West (see U.S. Bureau of the Census, 1978).

The decline in the proportion of the population living in large cities results in a steadily decreasing number of members in the House of Representatives who represent urban districts. In the 95th Congress, only 103 (or 24%) of the districts were predominantly urban while 138 (or 32%) were predominantly suburban, 121 (or 28%) rural, and 73 (or 16%)

Figure 2 Distribution of Seats by Northern Democrats, Southern Democrats, and Republicans, House of Representatives, 95th and 87th Congress

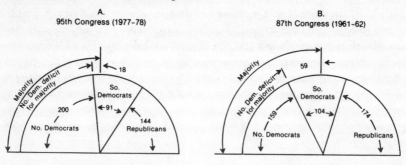

mixed. In terms of city size, of those 103 urban districts, only 90 included cities of 250,000 or more within their boundaries, either in whole or in part. Even among the seats held by northern Democrats, the 70 that were predominantly suburban slightly exceeded in number the 66 that were predominantly urban, and there were also 35 northern Democratic constituencies that were predominantly rural.

In the 1977 session of Congress the suburban northern Democrats were almost as supportive of urban positions (88%) as the urban northern Democrats (90%), and even the rural northern Democrats' votes were substantially pro-urban (80%). How long northern Democratic members from suburban and rural constituencies will continue to share, by and large, the policy outlook of the Democratic central-city representatives while these latter are ceasing to be the dominant contingent in the northern Democratic membership is an open question. But it is difficult to conceive of a rise in the Democratic suburban and rural level of pro-urban support, so the probability is that the level will drop.

The decline in the proportion of the population living in the Northeast and Midwest will result in a decreasing number of representatives with districts from those regions. A New York *Times* study projected that when Congress is reapportioned after the 1980 census, the states in the East and Midwest will lose, and those in the South and West will gain. Likely losers are New York (4 seats), New Jersey (1 seat), Ohio (2 seats), Michigan (1 seat), Illinois (2 seats), Pennsylvania (2 seats), Indiana (1 seat), and Missouri (1 seat). The projected gainers include Florida (5 seats), Texas (2 seats), New Mexico (1 seat), Arizona (1 seat), Colorado (1 seat), Utah (1 seat), Oregon (1 seat), Tennessee (1 seat), North Carolina (1 seat), and Arkansas (1 seat). Within states the major losers are likely to be districts in St. Louis, Chicago, Detroit, Pittsburgh, Philadelphia, Jersey City, Newark, and New York City. The gainers would be in areas close to or including Phoenix, Albuquerque, Denver, Houston, Little Rock, Orlando, and Tampa (see Reinhold, 1976). In short, the loss of seats would be in the regions (the East and Midwest) that gave a relatively high level of support to urban programs, and the gains in those regions (the West and South) where, except for the western Democrats, there have been only low levels of urban support.

How long western Democrats will continue to provide high levels of urban support is a crucially important question. In 1977 western Democrats voted almost as pro-urban as eastern and midwestern ones, especially in the House. Yet western *Republicans* were shown to be the second least pro-urban group in the House and Senate, whose anti-urban stance was exceeded only by the southern Republicans. If snowbelt Democrats in coalition with eastern and potentially with midwestern Republicans engage too strongly in what has been called "aggressive regionalism,"[11] they may cause western Democrats to start perceiving themselves not as allies, but as targets of their pro-urban Democratic colleagues from the snowbelt. And these western Democrats might then begin to vote more as sunbelters in protection of real or hypothetical anti-urban sectional interests and less as traditionally pro-urban northern Democrats.

The impact of present population trends on the Senate is more difficult to nail down. Since the Senate is never reapportioned, the size of its regional groups will remain the same. Senators in general, and even Democratic senators from the more urban states, will however inevitably have to recognize the increasingly suburban character of their overall constituencies. Politically, they may not be able to afford the reputation of being out-and-out champions of big cities and of the disproportionately large concentrations of poor and of blacks who live there. On the other hand, 52 senators do represent states that have at least one city of 250,000 or more, and these senators will not be able to neglect urban interests completely.

Finally, the increasing suburbanization and the westward and southward flow of the population will probably affect the intensity of presidential leadership in favor of increased federal aid to large cities. In a nation in which after 1980 fewer electoral votes will be coming from the East and Midwest and in which the suburban population will be in a position to outvote its big-city residents, presidents will probably not find it electorally profitable to assign their highest policy and budgetary priorities to programs that can be perceived as basically benefiting large cities. *Democratic* presidents, however, whose traditional followings have included the poor and the black and others who live in large cities, will no doubt find it much harder to ignore their needs than will Republican presidents. In 1976 President Carter, for example, received almost two-to-one majorities or better in such cities as New York, Boston, Newark, Philadelphia, Cleveland, Chicago, Detroit, Minneapolis, St. Louis, Oakland, and Baltimore. Substantial parts of those majorities came from black voters, who were estimated as having cast 90% of their votes for Carter nationally.[12] The large majorities built up in New York City, Philadelphia, Pittsburgh, Cleveland, Toledo, Milwaukee, St. Louis, and Kansas City accounted for Carter's statewide margins of victory in New York, Pennsylvania, Ohio, Wisconsin, and Missouri without which he would not have had the electoral votes to win the presidency. When Carter seeks reelection in 1980, he would as a Democrat need strong support among large-city and black electorates, and it is doubtful that the turnout and the size of his

1976 majorities among these groups would again be forthcoming if his administration is not perceived as significantly responsive to urban interests.

Nevertheless, in the long run the most probable impact of the decline in the population living in large cities and in the metropolitan areas of the East and Midwest, generally, is that Congress will not be enacting dramatically large additions to, expansions of, and increases in spending for urban grant programs. Furthermore, those additions, expansions, and increases in spending that Congress does enact will probably spread their benefits widely and thus interest the suburbs (and perhaps even poor rural areas) as much or more than large central cities. Congressional urban programs, on the other hand, which would target funds narrowly primarily to improve the fiscal conditions of hardship city governments and the physical and social conditions of the poor—especially the black, slum-dwelling poor—will be extremely difficult if not altogether impossible to enact.[13]

NOTES

1. The votes are by the Congressional Quarterly number: in the House, 19, 20, 22, 23, 24, 35, 51, 53, 54, 60, 61, 62, 63, 148, 165, 171, 199, 201, 203, 211, 212, 218, 219, 352, 353, 355, 358, 409, 433, 434, 438, 441, 442, 577, 694; and in the Senate, 38, 43, 46, 47, 48, 126, 127, 129, 130, 132, 133, 135, 137, 163, 165, 167, 170, 171, 174, 175, 177, 512, 555, 560 (see *Congressional Quarterly,* 1978).

2. In the House a constituency was classified as "urban," "suburban," or "rural" according to whether a majority of its population lived in a central city of a standard metropolitan statistical area, the "outside central city" portion of such a metropolitan area, or outside such a metropolitan area. Constituencies for which there was no central city, suburban, or rural majority were classified as "mixed" and excluded from further analysis with respect to the impact of constituency on urban voting.

3. Senate constituencies could not be classified in the same way as in the House since in only one state, New York, did a majority of the population live in central cities. The urban character of statewide constituencies was therefore classified as "more urban" if the state contained a city whose population was 250,000 or large and "less urban" if it did not. No other population cut-off for the size of a state's largest city was found to be statistically significant in accounting for differences in the urban support scores of senators.

The urban character of each state was also classified according to the percentage of its population living in central cities as follows: 0%-20%, "low urban"; 21%-40%, "midurban"; and 41%-60%, "high urban"; there was no statistically significant difference in the urban support scores of senators when their states were classified in this fashion.

4. Those readers interested in statistics should know that an analysis of variance and a multiple classification analysis confirmed the conclusions of what may be the

more intuitively meaningful analysis in the text based on point spreads. A multiple classification analysis (MCA) of party and constituency produced for the House adjusted beta weights of 0.64 for party and 0.16 for constituency and for the Senate, adjusted betas of 0.41 for party and 0.19 for constituency, thus reflecting the much heavier impact of party over type of constituency in both chambers.

An analysis of variance in the House testing for the impact of the size of the central city showed that for central city Republicans, size of the city was not statistically significant in accounting for differences in urban support. For the Democrats, size of the central city just barely reached significance at the 0.05 level (actual significance = 0.0493) in accounting for difference in urban support and produced an eta of 0.3350, thus signifiying that city size accounted statistically for about 11% (eta^2 = 0.1122) of the variation among the urban support scores of central city Democrats. For a description of all these statistical tests, see Nie et al. (1975: chs. 17 and 22).

5. Following the Congressional Quarterly Service, the eastern states were considered to be Connecticut, Delaware, Maine, Maryland, Massachusetts, New Hampshire, New Jersey, New York, Pennsylvania, Rhode Island, Vermont, and West Virginia; the midwestern states, Illinois, Indiana, Iowa, Kansas, Michigan, Minnesota, Missouri, Nebraska, North Dakota, Ohio, South Dakota, and Wisconsin; the southern states, Alabama, Arkansas, Florida, Georgia, Kentucky, Louisiana, Mississippi, North Carolina, Oklahoma, South Carolina, Tennessee, Texas, and Virginia; and the western states, Alaska, Arizona, California, Colorado, Hawaii, Idaho, Montana, Nevada, New Mexico, Oregon, Utah, Washington, and Wyoming.

6. The conclusion of the point-spread analysis in the text is again confirmed by statistical analysis of variance and multiple classification analysis. For the house an MCA of party and section produced adjusted betas of 0.64 for party and 0.26 for section, thus showing the much more significant impact of party. For the Senate, the MCA adjusted betas were 0.41 for party but 0.52 for section, showing that unlike in the House, section had a slightly more significant impact than party.

7. The conclusions of the point-spread analysis are confirmed by statistical analysis of variance and MCA a third time. For the House an MCA of party and region produced adjusted betas of 0.63 for party and 0.37 for region, thus showing the greater impact of party over region. For the Senate, however, the MCA adjusted betas were 0.51 for party and 0.68 for region, showing that, statistically speaking, region had a somewhat greater impact than party in urban voting.

8. And, indeed, on the 1978 votes for loan guarantees to New York City—which were supported energetically by the Carter administration—the margins of victory for the pro-urban position on the two crucial House votes were overwhelming ones of 291 to 109 (Democrats 236 to 25; Republicans 55 to 84) and of 247 to 155 (Democrats 203 to 59; Republicans 44 to 96). See Congressional Quarterly House votes 370 and 371 of 1978, *Congressional Quarterly Weekly Report* (1978a: 1510-1511).

The pro-urban margins in the Senate were similarly overwhelming ones of about 2 or 3 to 1 on defeating anti-urban amendments and of almost exactly 2 to 1 on final passage (final passage 53 to 27: Republicans 18 to 15; Democrats 35 to 12). See Congressional Quarterly Senate votes 193-197 of 1978, *Congressional Quarterly Weekly Report* (1978b: 1709).

9. To my knowledge, Pressman (1975) was the first political scientist to analyze in print the implications of the shift from categorical project grants to formula grants.

10. "Most of" because through deaths, resignations, and special elections, the number of northern Democrats, southern Democrats, and Republicans changes slightly over the course of a session of Congress.

11. See the remarks of the Texas Senator Lloyd Bentsen during the debate on the HCDA (*Congressional Record*, 1977).

12. As students of elections know, presidential election returns by large city are not reported in any standard reference. I am indebted for the 1976 totals to Alfred Toizer who is conducting a study at Temple University of the impact on the electoral vote outcome of presidential pluralities in 38 large cities. The estimates of the 1976 black vote are from Joint Center for Political Studies (1976).

13. For a possible though unlikely argument that a broad-based political coalition could be developed to support expanded federal aid for the problems of hardship cities, see Caraley (1977: ch. 20).

REFERENCES

BURNHAM, W. D. (1975) "Insulation and responsiveness in congressional elections." Political Science Quarterly 90 (Fall): 411-435.

CARALEY, D. (1977) City Governments and Urban Problems. Englewood Cliffs, NJ: Prentice-Hall.

——— (1976) "Congressional politics and urban aid." Political Science Quarterly 91 (Spring): 19-45.

CLAUSEN, A. (1973) How Congressmen Decide. New York: St. Martin's.

Congressional Quarterly (1978) Congressional Roll Call 1977. Washington, DC.

Congressional Quarterly Weekly Report (1978a) June 10: 1510-1511.

——— (1978b) July 1: 1709.

Congressional Record (1977) June 7: S9061-S9062.

Joint Center for Political Studies (1976) Focus 4(12): 4.

MAYHEW, D. B. (1966) Party Loyalty Among Congressmen. Cambridge, MA: Harvard University Press.

New York Times (1978) January 25.

——— (1976) January 23.

NIE, N. H. et al. (1975) Statistical Package for the Social Sciences. New York: McGraw-Hill.

PECHMAN, J. A. [ed.] (1977) Setting National Priorities: The 1978 Budget. Washington, DC: Brookings Institution.

PRESSMAN, J. (1975) "Political implications of the New Federalism," pp. 13-39 in W. E. Oates (ed.) Financing the New Federalism. Baltimore: Johns Hopkins University Press.

REINHOLD, R. (1976) "Population shift study gives "sunbelt" house majority after 80." New York *Times* (Jan. 23): 1: 20.

ROSENBAUM, D. E. (1978) "Califano emphasis on people rather than cities in aid to poor." New York *Times* (Jan. 25): 15.

SHANNON, W. W. (1968) Party, Constituency and Congressional Voting. Baton Rouge: Louisiana State University Press.

TRUMAN, D. β. (1959) The Congressional Party. New York: John Wiley.
TURNER, J. (1970) Party and Constituency (revised by E. V. Schneier, Jr.). Baltimore: Johns Hopkins University Press.
U.S. Bureau of the Census (1978) Current Population Reports, Series P-20, No. 331, "Mobility of the population of the United States: March 1975 to March 1978." Washington, DC: Government Printing Office.

PART II

MINORITIES AND POLICY

3

THE IMPACT OF BLACK ELECTED OFFICIALS
ON URBAN EXPENDITURES AND
INTERGOVERNMENTAL REVENUE

SUSAN WELCH

University of Nebraska-Lincoln

ALBERT K. KARNIG

Arizona State University

While several works have explored the conditions under which blacks are most likely to win election to office in urban areas (Kramer, 1971; Karnig, 1976; Cole, 1974; Karnig, 1979; Karnig and Welch, 1978; MacManus, 1978; Marshall and Meyer, 1975; Jones, 1976; Dye and Robinson, 1978), there have been few systematic analyses of the impacts, if any, blacks make once they reach these offices. This article explores the impact black mayors and city council members have on urban expenditures and inter-

AUTHORS' NOTE: *This article, aspects of which are drawn from a larger monograph entitled* Black Elected Officials and Urban Politics, *was prepared with support from National Institute of Mental Health Grant 1 RO1 MH31052-01 and from the University of Nebraska Research Council.*

governmental revenue in U.S. cities over 50,000 having at least 10% black population.

IMPACTS OF BLACK OFFICIALS

There are at least three kinds of possible impacts that black officials could make. One is to increase participation by blacks. It seems reasonable to expect that when blacks see that they can elect another black, their interest in the electoral process might increase. Only one study has looked at black participation as a function of black candidates or officeholders. Abney (1974) found that black turnout in Mississippi was modestly related to the presence of black candidates for office; the highest bivariate correlation of turnout with any of the sociopolitical variables he examined was with the number of black candidates, a correlation of .29. When other factors were controlled, this correlation was somewhat reduced but still indicated a modest relationship between turnout and black candidacies. Given the evidences of black voting solidarity found so far (see Feagin and Hahn, 1970), this could generate an increasing cycle of participation and candidate success. The exploration of the impact of black candidates and officeholders on black political participation would seem to be a fruitful avenue for research, but not one that we are prepared to undertake here.

To date, perhaps one of the most important benefits of electing blacks is symbolic. Some empirical evidence of this is found in Cole's (1974) New Jersey study. In cities with black mayors, 87% of the black community could identify the name of this officer, compared with 72% of blacks in municipalities with white mayors. Foster (1978) also found that more black school children know their mayor and have positive images of the role of mayor when the mayor is black rather than white. In Cole's (1974) sample of black New Jersey residents, only 15% disagreed with a statement that it is important that blacks hold elective office. This is fragmentary evidence, to be sure, but it does point to the possibility that the election of black public officials may help to stem the tremendous alienation toward government that has been found among blacks even more than white (Miller, 1974).

This symbolic impact, then, illustrates the function of "descriptive" representation, as defined by Pitkin (1972). That is, when blacks are elected to office, they provide descriptive representation for the black community, regardless of whether or not the black representative has substantive policy views in line with those of other blacks. Still, to increase confidence by blacks in government on a long-term basis, more than symbolic benefits need to be shown. That is, more "substantive" (Pitkin,

1972) representation must be evidenced. Substantive representation deals with the congruence between the policy wishes of the representative and the public.

In fact, we have limited evidence to suggest that black representatives do mirror the views of their constituents, not in all cases but in most. Mann (1974) has suggested that blacks on school boards, even more often than their white counterparts, adopt decision-making roles conducive to policy directives from the electorate. Further, Thompson (1963), and Kronus (1971) have found that there is a basic congruence between policy orientations of blacks of various social classes. If this is true, then a basic policy congruence could be expected between black elected officials and their constituencies. This convergence can result despite the fact that socioeconomic differences have been found to be larger between black school board officials and the black population than they are between parallel white groups (Wirth, 1975). Overall, then, we believe that it is reasonable to assume that black officials are generally sympathetic to the policy concerns of the black public and therefore constitute more than mere symbols of black representation.

What are these policy areas with which the black public is concerned? At this juncture, the major black urban policy concerns largely mirror the problems revolving around the living conditions of urban blacks; that is, inequalities of housing, health care, employment, income, as well as the quality of education in the city. It seems reasonable to assume that blacks are less committed to downtown beautification and new city amenities, for example. These assumptions are supported by data found in surveys of blacks in major cities after the urban riots of the 1960s. Along with police practices, most blacks ranked unemployment, housing, and education as serious concerns. Inadequate recreation was also seen as a problem (Advisory Commission, 1968). To the extent that large segments of the black population are primarily troubled by issues other than the core of socioeconomic issues just outlined, then our assumptions about policy preferences of the black community are that much in error.

The expectations that many people had about the impact that blacks might make were probably unrealistic (Nelson, 1972; Bullock, 1975). Nevertheless, it may be assumed that blacks place confidence in black officials because they expect black officials to understand their plight and act to do something about it. Therefore, it is appropriate to examine whether policy changes have been made in cities with black officials.

A black official has special problems: He or she must move with sufficient speed so that other blacks do not feel that he has "sold out," but there are also strong pressures on him from the white community to move cautiously (see Persons, 1977; Nelson, 1972; Davis and Van Horne, 1975; Levine and Kaufman, 1974; Levine, 1974). These whites frequently must be heeded, because they usually control the financial institutions, media, and other resources upon which black officials are dependent in proposed redevelopment, reform, or other plans. Balancing these pressures is not only a source of psychological strain for the official but also a cause of lost confidence by the black, the white, or both communities (see Nelson and Van Horne, 1974).

The special dilemmas and limitations encountered by the black officials do not necessarily mean that black representation is pointless. Some studies have shown that black officials have made an impact. At the city level, Cole (1976: ch. 7) has documented at least partial success by black officials in having their policy preferences adopted by city councils in New Jersey. And, Campbell and Feagin (1975) have pointed to a number of communities, even very poor ones, where the election of black officials has brought about major changes in policies affecting blacks: jobs, street paving, education, and other public services. Feagin's (1970) survey of 42 black officials in the South showed that almost all of them (83%) found they had as much or more influence in office as they had anticipated before being elected.

Most analyses of the impact of black leadership have been case studies (Nelson, 1972; Nelson and Meranto, 1977; Greer, 1971; Weinberg, 1968; Masotti and Corsi, 1969; Stone, 1971; Poinsett, 1970; Stokes, 1973; Levine, 1974; Persons, 1977). These studies—all but one focusing on the mayoral leadership of Carl B. Stokes of Cleveland or Richard G. Hatcher of Gary, Indiana—detail the political problems that the black mayor faces in trying to achieve his own policy objectives. Although the experiences of the two men were different, and in some ways it can be argued that Mayor Hatcher was the more successful of the two politically and in terms of policy, some generalizations can be drawn from their experiences. First of all, both men were successful in bringing to the city federal and private funds to help in the rehabilitation of the inner city. With these revenues, as well as with ordinary city revenues, new housing was built, job training and employment centers were run, and other socioeconomic programs were enhanced (Nelson and Meranto, 1977; Levine, 1974; Levine and Kaufman, 1974). Further, both mayors dramatically increased black employment by the city: By 1969, for example, 14 of Gary's 27 departments were headed by members of black and Hispanic groups (Levine, 1974: 79), and Davis and Van Horne (1975) report that Stokes hired or promoted 274 minority individuals to supervisory positions in the Cleveland government. Hatcher, particularly, was able to make giant strides in professionalizing city government, reducing corruption in government, and combatting organized crime within and outside of the governmental structure.

On the other hand, both mayors were unable to achieve a substantial part of their goals. Both were hampered by the desperate financial straits of their cities; in both cases the tax base was simply not enough to provide decent salaries for city employees and finance new and expanded programs for the benefit of the poor community.[1] In Cleveland, because of the city's financial problems, Mayor Stokes at one point fired 1,500 city employees, including many low-paid workers such as garbage collectors. Hatcher and Stokes also could not overcome the political constraints provided by the city council; in neither case did the mayor have a supportive council, though this changed somewhat in Hatcher's second term. In both cases the council was racially divided, and in Gary part of the council was under machine control and hostile to Hatcher's programs. Stokes could never make peace with the Cleveland police force, who were adamantly opposed to him, and in both Gary and Cleveland the white community was largely hostile. All of these factors, then, operate as severe constraints on a mayor attempting to implement an activist policy, one which would cost money and require substantial community support.

In studying the impact of black mayors, Keller goes slightly beyond the case study approach to compare three cities with black mayors (Gary, Cleveland, and Newark) with three somewhat similar cities having white mayors (Indianapolis, Cinncinati, and Trenton). His technique is to compare city expenditures in these cities from 1965 to 1973, looking particularly at expenditures on police, fire, roads, public welfare, parks and recreation, and housing and urban development. His initial hypothesis was that black mayors emphasize social welfare policies and spend more in that area than do cities with white mayors. He found, however, that black-run cities spend more than white-run cities do on police; in fact, as the black population increased, each city spent more on fire and police protection. Spending on roads did not differ in cities with black or white mayors. Cities with black mayors did not spend more on social-welfare programs, contrary to Keller's initial expectations. He argues that there are a variety of constraints on the ability of black mayors to spend for these kinds of programs, the constraints that we have discussed above. Because of the small number of cases, Keller cannot take into account the racial composition of the city council, for example, which might be an important determinant in direction of city expenditures.

PROBLEMS IN STUDYING THE IMPACT
OF BLACK ELECTED OFFICIALS

Studying the impact of black elected officials on public policy is a difficult chore at best. Such an analysis is fraught with methodological and conceptual difficulties. In the first place, policy changes, or lack thereof, may not be due to mayoral activity. Black mayors are limited in their policy initiatives by their political environment. What goes on during a mayor's term cannot necessarily be attributed to the policy goals of the mayor. The fiscal condition of the city, the city council, public opinion, the willingness of the state and federal governments and private foundations to support city undertakings all play a role in policy formation and implementation. Salanik and Pfeffer (1977) demonstrate that the mayor, black or white, has relatively little impact on expenditure patterns in cities.

The situation of the black mayor may sometimes be worse than that of the white. We can expect that blacks will most often be elected in cities where blacks are a majority or approaching a majority. These are the very cities in the worst financial condition, with middle-class whites fleeing the central city to the suburbs, industry deserting the area to locate in the sunbelt, and, in general, increasing needs far outrunning decreasing resources. Thus, many of the nation's black mayors have taken over in cities that have been in the decay spiral so long (i.e., Newark, Gary, East St. Louis) that it is almost inconceivable to imagine how they might be rehabilitated. Success, for a mayor in these conditions, may mean simply holding on to the status quo; improvement is out of reach, at least in the short run.

The white public may be hostile to any attempt at significant changes in resource distribution (Nelson and Van Horne, 1974). Those whites in cities that are the worst off might be expected to be the most hostile to change. Thus, attempts by a black mayor to mobilize public support will be difficult, at best, unless the community is largely black.

Measuring the impact of blacks on the city council is even more complex than assessing the effect of black mayors. Unlike the mayoral situation in which black control is easily perceptible, on the city council blacks may control any proportion of the seats. Their influence on the council is not, however, necessarily proportional to their numbers—it may be greater or lesser. Then, too, equitable proportions on the council is probably not so important to achieving policy goals as the absolute representation that blacks hold on the council. That is, we would expect blacks to have greater influence when they hold 60% of the council seats as compared with another council on which they hold 25% of the seats, regardless of their population proportion.

In evaluating the impact of black leadership, one must also take into account an "interaction effect" between the mayorship and the council. One might expect black mayors to achieve more of their policy goals, other things being equal, if they have a black majority on the council, than if the council majority is white. Mayor Stokes, for example, faced a hostile, white-dominated council that disagreed with many of his major policy initiatives, while Maynard Jackson, to cite another case, has a council evenly divided between black and white, thus giving him more room to bargain and negotiate (Persons, 1977). In any event, one must look at whether blacks control both mayorships *and* hold a dominant voice on the council, or hold one of these power positions, or are only a minority on the council.

The setting of the city in the intergovernmental context also may have a negative influence on the ability of the mayor to act in many instances (Preston, 1976). Many of the problems of the city are national problems (unemployment, for example); further, many cities do not control the most important city services, such as housing, education, and welfare. The discretion and resources possessed by the city, let alone by the mayor, to deal with these and other problems is minimal in many cases. Moreover, the mayor may well lack political influence necessary to enlist the aid of these other units. County services may be under the control of a county-wide political machine not responsive to the black mayor or the black community. The city's representatives in the state legislature and in Congress may not be allies of the mayor either. Thus, the mayor may well lack political strength as well as legal authority to deal with many of the socioeconomic problems faced by the black constituency.

A further set of problems are methodological. How does one find an appropriate set of policy variables? In a case study or modified case study approach one can look at internal shifts in resources; for example, see if urban renewal money is shifted from renewal for new downtown retail establishments to renewal for new housing for the poor and lower middle income. Potential shifts in education expenditures from neighborhood to neighborhood and program to program can be gauged, and so forth. In aggregate data analysis, these kinds of shifts are much harder to discern and to compare over a large number of cities. The most comparable intercity data are those collected by the U.S. Bureau of the Census; its *Government Finance* series records city expenditure in several functional areas: police, fire, highways, sewage, sanitation, public welfare, education, hospitals, health, libraries, parks, and housing and urban renewal. City revenue is also reported and classified by standard categories, e.g., tax revenue from property, sales, and other taxes and intergovernmental revenue, broken down by federal, state, and other. While these data do offer comparability among cities, there are also certain problems. One is that functional responsibilities are not the same across cities; for example, some city governments organize and finance an autonomous school district. Likewise, not every city has responsibilities in the area of welfare, roads, sanitation, and other areas (see Liebert, 1974). These discrepancies are most apparent in the areas of welfare and education. Thus, one might compare two cities with entirely different legal responsibilities for financing these functional areas. As Liebert (1974) has shown, these divergencies in functional responsibilities can make a difference in the cross-sectional analysis of comparative urban data.[2]

Another obstacle associated with determining the impact of black officials on public policy is the time span to be examined. It makes little sense to examine the policy correlates of black leadership at one point in time. Too many extraneous variables affect the policy output, and black leadership is only one of many factors. Then, too, one must allow for some lead time. Blacks coming into office in January 1978, for example, probably would not have any effect on the budget until at least January 1979, and perhaps longer if the fiscal cycle is July to July or September to September. Thus, an appropriate methodology would be an over-time study, utilizing a pre-black leadership basemark in the hopes that this will serve as a control for many of the other factors affecting a city's budget pattern. A further question, however, is what kind of a lead time is optimal. If the lead time is too short, no results will be apparent; if it is too long, the possibility exists that any short-term influences will no longer be measurable. Ideally, perhaps, a time series analysis could be utilized, with many readings taken over a long period of years.

After listing all of these problems, is it worthwhile to attempt the study of black impact on a cross-city basis? We believe it is, and have tried to design our study to avoid as many of the obstacles as we can.

RESEARCH DESIGN

We will use multiple regression and a longitudinal design to test for the effect of black representation on city budgetary allocations. To make better sense of the many expenditure variables under analysis, we categorized them into four groups. The first, social welfare expenditures, included those for health, housing, welfare, and education. A second category, labeled protective services, consisted of spending for fire and

police services. Park and library expenditures comprised our third category, amenities. Finally, a fourth category consisting of expenditures for
streets and highways, sanitation, sewage, and hospitals was labeled physical
facilities expenditures. In addition to analyzing each expenditure category,
we also analyzed these four aggregate scales. Additionally, we utilized
revenue totals for federal revenue, state revenue, and total intergovernmental revenue received by the city.

Our basic hypotheses were that the presence of a black mayor and
stronger council representation would lead to:

(1) more of an increase in spending for social welfare
(2) less of an increase in spending for amenities
(3) less of an increase in spending for physical facilities
(4) less of an increase in spending for protective services, especially fire
(5) more of an increase in intergovernmental revenue, especially
federal revenue.

We utilized three measures of black representation. First, we computed
the mean absolute black representation in 1970 and 1972 (i.e., 1970
representation + 1972 representation/2), the mean proportional representation in those two years (1970 representation + 1972 representa-
tion/twice the proportion black in the population), and finally the
presence of a black mayor in either of those two years. However, since the
absolute and proportional representation measures were highly correlated,
separate regressions were run for each, using the same dependent and other
independent variables.

Our baseline will be 1968-1969, a time when there were few black
mayors in any of these cities. Our end year will be 1974-1975. In addition
to being the most recent year available when the data was collected in
1977, this allows for a two- to four-year lag between mayoral incidence in
1970 and 1972 and the time of measurement. This should be long enough
to capture an effect, without being so long that short-term effects are
washed out. Of course, ideally, we would follow these measures over
another three to four years as data become available.

By using an over-time design, we have eliminated the need for many
control variables. We will, however, control for black population change
between 1960 and 1970 as one measure of change. We assume that cities
that had a bigger increase in black population between 1960 and 1970 will
continue to have a bigger change in the 1970-1974 period, thus possibly
affecting the budgetary allocations. We also control for percent black in
the city, mean income and education levels in the city, and total population change between 1960 and 1970.

We ameliorate the problem of different, functional responsibilities for the cities in our sample in two ways. First, we utilize an over-time design. The assumption is that the legal changes in city functional responsibilities in these six years were negligible, and those that did occur were random with respect to the other variables under consideration. Second, in our analysis of expenditures in each functional category, we eliminate from the analysis cities that had no expenditures in either the earlier or later period. We assume that if a city did not spend anything in a particular functional area in either of the years, then they did not have the authority to do so. One disadvantage of this procedure, of course, is that it reduces the number of cases under analysis. However, there are at least 118 cities in each expenditure category.[3]

In this analysis, we utilize only those cities over 50,000 population, since that is the only class of cities for which the census reports yearly budgetary data. This reduces the sample size to 139 cities for which we have data for both 1968-1969 and 1974-1975.

Two types of regression equations are used. First, we simply computed gain scores in each of our expenditure and revenue categories. These gain scores were then used as the dependent variables in a multiple regression. The regression weights of the black representation variables tell us whether those cities with black mayors (and council members) increased their expenditures in a given category more than cities without this black representation. This is a straightforward procedure, and one widely used. However, Bohrnstedt (1969) has pointed out that gain scores are usually highly correlated with the baseline score; given the regression toward the mean effect, those with high initial scores are likely to have lower gain scores than those with lower initial scores. An approach suggested by Bohrnstedt is to regress the time two score on the time one score. In a multiple regression, the regression weights of the other independent variables then allow one to assess their effects on the time two score controlling for the initial score. Frequently, however, the correlation between time one and time two scores is very high. This leaves little variation to be explained by the other independent variables. This is a virtue of the procedure, for if the time one score explains all of the variation in the time two score, then it is obvious that black representation or any other intervening variable could not have produced the time two score. For purposes of comparison, we will utilize both the gain score and the Bohrnstedt approach in our analysis.

Our dependent variables are presented in two ways. We have computed per-capita expenditure scores (expenditure/population) to assess the level of resources per capita is invested in each functional area. An analysis of these scores determines whether the absolute per-capita amount spent on, for example, education, increased more in cities with black mayors than with other cities. However, one drawback with per-capita scores in this kind of analysis is that cities with black mayors and council members might be found disproportionately in cities with the severest budget problems. This may mean that budgets in these cities did not increase overall at the same rate as budgets in other cities. Thus, despite priorities of black representatives, it could be possible that expenditures could not increase as fast as in other wealthier cities. Another measure, the proportion of the budget devoted to each expenditure category (i.e., education expenditure/total expenditure), is one way of dealing with that problem. This measure allows us to see if a city increased the proportion of its resources devoted to a particular functional area, regardless of the absolute dollars it had available to it. Thus, for each budget category, we have four dependent variables: per-capita, gain in per-capita, proportional, and gain in proportional expenditures.

FINDINGS

Tables 1 and 2 present the findings relevant to our basic hypotheses. While small, the coefficients reveal that the presence of black mayors does tend to result in an increase in social welfare expenditures, both proportionately and per capita. Along with that increase, Tables 1 and 2 show slower rates of growth for per-capita and proportionate expenditures for protective expenditures, amenities, and physical facilities. These general relationships are further substantiated when one examines the individual expenditures, for example, health (Welch and Karnig, 1979; Karnig and Welch, forthcoming).

We also examined per-capita revenues from intergovernmental sources totally and from the federal and state governments individually. One of the most frequently mentioned accomplishments of both Mayors Stokes and Hatcher was their ability to attract outside funding to their cities, particularly federal funds. Was this a common pattern or were these two exceptional cases? Table 3 indicates that black mayors do succeed in increasing their intergovernmental revenue more than do other mayors. All of the signs are positive, though only the relationship with gain in total intergovernmental revenues is significant. Black council representation bears a consistently negative relationship with the inflow of intergovernmental funds. It is difficult to discern a reason for this because high black council representation (absolute) should be associated with a high black population, and consequently with need factors that in part determine

(text continued on page 115)

Table 1 The Impact of Black Representation on Per Capita Expenditures By Category

Dependent Expenditure Variables (N)	R^2	Black Mayor[a]	Mean Council Representation	R^2	Black Mayor[a]	Mean Council Representation
General Expenditure (135)	.85	.00	.06*	.85	.03	.00
Gain In General Expenditure	.16	.04	.02	.16	.02	.03
Total Social Welfare (119)	.88	.05	.05	.87	.07*	.01
Gain Score	.28	.16*	-.01	.28	.17*	-.05
Protective Expenditure (135)	.71	-.09*	-.00	.69	-.08*	-.02
Gain Score	.11	-.12	.08	.11	-.11	.06
Amenities Expenditure (133)	.35	-.08	.02	.29	-.10	.09
Gain Score	.14	-.09	.03	.14	-.11	.10
Physical Facilities Expenditure (133)	.54	-.09	.01	.54	-.08	-.03
Gain Score	.04	-.13	.03	.04	-.12	-.03

a. Figures are standardized regression weights (betas). Black mayors appear twice because two regressions were run: one with black mayors and absolute council representation, one with black mayors and proportional council representation.

* Significant at .05 level.

Table 2 The Impact of Black Representation on Budget Proportions of Selected Expenditures

Dependent Expenditure Variables (N)	R^2	Black Mayor[a]	Mean Council Representation	R^2	Black Mayor[a]	Proportional Representation
Social Welfare (118)	.79	.08*	-.01	.79	.09*	-.03
Gain Score	.09	.09	-.01	.09	.10	-.05
Protective Expenditures (135)	.49	-.04	-.04	.49	-.06	.03
Gain Score	.07	-.05	-.08	.07	-.08	.03
Amenities Expenditures (133)	.37	-.01	.00	.38	-.03	.11*
Gain Score	.09	-.01	.09	.09	.02	-.03
Physical Facilities Expenditures (133)	.56	-.10	-.05	.56	-.10*	-.05
Gain Score	.03	-.09	-.05	.04	-.09	-.07

a. Figures are standardized regression weights (betas). Black mayors appear twice because two regressions were run: one with black mayors and absolute council representation, one with black mayors and proportional council representation.
*Significant at .05 level.

Table 3 The Impact of Black Representation on Per Capita Intergovernmental Revenue

Dependent Expenditure Variables (N)	R^2	Black Mayor[a]	Mean Council Representation	R^2	Black Mayor[a]	Proportional Council Representation
Total Intergovernmental Revenue						
(132)	.53	.10	-.06	.53	.10	-.06
Gain in IGR	.18	.13	-.08	.18	.13*	-.09
Total Federal Revenue (135)	.15	.10	-.07	.15	.11	-.10
Gain	.11	.07	-.10	.12	.07	-.08
Total State Revenue (132)	.64	.05	.02	.64	.06	-.00
Gain	.21	.09	-.03	.21	.10	-.05

a. Figures are standardized regression weights (betas).
*Significant at .05 level.

some state and federal funding. Nevertheless, neither proportional nor absolute council representation is positively related to the inflow of federal funds.

Thus far, our data indicate that black mayors have made an impact on the direction of urban public expenditures. With some deviation, compared with municipalities that did not have black mayors during the measurement period, in cities with black mayors, expenditures have grown faster in social services and increased more slowly in other areas of city life—amenities, protective services, and physical facilities. On the other hand, black council members seem to make much less of a consistent difference. Within every category of expenditure, the impact of black council representation is mixed.

Yet before we accept these findings, some further explorations need to be made. Perhaps cities with one kind of characteristics conform to these generalizations, but cities with other characteristics do not. For example, it might be that in northern cities, mayors have more of an impact than they do in southern cities, or it might be that cities with certain kinds of electoral systems make the difference. We have chosen to explore further the impact of three conditions: region, partisanship, and mayoral powers.

REGION

Our regional analysis has a drawback. Unfortunately, all the black mayors in this subset of cities are from the North, because black representation information refers to 1970 and 1972. Since then, of course, blacks have been elected mayor in New Orleans, Atlanta, and other southern cities. However in this analysis, we could make no comparison of the effects of northern and southern black mayors. We could, however, compare the black council representatives from these two regions. It' is possible, for example, that council members from one of the regions were behaving as expected, while those from the other region were acting in a contrary, or in a less patterned manner. To test this possibility, we examined the impact of black officeholders in the North and in the South separately. For the northern cities, regression coefficients were computed both with mayors and council members entered together and separately. The mayoral variable was, of course, not entered into the southern equations. Table 4 presents the results of this analysis.

The existence of southern black council members seems to have a small positive effect on all expenditure categories except amenities and protective services. In no case, however, is this influence statistically significant. Rather, we see a pattern in which the strength of the black delegation of

Table 4 Black Council Impact on Major Categories of Per Capita
City Spending By Region[a]

	Absolute Representation			Proportional Representation		
	North	North*	South	North	North*	South
General Expenditures	.12*	.12*	.02	.03	.05	.01
Gain	−.09	−.02	.17	−.08*	−.05	.10
Social Welfare	.05	.11*	.05	.00	.05	.02
Gain	−.01	.11	.14	−.09	−.04	.11
Physical Facilities	.08	.06	.05	.03	.03	−.04
Gain	−.02	−.04	.02	.00	−.01	−.07
Amenities	.16	.15	−.04	.20*	.20*	−.01
Gain	.19	.19	−.04	.25*	.25*	−.00
Protective Services	−.00	−.03	−.01	−.00	−.02	−.03
Gain	−.02	−.01	.09	.04	.03	.05
State Revenue	.02	.00	.18	−.17*	−.01	.07
Gain	−.05	−.07	.18	−.20*	−.07	.08
Federal Revenue	.34	−.33*	.03	−.02	−.14	.04
Gain	−.33	−.33*	.02	−.09	−.16	.04
Total Intergovernmental Revenue	−.21*	−.16	.04	−.15*	−.13	.02
Gain	−.19	−.15	.06	−.13	−.12	.02

a. Controlling for all factors controlled for in previous tables.
*Also controlling for the presence of a black mayor.
North 72 ≤ N ≤ 78
South 47 ≤ N ≤ 50

southern city councils is positively related, but in a very small way in most cases, to total expenditures, social welfare, and physical facilities expenditures. Southern black council representation is also associated in a reasonably strong fashion with state revenue gains and, still favorably though less closely, with gains in federal revenue and total intergovernmental revenue. Northern council members, in contrast, have a mixed relationship with both revenues and expenditures. The strongest relationships are with state and total intergovernmental revenue, and these are in the opposite direction as hypothesized: Larger black representation led to smaller gains in state revenue and total intergovernmental revenue.

These findings are mildly surprising. Southern council representation, more than northern council representation, has an impact more closely conforming to our expectations. When their impact is clearest, northern council representation has an impact opposite to that which we predicted. We might consider briefly why black council representation could be negatively related to the inflow of intergovernmental funds. A logical possibility is that these cities with large black representation also have a very high proportion of blacks. In the North, cities with high proportions of black population tend to be in the states that are suffering acute economic decline: higher unemployment, higher taxes, faltering services, population losses, and other aspects of financial disruption. Under these conditions, it is plausible that state aid to cities would not be increasing as rapidly as in states without these economic problems. Up until the mid-1970s, at least, federal aid, too, had been shifting away from these states toward the states of the sunbelt, especially in the South and Southwest, where there was marked economic and population growth during this period.

GOVERNMENTAL FORM

Turning from the impact of region to the impact of governmental form, we had hypothesized that mayors in cities where strong mayor systems existed would have more of an opportunity to make an impact than mayors in other cities. Mayors who could exercise a veto and who have strong appointive and budgetary powers have more opportunity to make an impact than do other mayors. We do not have a perfect measure of "strong" versus "weak" mayoral systems, but we can examine mayoral impact in cities where mayors have the veto and in cities where mayors do not. Again, it needs to be kept in mind that we are dealing with progressively smaller numbers of cases. In that light, the findings in Table 5 appear to be consistent. That is, in most of the expenditure and revenue categories, it seems to make little difference whether the powers of the mayor are strong or not. Much the same sort of relationship exists between the presence of black officeholders and the expenditures in veto and nonveto cities. One exception is that in strong-mayor cities black mayors seem more influential in bringing in intergovernmental revenue that they do in weak-mayor cities. This seems intuitively plausible, in that seeking to bring in outside funding is an activity in which a strong mayor might be able to take more initiative than mayors in weak-mayor systems.

A second structural characteristic that we believed might influence the ability of black officials to affect public policy is the degree of partisanship in the city. Two arguments might be made here. First, it could be argued that in a partisan city black mayors and council members would do

(text continued on page 120)

Table 5 The Impact of Black Elected Officials in Cities with Different Mayoral Powers

	Veto				Non Veto			
	Mayor	Absolute Council Representation	Mayor	Proportional Council Representation	Mayor	Absolute Council Representation	Mayor	Proportional Council Representation
General Expenditures	.04	.06	.08	.02	-.04	.04	.05	.04
Gain	.09	.01	.11	-.10	.04	.04	-.02	.02
Social Welfare	.06	.08	.11	.03	.03	-.02	.04	-.02
Gain	.22*	-.00	.22*	-.06	.18*	-.05	.18*	-.05
Physical Plant	-.10	.12	-.07	.02	-.06	-.05	-.07	-.04
Gain	-.16	.05	-.13	.04	-.08	-.01	-.09	.01
Amenities	-.14	-.04	-.15	.00	-.10	.09	-.11	.15*
Gain	-.18	-.03	-.19	.02	-.11	.10	-.13	.18*
Protective Services	-.07	.05	-.06	.01	-.11*	-.06	-.11*	-.02
Gain	-.09	.08	.01	-.06	-.12	.02	.08	-.13
Intergovernmental Revenue	.33*	-.20	.28*	-.14	-.05	.01	-.04	-.00
Gain	.39*	-.20	.35*	-.13	-.00	-.03	.00	-.06
Federal Revenue	.08	.01	.09	-.03	-.01	-.06	-.02	-.03
Gain	.09	-.08	.09	-.12	.06	-.09	.04	-.05
State Revenue	.10	-.06	.10	-.08	.07	.06	.07	.05
Gain	.18	-.17	.16	-.16	.12	.03	.13	.01

*Significant at .05 level.

Table 6 The Impact of Black Elected Officials in Partisan and Non Partisan Cities

	Partisan (45)				Non Partisan (90)			
	Mayor	Absolute Council	Mayor	Proportional Council	Mayor	Absolute Council	Mayor	Proportional Council
General Expenditures	.06	.08	.10	.06	-.04	.04	.02	-.02
Gain	-.02	.15	.02	.09	.04	.01	.05	-.05
Social Welfare	-.04	.21*	.04	.12*	.04	-.03	.04	-.03
Gain	-.17	.27	-.07	.15	.19*	-.07	.20*	-.08
Amenities	-.08	.14	-.05	.13	-.07	-.06	-.09	.06
Gain	-.18	.22	-.14	.20	-.08	-.07	-.10	.06
Physical Facilities	.12	.09	.15	.05	-.11	-.03	-.11	-.04
Gain	.14	.10	.17	.05	-.16	-.02	-.16	-.02
Protective Services	-.20*	.05	-.18	.02	-.11*	.02	-.10*	-.00
Gain	-.48*	.20	-.43	.12	-.08	.07	-.07	.05
Intergovernmental Revenue	.21*	-.02	.20*	.00	.18*	-.05	.13*	-.04
Gain	.44*	-.11	.38*	-.03	.15	-.04	.15	-.03
State Revenue	-.30*	.17	-.21	.05	.13*	-.02	.13*	-.03
Gain	-.29	.14	-.20	.02	.23*	-.05	.23*	-.06
Federal Revenue	.22	.06	.24	.02	.05	-.19	.03	-.13
Gain	.30	-.05	.30	-.07	-.01	-.18	-.01	-.13

better, because they are likely to be more cohesive (assuming that most if not all are Democrats) and to have some sort of common set of goals. On the other hand, it could equally plausibly be argued that black officials will do better in a nonpartisan system, because it is likely that in a partisan system the party organization is not supportive of black officials and their goals. Thus, it may be that in a nonpartisan system, black officials can more easily build coalitions of supporters. In order to see which, if either, of these assumptions was more valid, we examined the impact of black officials in cities of partisan and nonpartisan structures separately. Table 6 presents the results of this analysis. Because of the small "N," one cannot take the results in the partisan system too literally, especially those results for the mayors. Many of the variables having strongly negative betas (protective services and state revenue, for example) have only weak bivariate correlations. Still, a reasonable conclusion from Table 6 may be that the nonpartisan cities follow pretty much the patterns we have described for all the cities, i.e., consistent mayoral impact and inconsistent or very weak council impact. In the partisan cities, the situation *may* be different. It would seem, for example, that black council representation in partisan cities stimulates more spending for social welfare than it does in nonpartisan cities. Absolute black council representation also seems to have a small positive impact on amenities and protective service spending and on gains in state revenue. However, these results must be viewed as tentative in light of the small number of cases under consideration, and especially the small number of cities that have black mayors.

SOME CONCLUSIONS AND IMPLICATIONS

Earlier, we discussed many of the constraints faced by black elected officials in major urban areas. Frequently they come to office in communities that are faced with severe financial problems: shrinking tax bases and increasing demand for public services, particularly for the disadvantaged. Often black officials, particularly mayors, are opposed by influential segments of the white public, perhaps including the press and the economic elite. A hostile bureaucracy may provide further resistance to proposed changes. However, in the structure of most American cities, the mayor needs support from these other segments in order to accomplish policy goals. The mayor, especially, needs the support of the city council. Even in strong-mayor systems, a majority of the city council must be persuaded to go along with new public policy initiatives, while in weak-mayor and commission systems, the mayor may be, at best, the first among several equals in terms of making and implementing public policy.

Salanik and Pfeffer's (1977) discussion of mayoral constraints illustrates that even white mayors face severe limitations on their freedom to influence budgetary matters.

As for a black city council member, he or she faces even more constraints in trying to shape public policy. An individual council member does not have the ability to focus attention on a public issue the way the mayor does. The council member is one of 5 or 7 or even 50 council members, and may represent a tiny minority of opinion on any given issue. Unless the council member is blessed with personal charisma, a powerful political organization, or good ties to the local press, it is not likely that his or her voice is going to be heard consistently on policy matters.

Given these constraints, we were somewhat surprised that the findings concerning the black mayors were as clear-cut as they were. We would have been suspicious if strong and entirely consistent findings had occurred throughout the data, given the limitation on the freedom of action of local public officials. These findings are certainly consistent with Salanik and Pfeffer's (1977) findings that only a small percent of the variation in city budgets can be attributed to mayoral action. It does seem safe to conclude, however, that black mayors have made an impact on the direction of urban public expenditures. With some deviations, in cities with black mayors, expenditures have increased faster in social services and increased more slowly in other areas of city life—amenities, protective service, and physical facilities—than in cities that did not have black mayors during this time. The priorities of black mayors, then, seem to be in the areas in which the black communities have raised the most protest: in education, welfare, housing, and health care. Thus, despite the constraints on mayoral leadership, it does seem that, overall, having a black mayor makes a difference, even when controlling for numerous city characteristics that may have had an impact on city budgets: black population and population change and income and educational levels of the city.

These findings are still more impressive when one remembers that different black communities have different needs. Certainly some of our cities are those where the most pressing need of the black community was for new sanitation facilities in the neighborhood or increased police protection. To the extent that black mayors responded to those needs, our findings would appear diminished, though in fact the black officials were making a positive impact.

How about black council members? Here the difference is much less clear. As the absolute and proportional size of the black membership on the council increases, we do not see the same shift to social welfare priorities. In fact, within each category of expenditure, the direction of the impact is mixed. What explanations do we have for this lack of impact? First, of all, in almost all of these cities (98%), blacks are a minority on the council. Therefore, even if they voted in unison to give higher priority to social welfare expenditures and less to spending on, say, fire protection, they may not be able to carry the day. In some cases, of course, they might be joined by sympathetic whites or other minority council members. Even so, in most of these councils, blacks are not even just a vote or two away from having the majority of the council members. For example, in 53% of the cities, blacks comprise less than 10% of the membership of the council (of which 31% have no representation), in 31% they have between 10% and 20%, and in only 17% of the cities do they have more than 20% of the council representation. Therefore, it is easy to see that, in most cities, blacks are far from being a dominant force on the council. Thus, it might be argued that it is a rational strategy for many black council members to try to get as much of a particular good or service for his or her neighborhood (i.e., a new park, fire substation, library branch, or whatever) rather than to hold out for shifting expenditures from these categories to other more basic human services ones. If that is the strategy, then one would not expect to find a positive relationship between the strength of the black council contingent and increased human service or decreased other expenditures.

Examining the impact of black elected officials by types of cities brought about no startling changes in our conclusions based on the universe of cities. Black council members did seem to make more of an impact in southern cities and in partisan ones, but these findings must be tentative. Mayoral powers (as measured by the veto power) seemed to make little difference in the impact of black officials.

This research is only the first step in exploring the impact of black elected officials on urban public policy across many U.S. cities. Two areas of exploration suggest themselves for the next step. First, an analysis of intracity shifts in expenditures would be of considerable value. Recently, there have been several explanations of intracity distribution of resources (Mladenka and Hill, 1977; Levy et al., 1974; Lineberry, 1975; Jones, 1977; Lineberry and Welch, 1974; Antunes and Plumlee, 1977). The methodologies used in these studies might be applied to examining a wider range of cities over a several year time span to see if the presence of black elected officials makes a difference in how resources are allocated within the city. For example, a black mayor may not be able to increase total expenditures for education, but may be able to see that more resources are spent in the lower socioeconomic neighborhood schools or that a larger proportion of library expenditures are for branch libraries and library materials in these same neighborhoods.

A second kind of analysis that suggests itself is a close look at minority hiring over time in cities where blacks have been elected to office. The cases of Hatcher and Stokes suggest that black mayors do make an attempt to hire more blacks and other minorities in responsible positions within the city bureaucracy. The case of the Chicano takeover of the government of Crystal City, Texas, suggests that a similar pattern occurred there (Shockley, 1973). Whether this is a widespread pattern is not clear, but if it is it would certainly be a major impact of black elected officials.

In sum, while it is clear that black elected officials are not miracle workers, it is also apparent that they have made an impact on the direction of city expenditures. At this aggregate level, the impact is small. Still, with city budgets that reach into the tens of millions of dollars, a small percentage shift from one category to another can, in fact, mean hundreds of thousands of dollars redirected to another function. Thus, a closer look at this important potential impact of black elected officials is certainly warranted.

NOTES

1. It should be noted that in Gary, U.S. Steel provided over 40% of the city's property tax revenue, but also contributed greatly to the problems of the city through its air and water pollution and its discriminatory hiring practices (Levine, 1974; Greer, 1971).

2. When Liebert replicated the Lineberry and Fowler (1967) study taking into account the limited functional responsibilities of some cities, he came to quite different conclusions than had Lineberry and Fowler. His results indicated that government plays no intervening role between population characteristics and expenditure rates, with one exception.

3. When examining the overall expenditure variables, we controlled for whether the city had spending authority in the area of education and welfare. That is, we coded cities as 1 if they were in states where cities had legal responsibility for schools, 0 if not. We followed the same procedure concerning welfare.

REFERENCES

ABNEY, F. G. (1974) "Factors related to Negro voter turnout in Mississippi." Journal of Politics 36: 1057-1063.

ANTUNES, G. and J. P. PLUMLEE (1977) "The distribution of an urban public service." Urban Affairs Quarterly 12: 313-332.

BOHRNSTEDT, G. W. (1969) "Observations on the measurement of change," in E. F. Borgatta (ed.) Sociological Methodology. San Francisco: Jossey-Bass.

BULLOCK, C. S., III (1975) "The election of Blacks in the South: preconditions and consequences." American Journal of Political Science 19: 727-740.

CAMPBELL, D. and J. FEAGIN (1975) "Black politics in the South: descriptive analysis." Journal of Politics 37: 129-159.

COLE, L. (1976) Blacks in Power. Princeton, NJ: Princeton University Press.

——— (1974) "Electing Blacks to municipal office." Urban Affairs Quarterly 10: 17-39.

DAVIS, L. G. and W. VAN HORNE (1975) "The city renewed: white dream–black nightmare." Black Scholar 7 (November): 2-9.

DYE, T. and T. ROBINSON (1978) "Reformism and black representation on city councils." Social Science Quarterly 59: 133-144.

FEAGIN, J. R. (1970) "Black elected officials in the South: an exploratory analysis," in J. R. Van der Slik, (ed.) Black Conflict with White Americans. Columbus, OH: Charles E. Merrill.

——— and H. HAHN (1970) "The second reconstruction: black political strength in the South." Social Science Quarterly 51 (June): 42-56.

FOSTER, L. S. (1978) "Black perceptions of the mayor: an empirical test." Urban Affairs Quarterly 14: 245-252.

GREER, E. (1971) "Richard Hatcher and the politics of Gary." Social Policy (Nov.-Dec.): 23-28.

JONES, B. D. (1977) "Distributional considerations in models of government service provision." Urban Affairs Quarterly 12: 291-312.

JONES, C. (1976) "The impact of local election systems on black political representation." Urban Affairs Quarterly 11: 345-354.

KARNIG, A. K. (1979) "Black resources and city council representation." Journal of Politics 41: 134-149.

——— (1976) "Black representation on city councils." Urban Affairs Quarterly 12: 223-242.

——— and S. WELCH (forthcoming) Black Elected Officials and Urban Public Policy. Chicago: University of Chicago Press.

——— (1978) "Electoral structure and black representation on city councils: an updated examination." Presented at the meeting of the Midwest Political Science Association, Chicago, April.

KELLER, E. J. (1977) "The impact of black mayors on urban policy." Presented at the meeting of the American Political Science Association, Washington, DC, September 1-4.

KRAMER, J. (1971) "The election of blacks to city councils." Journal of Black Studies 1: 443-476.

KRONUS, S. (1971) The Black Middle Class. Columbus, OH: Charles E. Merrill.

LEVINE, C. H. (1974) Racial Conflict and the American Mayor. Lexington, MA: Lexington Books.

——— and C. KAUFMAN (1974) "Urban conflict as a constraint on mayoral leadership: lessons from Cleveland and Gary." American Politics Quarterly 2: 78-106.

LEVY, F. S., A. J. MELTSNER and A. WILDAVSKY (1974) Urban Outcomes. Berkeley: University of California Press.

LIEBERT, R. J. (1974) "Municipal functions, structure and expenditures: a reanalysis of recent research." Social Science Quarterly 54: 765-783.

LINEBERRY, R. L. (1975) "Equality, public policy and public services: the underclass hypothesis and the limits to equality." Presented at the meeting of the American Political Science Association.

——— and E. FOWLER (1967) "Reformism and public policies in American cities." APSR 61: 701-716.

LINEBERRY, R. and R. WELCH (1974) "Measuring the distribution of urban public services." Social Science Quarterly 54: 700-712.

MacMANUS, S. (1978) "City council election procedures and minority representation: are they related?" Social Science Quarterly 59: 153-161.

MANN, D. (1974) "The politics of representation in urban administration." Education in Urban Society 6: 297-317.

MARSHALL, H. and D. MEYER (1975) "Assimilation and the election of minority candidates: the case of black mayors." Sociology and Social Research 60 (October): 1-21.

MASOTTI, L. H. and J. R. CORSI (1969) Shoot-Out in Cleveland: Black Militants and the Police, July 23, 1968. New York: Praeger.

MARTIN, M. [ed.] (1966) The Public Welfare Directory: 1966. Chicago: American Public Welfare Association.

MILLER, A. (1974) "Political issues and trust in government: 1964-1970." American Political Science Review 68: 951-972.

MLADENKA, K. R. and K. Q. HILL (1977) "The distribution of benefits in an urban environment." Urban Affairs Quarterly 13: 73-93.

National Advisory Commission (1968) Report on Civil Disorders. Washington, DC: Government Printing Office.

NELSON, W. E. (1972) Black Politics in Gary: Problems and Prospects. Washington, DC: Joint Center for Political Studies.

——— and P. J. MERANTO (1977) Electing Black Mayors. Columbus: Ohio State University Press.

NELSON, W. E. and W. VAN HORNE (1974) "Black elected administrators: the trials of office." Public Administration Review (November-December): 526-533.

PERSONS, G. (1977) "Black mayoral leadership: changing issues and shifting coalitions." Presented at the meeting of the American Political Science Association, Washington, DC, September 1-4.

PITKIN, H. (1972) The Concept of Representation. Berkeley: University of California Press.

POINSETT, A. (1970) Black Power Gary Style: The Making of Mayor Richard Gordon Hatcher. Chicago: Johnson.

PRESTON, M. (1976) "Limitations of black urban power: the case of black mayors," pp. 111-134 in L. Masotti and R. Lineberry (eds.) The New Urban Politics. Cambridge, MA: Ballinger.

SALANIK, G. R. and J. PFEFFER (1977) "Constraints on administrator discretion: the limited influence of mayors on city budgets." Urban Affairs Quarterly 12: 475-498.

SHOCKLEY, J. S. (1973) Chicano Revolt in a Texas Town. South Bend, IN: University of Notre Dame Press.

STOKES, C. B. (1973) Promises of Power: A Political Autobiography. New York: Simon and Schuster.

STONE, C. (1971) Black Political Power in America. New York: Dell.
THOMPSON, D. (1963) The Negro Leadership Class. Englewood Cliffs, NJ: Prentice-Hall.
WEINBERG, K. (1968) Black Victory: Carl Stokes and the Winning of Cleveland. Chicago: Quadrangle Books.
WELCH, S. and A. KARNIG (1979) "The impact of black elected officials on urban social welfare expenditures." Policy Studies Journal 7: 707-714.
WIRTH, C. (1975) "Social bias in political recruitment: a national study of black and white school board members." Presented at the meeting of the Southern Political Science Association.

4

THE COMMUNITY ACTION PROGRAM AND THE
DEVELOPMENT OF BLACK POLITICAL LEADERSHIP

PETER K. EISINGER

University of Wisconsin–Madison

The prime years of the Community Action Program (CAP) of the federal War on Poverty lasted less than half a decade. But even as the program began to undergo the first of a series of eviscerating transformations in the late 1960s, one of its sharpest critics was nevertheless willing to suggest that community action would leave an important and enduring imprint on the structure of black politics. In his celebrated polemic, *Maximum Feasible Misunderstanding*, Moynihan wrote, "Very possibly the most important long run impact of the community action program of the 1960s will prove to have been the formation of an urban Negro leadership echelon at just the time when the Negro masses . . . were verging towards extensive commitments to urban politics" (1969: 129). Now, nearly a decade after Moynihan's prediction, it is appropriate to begin to explore the degree to which this has in fact been the case.

In the period since the publication of Moynihan's book, a number of observers have offered general support for its prediction. In a 1969 study

AUTHOR'S NOTE: *I wish to thank several graduate assistants for their faithful help on this project, including Tim Kaufman-Osborn, Dave McConnell, and Darryl Solochek. Support for this research was provided by the Institute for Research on Poverty at the University of Wisconsin–Madison. Responsibility for the finished product, however, is mine alone.*

done under contract to the Office of Economic Opportunity, for example, the firm of Barss, Reitzel and Associates concluded that "current information indicates that this [ghetto leadership] vacuum has been at least partially filled by leaders with a high degree of contact with CAP—if not indeed created by it" (Brecher, 1973: 102; see also Kramer, 1969). In *Regulating the Poor,* Piven and Cloward argue that the Great Society programs worked with "startling success" to integrate blacks into the existing political system: "In many cities the Great Society agencies became the base for new black political organizations. ... In some areas with large numbers of black voters, the leaders of these new organizations began to seek elective office" (1971: 274). In a major retrospective on the impact of community action, Peterson and Greenstone echoed the foregoing conclusion, arguing that, most fundamentally, CAP "contributed to black incorporation in the body politic," (1977: 272) helping, among other things, to underwrite organizationally the election of blacks to political office (see also Strange, 1972). More recently, Browning et al. found in their study of minority politics in the San Francisco area that a third of the victorious minority candidates had prior experience in community action, Model Cities, or other federal poverty programs. For more than half of this group, "their identification with the program was a major factor in increasing their visibility and establishing their credibility as minority leaders" (1978: 18).

The evidence on which most of these conclusions have been based, however, is largely a product of case study material. The data are sparse, geographically limited, and in all but the Bay Area study out of date. A systematic examination of the importance of community action in the dramatic emergence of a corpos of black political leaders is lacking not only in the literature evaluating the War on Poverty but also in recent studies of black elected officialdom in particular (e.g., Cole, 1976; Feagin and Campbell, 1975; Conyers and Wallace, 1976). Thus the purpose of the present study is to offer a preliminary analysis of more systematically generated data regarding the role of community action in the background of a nationwide sample of black elected officials in state and local government.

THE COMMUNITY ACTION PROGRAM

The Community Action Program was established by Congress in Title II of the Economic Opportunity Act of 1964. As Levitan (1969) has observed, CAP was a catch-all for projects to combat poverty: All sorts of programs, ranging from day care to community organizing to consumer education to birth control clinics, could be funded through it. In addition to supporting and shaping the delivery of certain types of services in target poverty areas, many CAPs engaged in political activities. The most common of these involved efforts to pressure local government bureaucracies to take greater account of the needs and desires of minorities and the poor. At the peak of the program in the late 1960s, there were more than 1,000 community action agencies in the United States. Of these agencies, 75% were located in predominantly rural areas, but two-thirds of the funding went to urban CAPs. In the public mind the program quickly became associated with the problems of big-city blacks (Christensen, 1975).

Although the congressional injunction to include poor people in the operations of community action agencies was contained only in the ambiguous clause calling for "maximum feasible participation of the residents of the areas and members of the groups served," the phrase nevertheless provided the main opportunity for the training of what were at the time "indigenous" leaders. "Maximum feasible participation" was initially interpreted as requiring, insofar as possible, the inclusion of representatives of the poor (who were frequently either poor themselves or simply black) in both policy-making and administrative positions. In 1966 Congress established explicit guidelines to guarantee that representatives of the poor would constitute at least one-third of the elected community action agency boards of directors, who were responsible for making basic policy and funding decisions. The CAP agencies, through which specific programs were funded, also offered job opportunities at the administrative and managerial levels for blacks and other minorities.[1] *Thus, community action agencies provided highly visible settings in which people traditionally excluded from responsible public positions could gain political or administrative experience as well as public reputations.*

But the heyday of the program was brief. In 1967, community action agencies were stripped of their independence from local government. All through the years of the Nixon administration the Office of Economic Opportunity (OEO), CAP's occasionally reluctant protector, was under assault. During one 14-month period, OEO was without legal authority after Nixon vetoed the agency's authorization. In 1974 Congress abolished OEO and replaced it with the Community Services Administration. Remaining CAPs were placed under the Community Services Administration. Shorn of their advocacy role, they became little more than minor players in the local government service delivery system. For the cadres of poverty warriors schooled in the early years of community action, other avenues, including electoral politics, seemed to offer more significant routes to power and influence.

THE SAMPLE

Although elected politicians surely comprise only a portion of the black community's "leadership echelon," a focus on this group offers a reasonable starting point. Between 1964, the year in which the Economic Opportunity Act was passed, and 1977 the number of black elected officials in the nation at all levels rose from approximately 70 (Williams, 1977) to 4,311 (Joint Center for Political Studies, 1978). The development of such a substantial pool of public figures in so short a period raises questions about the means by which such people were identified, trained, and supported politically. To the extent that community action played a role in fulfilling these leadership development functions, one might conclude that government policy and public resources were successfully employed to aid and encourage the political mobilization and representation of a disadvantaged group.

The data on which this article is based were gathered in the summer of 1977 by telephone interviews with a nationwide sample of black elected officials. The sample was drawn in equal parts from two comprehensive rosters of black elected officials put out by the Joint Center for Political Studies in 1970 and in 1976. This strategy was designed to maximize the possibility of analyzing the effects of community action experience on the emergence over time of the black leadership pool. Approximately equal numbers of mayors, aldermen or city councilmen, and state representatives were randomly selected. Letters were sent to respondents telling them that they had been selected for a study of the work histories of elected officials. Each letter was then followed up by a telephone interview.

Of the total of 285 names drawn, 210 were successfully interviewed, yielding a response rate of 74%.[2] These respondents represent 9% of the universe of black officials in the three offices in these two years (N = 2,254). For most purposes the samples have been combined in the analysis that follows. Of the 210 respondents, 54 were no longer in political office.

There are several basic questions of importance for this study. First, did significant numbers of black elected officials have experience in the Community Action Program prior to their initial election? Second, do those who had CAP experiences differ in any important ways from other black politicians? Finally, did CAP experience seem to serve the leadership development functions of identification, training, and support?

DIMENSIONS OF CAP EXPERIENCE

Respondents were asked whether they had been involved as paid workers, administrators, board members, or volunteers in any of a wide variety of specific federal programs, in grass roots and political organizations, or in state and local government prior to their initial election to public office.[3] For each positive response, details regarding the location, length of time, and specific nature of the individual's involvement were elicited. Participation in a federally funded Community Action Program emerged as a significant preelection experience: 42 elected officials, representing 20% of the total sample, reported that they had been involved in one capacity or another in a community action agency.[4] (An additional 7 officials had experience in community action *after* their initial election to office, but these were not included in the CAP group in the analysis.) The length of involvement in CAP of the 42 respondents (called CAPers for short) with preelection experience ranged from 1 to 12 years, averaging 3.9 years.

The incidence of prior community action experience among black elected officials has steadily increased over time (see Figure 1). The 42 officials with CAP experience represent 23% of the 180 politicians in the sample elected since 1964. The proportion of CAPers has increased in each succeeding "class"—i.e., all those elected for the first time in any given year—suggesting that the influence of community action experience has been more than a short-run epiphenomenon of the mid-1960s.

THE DISTINCTIVENESS OF THE CAP GROUP

Tracing the independent effects of community action involvement on the political careers of the respondents is an extremely difficult task. The chief problem lies in the fact that most of the 210 respondents had a multiplicity of preelection experiences that might have provided political visibility, training, and support. Involvement in the civil rights movement, for example, appears to have the kind of universality among black officials that service in the *Résistance* was once claimed to have among French public figures. Of the entire sample, 74% said they had significant experience in civil rights organizations (mainly the NAACP). Of the sample, 24% had been members of local government commissions or boards, and 12% had served their state government in some capacity. Others had worked in a variety of federal programs administered at the local level such as Model Cities. Since 165 respondents had experience in more than one of these settings (60 had experience in four or more; only 20 had experience in

Figure 1   Gross Overtime in Proportion to Black
Elected Officials with CAP Experience

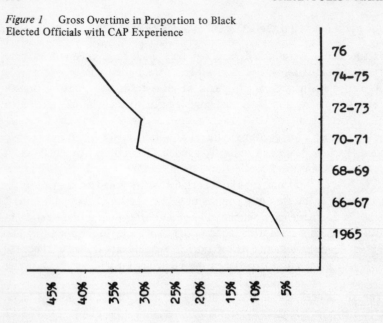

none of them), the chances that experiences would contaminate one another were high. Elaborate controls, even when possible, reduce the cells to miniscule proportions.

To deal with the problem of controls, I have chosen to compare three different groups: CAPers (n = 42), civil righters (n = 118), and those with neither CAP nor civil rights experience (n = 50). Among the CAP group, 38 (90%) also had civil rights experience, making a pure comparison between civil rights and CAP backgrounds essentially impossible. Nevertheless, juxtaposing the 42 CAPers and the 118 civil righters provides a basis for determining whether the addition of CAP experience to that of the civil rights movement produces any difference.

The three groups differ among themselves on several descriptive dimensions. As Table 1 shows, a majority of those with CAP backgrounds were state legislators, whereas slightly less than one-third of the civil righters and only one-tenth of the residuals occupied such office. The disproportionate tendency of people with CAP backgrounds to be found in state office is an important finding and is taken up more fully later.

In comparison with the other two groups, CAPers tended to hold office in (or from, in the case of state legislators) urban settings (see Table 2). Of the 22 CAPers in state legislatures, for example, 18 represented districts in cities larger than 100,000. Indeed, 10 of those 18 came from cities of over

Table 1 Distribution by Office

	CAP		Civil Rights		Neither	
Mayor	24%	(10)	32%	(38)	46%	(23)
State Representative	52%	(22)	32%	(38)	8%	(4)
Alderman	24%	(10)	36%	(43)	46%	(23)
N =		42		118		50

NOTE: χ^2 = 21.69. Significant at the .001 level.

Table 2 Distribution by Size of Place

	CAP		Civil Rights		Neither	
>10,000	29%	(12)	41%	(48)	66%	(33)
10–100,000	19%	(8)	25%	(29)	22%	(11)
<100,000	52%	(22)	35%	(41)	12%	(6)

NOTE: χ^2 = 20.068. Significant at the .001 level.

half a million. In contrast, however, the CAP mayors (6 out of 10) were concentrated in tiny villages under 2,500 in population. Although nearly half the entire sample is composed of small town and rural politicians (n = 93), only 29% of the CAPers occupied offices in or from places under 10,000 in population. It is important to recall here that, nationally, three-quarters of the CAPs were rural operations. These data indicate, however, that it was the urban component of the program that provided an avenue to elective office. Although the three groups are distributed regionally in relatively equal proportions—nearly half of each group comes from the South—even the southern CAPers tended to come from large urban places, whereas southern politicians in the other two categories tended to come from small towns and rural areas. Similar urban-rural differences obtain in the North.

The three groups differ only slightly in terms of age, and the CAPers and civil righters can be distinguished from the residuals in educational achievement (see Table 3). These data suggest that CAP provided an avenue to public service for a particular generation of young and relatively well-educated activists. Black politicians who came up through CAP also exhibit somewhat more ambitious career patterns than their counterparts in the other two groups. Consider, for example, the initial level at which members of these three groups entered electoral politics. Table 4 shows that although each of the three groups had similar low proportions of those who began their elective careers as mayors, the CAP group was

substantially more likely than the other two to enter elective politics as
state legislators. Civil righters and residuals tended to begin at the lowest
level office, namely, that of city councilman.

The three groups also exhibit different mobility patterns once they
have achieved elective office. Mobility, as it is conceived here, is a function
of the proportion of officials in a particular group who move out of their
first office to another. For each of the three groups, mobility (M) out of
each office was measured in terms of the percentage change:

$$(S/F) - 1 = M,$$

where S is the number of officials in a given office at the time the sampling
rosters were compiled and F is the number of officials who held that office
at their initial entry into elective politics. An M score of zero indicates no
mobility, positive signs indicate an increase in the number of officials from

Table 3   Mean Age and Education

	CAP	Civil Rights	Neither
Mean Age	46	52	50
Mean Years of Education	15.5	15.2	13.2

Table 4   Initial Level of Entry to Elective Politics

	CAP		Civil Rights		Neither	
Mayor	10%	(4)	14%	(16)	12%	(6)
Alderman	36%	(15)	48%	(57)	70%	(35)
State Representative	40%	(17)	31%	(37)	8%	(4)
Other (county, school board)	14%	(6)	7%	(8)	10%	(5)

NOTE: χ^2 = 49.78. Significant at the .001 level.

Table 5   Mobility Scores

	CAP	Civil Rights	Neither
Alderman	-.67	-.74	-.66
Mayor	1.50	1.38	2.83
State Representative	.29	.03	0

a particular group in a given office, and negative signs indicate a decrease. Table 5 presents mobility scores for each of the three groups.

Slightly more than half the entire sample (n = 107) began their careers in electoral politics as an alderman. All three groups show similar rates of mobility out of that office. The CAP and civil rights groups exhibit nearly equal rates of increase in the proportion of mayors among them. The residual category, however, stands apart here, its original number of mayors nearly quadrupling (from 6 to 23).

Neither the civil righters nor the residuals experienced any increase, as groups, in the number of state legislators. But the CAP group, whose original complement of state legislators was 17, showed an increase to 22, a gain of nearly 30%. Thus, not only do CAPers tend disproportionately to begin their elective careers as state legislators but they also tend to move to that office from others in disproportionate numbers.

Once in office, CAPers also appear to display a surer sense of ambition and commitment to public life. Respondents still in office were asked what they planned to do after their current term expired. The results are shown in Table 6. Most CAPers plan to run again for some office. But civil righters and the residuals are less sure of their plans, and a significant number of the latter plan to retire from public office.

COMMUNITY ACTION AND LEADERSHIP DEVELOPMENT

One of the first problems faced by those who aspire to elective office is how to establish a public identity. The tasks of gaining name recognition and of making a reputation as one who might appropriately fill a responsible public role are often accomplished by service in civic or auxiliary governmental or party organizations.[5] To the degree to which such

Table 6 Ambition: What Officials Plan To Do after Current Term

	CAP		Civil Rights		Neither	
Run for same office again	53%	(18)	31%	(28)	36%	(15)
Run for another office	12%	(4)	13%	(12)	7%	(3)
Retire from politics	9%	(3)	6%	(5)	26%	(11)
DK.	26%	(9)	50%	(45)	31%	(13)
	100%	(34)	100%	(90)	100%	(42)

NOTE: χ^2 = 95.53. Significant at the .001 level.

institutions provide these opportunities for achieving visibility, we may say that they perform an *identification function*.

A second problem involves the acquisition of skills and training that might carry over into a career in electoral politics. Many politicians gain such experience in their prepolitical careers, particularly in the law,[6] but others rely on civic, political, or governmental institutions to prepare them. Much of this training is not, of course, pursued consciously with an eye toward a political career, but we may nevertheless speak of the *training functions* inherent in institutional roles and organizational affiliations.

Finally, individuals who aspire to political leadership require support for their efforts in the way of organizational resources and manpower. To the extent that institutions and organizations fulfill these requirements, we may speak of their *support function*.

To a significant degree CAP seems to have performed all three functions for those black officials who were involved in that program. Whether community action was a more effective setting for the performance of these leadership development tasks than were alternative institutions, however, is not entirely clear. But that is a question we shall examine in a moment.

The overwhelming majority (n = 36, 86%) of those officials who served in CAP did so in the same town or city in which they subsequently ran successfully for office. Such agencies, then, did provide a potential base for establishing local visibility. Furthermore, most of those who had experience in community action agencies played roles there of a highly visible nature: 26 of them had served as elected board members for their agencies. Nine others had served as administrators of programs funded by the community action agencies or in the agencies themselves. Both types of positions were often fraught with controversy, involving their incumbents in intense neighborhood struggles. In many places these figures gained substantial personal notoriety.

Membership on the elected boards or in the local CAP administrative hierarchy, both at the director level as well as in the professional and middle level range, also provided a certain amount of training in the mechanics of seeking and holding public office. Board members, for example, had had to campaign in order to be elected.[7] Occasionally, their neighborhood jurisdictions were the size of substantial cities. Once on the board of a community action agency, members had to learn the fine and often disputed distinctions between their own policy-making role and the administrative tasks allotted to others. In addition, many became expert advocates and bargainers. Administrators learned the workings of local government and the byways of cooperative federalism. Budgeting, grants-manship, personnel practices, dealing with an occasionally militant clientele, and bargaining were other skills they had to master.

In order to discover the nature of the benefits that CAPers and others thought they had gained in their various preelection activities that carried over to political office, respondents were asked which of their preelection involvements were particularly important preparatory experiences and what they had learned in each of those. The results are shown in Tables 7 and 8.

The major finding in Table 7 is that no single organization or experience emerges as the clearly dominant preparatory ground for black political officials. Community and neighborhood organizations—mainly various sorts of block clubs and neighborhood improvement associations—are the involvements most frequently cited for the sample taken in its entirety; but these were mentioned only 12% of the time. The CAP ranks as the seventh most important experience among the 13 specific categories. However, among those with CAP backgrounds, the federal program clearly offered the most important political benefits.

As for what exactly these officials believed they had gained from their preelection experiences, CAPers were marginally more likely to stress political exposure and leadership training than any other benefit. "I became known in the community through my work on the _____ CAP board," was a typical comment. "I gained training as a representative," commented another official. "Political office was just the logical next step for me," said another.

Equal proportions of all three groups stressed the knowledge they had gained of the mechanics of government, ranging from familiarity with local government personnel and procedures to budgeting to getting grants from the federal government. Some also stressed the understanding they had gained of interest group politics and believed they had learned how and where to bring pressure to bear on government at its most vulnerable points. Civil righters were somewhat more likely than the other two groups to mention that their involvement in preelection activities (the most important of which were *not* civil rights organizations for all but 12 of the 118) was important for teaching them about the needs of their community. The residuals, many of whom we may recall had no preelection involvement in any public program or agency or movement organization, were much more prone than either of the groups to suggest that they had entered political office wholly unprepared by anything in their previous experience. Except for the fact that the CAPers appear to have entered political life somewhat better prepared than others, however, the differ-

Table 7 The Most Important Preparatory Experiences for Politics

	CAP		Civil Rights		Residuals		Totals	
CAP	28%	(13)	—		—		6%	(13)
Civil Rights	9%	(4)	9%	(12)	—		8%	(16)
Community and neighborhood groups	4%	(2)	12%	(16)	19%	(7)	12%	(25)
Party Organizations	11%	(5)	10%	(13)	6%	(2)	9%	(20)
School, internships	9%	(4)	3%	(4)	—		4%	(8)
State Government	—		4%	(5)	—		2%	(5)
Labor Unions	2%	(1)	5%	(7)	—		4%	(8)
Church	—		3%	(4)	3%	(1)	2%	(5)
Local Government	4%	(2)	9%	(12)	22%	(8)	10%	(22)
Federal Programs	—		2%	(3)	—		1%	(3)
Occupation	6%	(3)	8%	(10)	25%	(9)	10%	(22)
National Government	—		*	(1)	3%	(1)	*	(2)
Civic and Fraternal Organizations	4%	(2)	7%	(9)	17%	(6)	8%	(17)
"All of My Experiences" (none singled out)	23%	(11)	26%	(34)	6%	(2)	22%	(47)
							N =	213

*N is greater than the sample because of multiple responses.

Table 8 The Impact of Prelection Experiences as Preparation
for a Political Career

	CAP		Civil Rights		Neither	
Provided exposure, motivation, training	24%	(12)	22%	(28)	14%	(7)
Taught mechanics of government and political process	22%	(11)	25%	(32)	24%	(12)
Taught knowledge of issues, community needs	18%	(9)	29%	(37)	14%	(7)
Learned how to deal with people	12%	(6)	8%	(10)	4%	(2)
Gained useful contacts	4%	(2)	5%	(7)	4%	(2)
Other	20%	(10)	2%	(3)	12%	(6)
Nothing learned or gained in any prior experience	2%	(1)	9%	(12)	29%	(15)
N =		51		129		51

ences in the distribution or rank ordering of benefits among the three groups are not particularly striking.

Community action agencies also provided some limited resource support for politicians, although other organizations were probably more important in this regard. Voter registration and education projects sponsored by CAP organizers were widespread phenomena in the early years of the program, both of which helped ghetto politicians indirectly, and aspiring officeholders occasionally used mimeograph machines and mailing lists supplied by CAPs.

Community action agencies did not, by and large, offer political endorsements, however, or did they seem to supply major campaign

Table 9 Organizational Source of Major Campaign Personnel
(Managers, Fund Raisers, Advisers)

	CAP		Civil Rights		Neither	
Grass Roots Organizations Model cities, CAP, neighborhood organizations, civil rights groups	87%	(13)	78%	(43)	40%	(4)
Party	13%	(2)	22%	(12)	60%	(6)

NOTE: $\chi^2 = 57.70$. Significant at the .001 level.

personnel to any great degree. Neighborhood and party organizations, in that order, most commonly supplied help for those who had any sort of organizational backing. Although CAPs did not, for the most part, supply campaign managers or other important campaign personnel, officials who had CAP experience nevertheless tended to draw on grass roots organizations for such people rather than on party organizations. Although two-thirds of the CAPers had worked actively for a political party prior to their initial election,[8] Table 9 suggests that those who drew on preexisting organizations for important campaign workers eschewed the local party apparatus in favor of neighborhood, civil rights, and, in two instances, CAP groups. Although the numbers are small here, they offer a certain contrast with the other two categories of black officials.

DISCUSSION

It is clear that the Community Action Program of the War on Poverty has played a moderately significant role in the supply and training of black elected officials in state and local government. Black officials with CAP experience account for nearly a quarter of all blacks elected to state legislative lower houses, city hall, and city councils since 1964. These people appear to be slightly more politically ambitious than black officials without such prior experience and are more prone to rely on grass roots organizations rather than on party organizations for political help. Above all, they are heavily concentrated in urban areas.

That urban rather than rural CAPs tended to produce black officials is not surprising: Christensen (1975) argues that rural CAPs, in particular, tended to be dominated by traditional local elites who controlled the representatives of the poor, carefully chose administrators acceptable to them, and used the program for purely economic and welfare ends rather than political mobilization. Such settings were thus less conducive to the emergence of independent, new black politicians than were the more turbulent urban CAPs.

That the urban leaders who had CAP experience were primarily attracted to the state legislatures rather than to city hall requires some comment. In part, one suspects that CAP activists gained special insights during their involvement in the poverty program into the limitations of city government as an instrument of social change, making city office a less attractive goal. In addition, CAP agencies and city government in many places developed a deeply antagonistic relationship, particularly where militant poverty warriors sought to pressure city bureaucracies and officials to be more responsive to minority groups and where CAP organizers sought to develop independent ghetto political movements. Under such circumstances, city government may have been seen as a hostile environment in which to launch a political career.

State politics was a natural choice for other reasons, however. The CAP experience did not facilitate the making of a citywide reputation, except in very small places (recall that 6 out of the 10 CAPer mayors were village mayors). In larger places the target clienteles of CAP agencies were distinct, ghettoized subpopulations, set apart by virtue of race and poverty. In most instances the poverty population constituted a minority of the city's inhabitants. If such populations generally provided too narrow a base on which to make a run for city hall, their residential concentration made them ideal constituencies for the support of legislative representatives.

Many aspirants to office were further encouraged to run for the state legislature rather than a city council seat by the fact that most of the city councils to which they had access are elected at large. Of the cities, (accounting for 12 state representatives in our sample) have at-large elections, only 3 cities have straight ward elections, and the remainder have a mixture of both. To run in an at-large system is to confront the problem of expanding one's localized reputation and support base to encompass the city as a whole. Even in such ward cities as New York and Cleveland, however, it made sense to run for state office rather than the city council: In both places, poverty area populations across the boundaries of city council districts, so state legislative office encompasses a larger constituency.

Has Moynihan's prediction, then, finally been proven correct? These data do not demonstrate that the community action program *formed* a black leadership cadre, but they certainly indicate that CAPs strongly *facilitated* the emergence of such a group. For many aspiring black politicians, community action offered the right sort of organization at the right time. It was accessible to people without a carefully wrought set of credentials. Converging as it did with the rise in black voter registration after 1965, the development of the Community Action Program offered public visibility and access to the political process *at public expense* to people who would, in most cases, have been hard-pressed to amass on their own the resources necessary to achieve such benefits. The CAP afforded a kind of controlled competition for visibility by excluding for the most part those aspirants to a political career who already had resources or popular followings. Thus, for example, CAPs offered a more congenial setting in which to rise than political party organizations, in which resource-rich individuals could command and monopolize the party's attention. By and large, CAP agencies also offered a more structured environment for learning the job of politician than did the often less formal, more diffusely organized, more sporadic civil rights movement.

In light of these observations, it becomes necessary to modify somewhat the generally gloomy assessments of the impact of community action. A number of studies have suggested that in the effort to resolve the conflicts between the two community action aims of ordinary (and politically safe) service delivery on the one hand and institutional change and political mobilization (by nature abrasive and challenging to established authorities) on the other, most CAPs opted for the former.[9] At best, it was argued these new service delivery mechanisms provided a few jobs in the ghetto, although even here most of the positions went to those who were already upwardly mobile.

But the nurturance of a black leadership cadre is an altogether different sort of achievement, transcending both the service delivery achievements of community action agencies and their modest attempts to underwrite a pressure group politics for the poor. Leadership development was not, as far as we can tell, a planned function of the Community Action Program. It evolved along a lengthy time dimension and thus could not have been evident at the point at which initial assessments of the Community Action Program were made. To the degree to which the program helped to train a significant portion of a generation of black political figures and provided them an entree to political life, the impact of the program is likely to endure long after its modest service delivery innovations and community organizing efforts have been forgotten.

NOTES

1. To my knowledge there are no reasonable estimates of the number of poor and/or minorities who were employed by CAPs in responsible positions or who served on boards. It is likely that the number ran into the tens of thousands.

2. Of the 75 respondents not included in the analysis, 11 had died, 48 could not be located, 14 refused to be interviewed, and 2 provided unusuable interviews. The 210 respondents who were successfully interviewed represented 32 states.

3. These included Model Cities agencies, Headstart, neighborhood organizations, federally funded CAP agencies, city government, state government, civil rights organizations, manpower training centers, and Job Corps. In addition, information about civic, fraternal, and other involvements was elicited.

4. Although these 42 politicians provide the central focus of this study, it is worth noting that an additional 28 elected officials had had experience in other programs associated with the War On Poverty or the Great Society, including Headstart and Model Cities.

5. For a study on city councilmen, see Prewitt (1970); for data on state legislators' involvements prior to state office, see Wahlke et al. (1962).

6. Of the CAPers, 12% were lawyers, as were 13% of the civil rights group. Only one of the residuals was a lawyer. This profession does not appear to provide a major entry path to politics for black local officials.

7. Community action agency board elections were characterized by extremely low voting turnouts, however. Typically, less than 5% of the eligible population managed to come to the polls (Levitan, 1969).

8. Of the civil righters, 74% had prior party experience as did 44% of the residuals.

9. This observation has been made by a number of scholars, including Rose (1972) and Clark and Hopkins (1969).

REFERENCES

BRECHER, C. (1973) The Impact of Federal Antipoverty Policies. New York: Praeger.

BROWNING, R., D. MARSHALL, and D. TABB (1978) "Minorities and urban electoral change: a longitudinal study." Presented at the Western Political Science Association meetings.

CAMPBELL, D. and J. FEAGIN (1975) "Black politics in the South: a descriptive analysis." Journal of Politics 37: 129-162.

CHRISTENSEN, T. L. (1975) "The urban bias of the poverty program," in D. B. James (ed.) Analyzing Poverty Policy. Lexington, MA: Lexington Books.

CLARK, K. B., and J. HOPKINS (1969) A Relevant War Against Poverty: A Study of Community Action Programs and Observable Social Change. New York: Harper & Row.

COLE, L. A. (1976) Blacks in power. Princeton, NJ: Princeton University Press.

CONYERS, J. E., and W. L. WALLACE (1976) Black Elected Officials. New York: Russell Sage.

Joint Center for Political Studies (1978) Focus (March).

――― (1976) National Roster of Black Elected Officials. Washington, DC: Author.

――― (1970) National Roster of Black Elected Officials. Washington, DC: Author.

KRAMER, R. M. (1969) Participation of the Poor. Englewood Cliffs, NJ: Prentice-Hall.

LEVITAN, S. (1969) The Great Society's Poor Law. Baltimore: Johns Hopkins University Press.

MOYNIHAN, D. P. (1969) Maximum Feasible Misunderstanding. New York: Macmillan.

PETERSON, P. E., and J. D. GREENSTONE (1977) "Racial change and citizen participation: the mobilization of low-income communities through community action, in R. Haveman (ed.) A Decade of Federal Anti-Poverty Programs. New York: Academic Press.

PIVEN, F. F., and R. CLOWARD (1971) Regulating the Poor: The Functions of Public Welfare. New York: Pantheon.

PREWITT, K. (1970) The Recruitment of Political Leaders: A Study of Citizen-Politicians. Indianapolis: Bobbs-Merrill.

ROSE, S. (1972) The Betrayal of the Poor: The Transformation of Community Action. Cambridge, MA: Schenkman.

STRANGE, J. H. (1972) "The impact of citizen participation on public admin-istration." Public Administration Review 32 (special issue): 457-470.

WAHLKE, J., H. EULAU, L. FERGUSON, and W. BUCHANAN (1962) The Legisla-tive System. New York: John Wiley.

WILLIAMS, R., Jr. (1977) Mutual Accommodation: Ethnic Conflict and Coopera-tion. Minneapolis: University of Minnesota Press.

PART III

FISCAL CRISIS AND POLICY

5

A UNITARY MODEL OF LOCAL TAXATION AND EXPENDITURE POLICIES

PAUL E. PETERSON

University of Chicago

Two models of local policy formation can be set forth. Although they are complementary rather than competing models, for heuristic purposes it is useful to present them as contrasting approaches. Since the first, bargaining, model is well known, I shall concentrate in this article on elaborating and applying a second, unitary, model of policy making. The article is divided into four main parts. After briefly identifying the limitations of the bargaining model, the first part develops the theoretical rationale for

AUTHOR'S NOTE: *Reprinted from* British Journal of Political Science *(July 1979)* © *1979 Cambridge University Press. Published under the title "A Unitary Model of Local Taxation and Expenditure Policies in the United States." This is a revised version of a paper originally presented at the Workshop on Public Policy, Institute of Local Government, University of Birmingham, in June 1978 and then given at the annual meeting of the American Political Science Association. New York City, in September 1978.*

The research was undertaken while serving as a Fellow of the John Simon Guggenheim Foundation and of the German Marshall Fund of the United States. Susan Sherman executed the regression analyses and she and Deborah Woods provided other valuable research assistance. The London School of Economics and Political Sciences generously made available office space and other supporting services. Helpful comments have been received from Benjamin Page, J. David Greenstone, L. J. Sharpe, Peter Self, Paul Kantor, Nelson Polsby, and George Jones.

the unitary model. The second part uses the model to analyze empirically the differences in the revenue sources for national, state, and local governments. The third part does the same for expenditure policies and, in the course of the analysis, distinguishes among three types of public policy—developmental, allocational, and redistributive. In the fourth part, hypotheses deduced from the model are tested by means of a regression analysis of state and local expenditures.

TWO MODELS OF POLICY FORMATION

THE BARGAINING MODEL

The bargaining model is well known. Local public policy is a function of the processes of conflict and bargaining among disparate groups, agencies, and factions within the local political system. Because the public officials formally responsible for the formulation and implementation of these policies are elected to office, it is in their interest to listen to the competing claims of bureaucrats, influential citizens, and ordinary voters. There are oligarchical and polyarchical versions of this model, and one or another may be the most appropriate in a particular local context (Agger, Goldrich and Swanson, 1964; Banfield, 1961; Dahl, 1961).

In offering explanations for their findings, students of taxation and expenditure policies have drawn freely from this bargaining model. For example, Lineberry and Fowler (1967) have said that the lower correlations between demographic variables and expenditures in reform, as compared to nonreform, cities is due to the lesser "responsiveness" of reform systems. When Clark (1968) found higher expenditure levels in more decentralized political systems, he concluded that decentralization allowed easier access to officials by a wider number of pluralist claimants for public benefits. And even economists now include numerous "taste" variables (per cent nonwhite, per cent foreign stock) in regression analyses of variations in state and local expenditure patterns (Weicher, 1970). Without apology, these economists make the crude assumption that every resident (of whatever age) has equal influence in shaping the collective "taste" function of the local community.

Yet, with all the variety of applications of bargaining models, the massive and frequently contradictory findings on expenditure patterns among states and localities within the United States remain much of a muddle. Two decades after the pioneering efforts in this tradition, no internally consistent set of propositions has begun to emerge (Brazer, 1959; Fabricant, 1952). In part this is due to the bargaining model itself.

It is so flexible that it can be folded and stretched to cover almost any finding. High correlations show high government responsiveness; low correlations show low government responsiveness. If one governmental characteristic has no explanatory power, then the analyst need only search for a means of quantifying another. In the end the model becomes less of a theoretical construct guiding the selection and analysis of data than a coverlet loosely resembling the society's democratic myths (a big red, white, and blue blanket, as it were) that can be tossed over almost any empirical result.

Almost, I say, because a second problem has been the difficult of incorporating within the bargaining model the numerous instances when so-called environmental variables—income, property values, urbanization, and so on—account for much of the variation. Indeed, Dye's (1966) work on state revenue policy, in which he concluded that variables endogenous to most bargaining models of policy making had little impact on policy at all, has been a continuing embarrassment.

Finally, the whole research tradition has been hopelessly enmired in a seemingly insoluble dilemma of finding comparable units of analysis. When governmental units whose functional responsibilities are similar have been compared, it has been inappropriate to introduce political variables into the analysis. When Dye chose to do so, it was not surprising that he found political variables had little impact. On the other hand, in comparisons of expenditures by governmental units for which meaningful indicators of political process variables can be obtained, the expenditure data themselves are incomparable because these units do not have similar functional responsibilities. Until a scholarly consensus is reached on the methodological questions, the debate on the relative importance of political and environmental variables will continue on its meaningless course.[1]

CITY INTERESTS

Although internal conflicts and competing preferences are not denied, the unitary model treats them as theoretically unimportant (Peterson, 1976). Instead the model assumes that the political system, taken as a whole, has its own set of interests which constrains the choices that policy makers take. The model has been used most successfully in the study of foreign policy and international relations, where each nation-state is assumed to have certain strategic interests which it tries to maximize in an ever-changing international environment. Although environmental factors preclude any nation-state from realizing its interests to the maximum, the attempt to do so limits each nation-state's policy alternatives. It can be assumed that the policy makers within each nation-state rationally search among policy alternatives for the very limited set that are most likely to maximize the nation's interests in a particular environmental context (Allison, 1971).

This model has also been used in studies of the market behavior of firms and corporations. Once again, it is assumed that the system—this time, a firm—has a strategic interest which it is trying to maximize in an ever-changing and competitive environment. Although most firms and corporations have internal factions and competing cliques, these are thought to be theoretically unimportant in explaining the firm's market behavior. Instead, it is the firm's interest in maximizing profits that constrains policy choice, and it is by that criterion that policy choice will be narrowed to a limited range of alternatives.

Although a comparable unitary model has seldom been applied to local political systems, there are good reasons for believing such a model could prove particularly useful. Local governments operate in an ever-changing environment to which they must be prepared to respond. Just as the nation-state must be prepared to counteract forces in the international arena, so a local government must anticipate not only the immediate changes in surrounding towns and communities but even the longer term trends shaping relationships among states and regions in the country as a whole. Second, a local government has little control over these environmental factors. Just as the individual firm in a competitive economy cannot control its sources of supply or the demand for its products, so local governments cannot control the movement of capital and labor across their boundaries. It is an open system which can be easily permeated by external forces, thereby increasing the need for sensitivity to significant external changes. Finally, a local government has an overriding set of interests that it must constantly strive to protect. Just as the nation-state wishes to maximize its power in the international system, and the private firm wishes to maximize its profits, so the local community wishes to maximize its economic well-being, its social standing, and its political position relative to other local units (Weber, 1958).

Although all three of these objectives are important to local communities, very likely the most important of the three—at least for revenue policy—is the community's economic prosperity. First, economic prosperity is necessary for protecting the fiscal base of a local government. In the United States, taxes on local sources and charges for local services remain an important basis of local government revenues. Although transfers of revenue to local units from the federal and state governments increased throughout the post-war period, as recently as 1974-1975 local governments still raised almost 60% of their own revenue (U.S. Department of Commerce, Bureau of the Census, 1976). Raising revenue from one's own economic resources requires continuing local economic prosperity. Second, good government is good politics. By pursuing policies which contribute to the economic prosperity of the local community, the local politician selects policies that rebound to his own political advantage. Bargaining models often depict the politician on a crucifix of cross-pressures, searching for solutions that will best compromise differences. Eager to avoid such a trap, politicians assiduously promote goals that have widespread benefits. And few policies are more popular than economic growth and prosperity. Third, and most important, local officials usually have a sense of community responsibility. They know that, unless the economic well-being of the community can be maintained, local business will suffer, workers will lose jobs, cultural life will decline, and city land values will fall relative to other areas. To avoid such a dismal future, public officials try to develop policies that assist the prosperity of their community—or, at the very least, do not seriously detract from it. Quite apart from any effects of economic prosperity on government revenues or local voting behavior, it is quite reasonable to posit that local governments are primarily concerned about maintaining the economic vitality of the area for which they are responsible.

In a unitary model this becomes the strategic objective which governs policy choice. Governments can be expected to take decisions which best maximize this particular goal—within the numerous environmental constraints with which they must contend. As policy alternatives are proposed, each is evaluated according to how well it will help to achieve this objective. Although information is imperfect and local governments cannot be expected to select the one best alternative on every occasion, policy choices will be constrained to those few which can plausibly be shown to be the most conducive to the community's economic prosperity. Internal disputes and disagreements may affect policy on the margins, but the major contours of local revenue policy will be determined by this strategic objective as shaped and limited by factors in the community's environment.

In attempting to maximize their economic prosperity, local communities are in a competitive position one with the other. Each must attract productive capital and labor to its area, and to achieve that end the conditions for productive economic activity must be as favorable in its own locality as in its competitors'. Otherwise, there will be a net outward flow of productive resources, leaving the community with a declining economic future. Local governments can do little to control the flow of productive resources directly; for example, they cannot establish tariff walls or control human migration in the same way that nation-states can. It is all the more important, therefore, that their taxation and expenditure policies be designed in such a way as to protect and enhance the productive capacity of the area. We shall see later that the results are local tax policies which emphasize the benefits received rather than the ability-to-pay principle and expenditure policies which permit only modest programs for redistribution.

CITY INTERESTS AND FISCAL POLICY

Local taxation and expenditure policies can have significant consequences for the economic health of a community. Although monetary policy, international trade agreements, and other crucial questions are reserved for national policy makers, economists have shown that decisions made locally can have their own economic consequences. When a government increases its expenditures on desired public services, such as schools, property values are enhanced (Oates, 1969; Pollakowski, 1973). Conversely, as heavier taxes are laid on local property, land values decline by the capitalized value of the tax increase (King, 1977; McDougall, 1976; Oates, 1973; Pollakowski, 1973; Rosen and Fullerton, 1977). If state governments provide relatively substantial payments to welfare recipients, persons in need of such assistance will migrate into the area (Cebula, 1974). And if governments restrict the entry of low-income residents into their community, land values rise (Babcock, 1966; Mills and Oates, 1975). Although research on these questions is only beginning, a quite consistent set of findings is beginning to emerge which affirms a connection between the local polity and the local economy.

A theoretical explanation for such a connection is provided by a line of reasoning originally stated, however imperfectly, by Tiebout (1956) who has also (implicitly) constructed a unitary model of policy formation. Tiebout notes that residents can migrate freely from one community to another and, as a consequence, they will calculate the impact of local government decisions in choosing their places of residence. To protect the prosperity of their local economy, local governments must consider the preferences of potential migrants. Governments who use their revenue policies to maximize their economic prosperity operate efficiently. They provide each resident with exactly that package of taxes and benefits which he most prefers. Each resident receives desired benefits in return for the taxes he pays, and (necessarily) each resident pays in taxes an amount that covers the average cost of producing the benefits received. In this ideal world of Tiebout's, the government achieves a revenue policy that maximizes the community's economic welfare. Because each resident is getting what he wants from government in return for the taxes he pays, government revenue policy provides the maximum inducement for living and working within the community.

Unfortunately, it is almost certain that no local government ever achieves Tiebout's hypothesized ideal. In the first place, government services are necessarily similar for large numbers of residents. Roads, streets, parks, schools and police protection cannot be varied infinitely to suit each person's taste. Because many government services have the property of being at least to some degree a collective good, what is provided to one is provided to many, if not to all. Yet the bundle of public services is such a complex basket that it is doubtful that any two households have exactly the same preferences.

Second, public services cannot be provided efficiently because no pricing mechanism pinpoints misallocations of public resources. Within the community the local government monopolizes the distribution of public services.[2] To obtain a comparable bundle of services at a lower price, residents have to bear both the search costs of finding the more efficient community and the costs of migration. Residents will tolerate inefficiencies that do not exceed these moving costs.

Third, local governments cannot charge consumers according to the amount of a public service each consumes. Because residents of a community have differing tastes, they consume public services differentially. And, in most cases, local governments are unable to allocate the costs among residents in such a way that each pays according to the benefits he receives.

Because of these constraints, it is unlikely that any local government system will closely approximate Tiebout's ideal world where, in the aggregate, government services match citizen preferences. And it is just as unlikely that any local government ever maximizes the relative attractiveness of its land areas to potential migrants. Instead, the marginal cost of the local public service is always greater than the perceived marginal benefits of the average taxpayer. His marginal benefit/tax ratio is always less than 1:0. Some portion of the marginal tax imposed on him will always be perceived as a surcharge imposed as a cost of living in that particular community. Note that by "average taxpayer" I am referring to the taxpayer who pays the mean dollar in local taxes, not the voter whose preferences fall at the median. From the point of view of the economic well-being of the community, it is the taxpayer's potential for migration elsewhere that is relevant and, in this regard, each taxpayer's contribution is weighted according to the amount of taxes paid.[3]

However, if this average taxpayer always receives less from the community in benefits than he contributes, at the same time he never receives from a local government all the services that he is willing to purchase. A local government is never able to supply all the public goods that each taxpayer is willing to purchase at any given price. In most contexts local governments cannot service any one person in a community without at the same time servicing others. If each taxpayer's particular demands were supplied, many others would receive the same service, even though they had little economic demand for it. The aggregate of public services supplied would far exceed the aggregate demand at that price. The benefit/tax ratio would fall precipitously. Consequently, the supply of government services to the average taxpayer is always less than his economic demand for them. His supply/demand ratio is always less than 1:0.

The overall level of government expenditures in a local community is a function of the conjoint effects of these benefit/tax and supply/demand ratios, as diagramed in Figure 1. Expenditures continue until the ratio of benefits to taxes for the average taxpayer equals his supply/demand ratio. In Tiebout's world these two ratios are unitary, as every taxpayer obtained the services he demanded and at the same time received benefits equivalent to the taxes paid. In a world of imperfect information and imperfect mobility, the intersection of these two ratios is at a point well below unity, but local governments nonetheless are constrained to offer a level of service at approximately the point where these two ratios meet. To depart drastically from this equilibrium point would endanger the economic well-being of the community. It is also in the interest of the community to shift the point of equilibrium to as high a level as possible. For example, if the equilibrium in Figure 1 can be shifted upward from E_1 to E_2, then taxpayers will have more of their demands supplied at a lower cost to themselves. When that is achieved, the community becomes a more desirable locale and productive labor and capital is attracted to the area.

The unitary model has been developed with special reference to local governments, because it is the local community which is most easily penetrated by forces in the external environment. The smaller the land area which the community encompasses, the more of its products are produced for an export market, and the easier it is for labor and capital to relocate. To a lesser extent, the force of the argument applies to state governments as well. For the most part, they too are unable to control capital and labor flows across their boundaries, and thus they are also constrained by the environmental context in which they operate. However, states are territorially larger units of government than localities, and

Figure 1 Ratios of the supply of local public goods to effective demand, and of the benefits received from local public goods to taxes paid by average taxpayer, at varying expenditure levels.

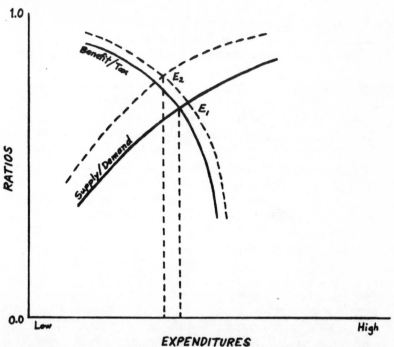

therefore the costs of moving across state boundaries are greater for any individual or firm. To that extent states are less constrained than localities, and therefore differences in the behavior of states, as compared to localities, are to be expected. The government least subject to these external constraints is the federal government, which through its control over economic policy, currency regulations, tariffs, passports, and visas has the greatest latitude with respect to the policies that are the focus of my analysis. Consequently, comparisons across governmental levels should reveal varying patterns of taxation and expenditure policy.

These differences in the degree to which the three levels of government in the United States are constrained in their policy making allow for the development of hypotheses concerning taxation and expenditure policy. In the following section I shall look at intergovernmental differentials in the way they raise their revenues and in the third part I shall examine the purposes for which they expend locally generated revenues.

REVENUE SOURCES FOR NATIONAL, STATE,
AND LOCAL GOVERNMENTS

There are two highly contrasting principles according to which governments can raise the revenues needed to provide public services. The one principle states that citizens should be taxed according to their *ability to pay*. It has been argued by many that tax payments should increase with income, wealth, and profits earned, and liberals have argued that not only should the payments increase proportionately with ability to pay but disproportionately or progressively, so that ever-increasing proportions of one's resources are paid in taxes as taxable resources increase. A contrasting principle is that citizens should pay for government services according to the level of *benefits* that they receive. In this way, each consumes no more services than he pays for at the price necessary to recover the costs of producing the service. If the first principle is defended in the name of equality, the second provides an equally compelling criterion of efficiency.

According to the unitary model, local governments will prefer efficiency over equality. Local units will attempt to raise revenues not according to their ability to pay but according to the level of benefits they receive from local services. The emphasis on efficiency at the expense of equality is due not to any antiegalitarian commitments of local policy makers but, if the unitary model is correct, to the constraints under which local governments operate. In order to protect the economic well-being of the community, the government must maximize the benefit/tax ratio for the average taxpayer. Indeed, it is especially important that the benefit/tax ratio of the more prosperous taxpayers who contribute disproportionately to the local economy be comparable to that in competing local areas. Yet, if residents are taxed according to their ability to pay, the benefit/tax ratio for higher income residents will be particularly low. On the other hand, if residents are taxed according to level of services received, the ratio of benefits to taxes for the average taxpayer increases in value.

Although many constitutional and statutory limitations prevent local governments from applying the *benefits-received* principle rigorously, they are allowed to levy user charges. These user charges are a close approximation of the benefits-received principle, because each consumer may be charged for the amount of a governmental good or service he consumes. And this charge can be levied at a price which covers the full cost of providing the good or service. However, local governments face many obstacles in levying user charges. In many cases, the beneficiaries of government services are difficult to ascertain precisely. In other situations, benefits cannot be easily supplied to some residents without providing them to all. Indeed, these are among the reasons for the services becoming a government function in the first place. And even where user charges are practicable, other constraints exist. Courts have ruled that where charges are levied, the charge must be no more than the amount necessary for providing the service. And what service is being provided is often defined narrowly by the judiciary. Finally, user charges are not deductible against federal income taxes in the same way that property, income, and sales taxes are. Consequently, this particular form of raising local revenues is not subsidized by the federal government to the very considerable extent that other forms are.

But even though local governments are restricted in applying the benefits-received principle to revenue raising, they seem to rely on this principle much more than either the state or the federal government do. As can be seen in Table 1, over the past two decades local governments have relied on user charges to raise over a quarter of their locally generated total revenues, whereas state governments rely on them for only 12% of their revenue, and the federal government depends on user charges for only 6%. To be sure, many localities fail to exploit user charges fully, and therefore do not achieve as close an approximation of the benefits-received principle as legal requirements allow. For example, Oakland officials set user charges at levels determined by precedent or by the practice in neighboring communities, and not necessarily at a level which fully recover costs (Meltsner, 1971). And the Advisory Commission on Intergovernmental Relations (1974), even while noting that "there has been a steady growth in the fiscal importance of local user charges," has urged their more widespread use as a mechanism "for diversifying local revenue structures when specific beneficiaries of particular government services can be ... identified." But, even if the potential for user charges has not been tapped fully, disproportionate and continuing dependence on such charges by local governments is nonetheless noteworthy.

Even if exploited fully, user charges have only a limited capacity for generating revenues. As a result, most local revenues are not generated by user charges but by a tax. As far as possible, local governments nonetheless continue to prefer the benefits-recieved to the ability-to-pay principle. In the first place, the tax that has become the distinctive prerogative of local governments is the property tax (see Table 1). Admittedly, the increasing dependence of local governments on intergovernmental transfers from the state and federal governments reduces their dependence on any form of local taxation. And it is true that states no longer depend on the property tax for their revenues. However, as a source of locally generated revenue, the significance of the property tax has abated hardly at all. From 1957 to 1973, the percentage of local revenue raised by the property tax declined

Table 1 Revenues Raised from Own Resources by Level of Government, 1957, 1962, 1967 and 1973*

Revenue Source	Local Government (per cent)				State Government (per cent)				Federal Government (per cent)			
	1957	1962	1967	1973	1957	1962	1967	1973	1957	1962	1967	1973
User charges†	28.3	26.4	26.3	26.1	16.5	12.8	13.9	12.4	7.9	7.0	6.6	5.8
Property tax	58.0	58.3	56.7	54.1	2.3	2.1	1.8	1.4	–	–	–	–
Income tax	.9	1.0	2.1	3.0	7.5	9.1	10.5	16.1	40.9	42.8	38.1	41.7
Corporation tax	–	–	–	–	4.8	4.3	4.8	5.6	24.3	19.3	21.0	14.6
Sales, gross receipts‡	5.5	5.1	4.8	6.4	45.8	43.7	42.8	40.3	12.8	12.6	9.8	8.0
Death, gift, other	.5	2.0	2.0	1.8	4.3	7.2	6.5	5.4	2.1	2.6	2.4	2.6
Miscellaneous, general revenue	4.9	5.2	6.0	6.4	3.3	3.1	3.6	3.9	2.0	2.2	3.2	3.1
Insurance	2.0	2.0	2.1	2.2	15.5	17.6	16.1	15.1	10.0	13.6	18.9	24.3
Total (%)	100.1	100.0	100.0	100.0	100.0	99.9	100.0	100.2	100.0	100.1	100.0	100.1
Total ($m)	21,357	31,598	44,419	81,216	20,728	30,117	46,794	97,108	87,066	106,441	161,351	247,849

*Sources: U.S. Bureau of the Census, U.S. Census of Governments 1957, *Compendium of Government Finances* (Washington D.C.: US GPO, 1959), Vol. 3, No. 5, Table 2, p. 17 ('Tax Revenue by Type of Tax, by Type of Government, 1957'). U.S. Bureau of the Census, U.S. Census of Governments 1962, *Compendium of Government Finances* (Washington, D.C.: US GPO, 1964), Vol. 4, No. 4, Table 3, p. 28 ('General Revenue by Source, by Type of Government: 1962'). U.S. Bureau of the Census, U.S. Census of Governments 1967, *Compendium of Government Finances* (Washington, D.C.: US GPO, 1969), Vol. 4, No. 5, Table 3, p. 26 ('General Revenue by Source, by Type of Government: 1966-67'). U.S. Bureau of the Census, *Government Finances in 1972-73*, Series GF 73, No. 5 (Washington D.C.: US GPO, 1974), Table 4, p. 20 ('Governmental Revenue by Source, by Level of Government: 1972-73').
†Includes motor vehicle, current charges and utility.
‡Includes liquor revenue.

only from 58% to 54%. Significantly, 82% of all revenue raised in 1972 from local tax sources still came from the property tax.

This dependence of local governments on the property tax has been a matter of some debate among economists (Netzer, 1966). But whatever the objections to the property tax, local governments continue to prefer it over the income or sales tax, simply because it is a tax on those products least equipped to escape its application. Consider the difficulties posed by the major alternatives. Taxes on sales encourage residents to purchase products outside the jurisdiction. Taxes on profits earned within a territory provoke businesses into carrying on their most profitable activities elsewhere. Taxes on locally earned income give residents an incentive to seek employment externally. By comparison, the property levy taxes immobile land and structures attached thereto; the things taxed cannot be readily transported to a new locale. And their users must undergo the substantial costs of permanent physical migration to avoid the tax's application to them.

Second, local governments hardly tax the profits of local businesses at all. Indeed, the U.S. Census does not even have a separate classification for such a local tax. The reasons are not difficult to discover. According to traditional economic theory, the corporation tax is an excise tax paid by the consumer, whose products are surcharged by an amount equivalent to the tax. But this assignment of the corporation tax burden is applicable only if the corporation tax is applied uniformly throughout a self-contained economic system. If such taxes were levied differentially by local governments, any price increases passed on to the consumer would meet effective competition from businesses located in low tax areas. Businesses in high tax areas would be driven from the marketplace. Few local governments are eager to kill their golden geese by such a tax.

Third, the remaining taxes that local governments utilize are seldom progressive and at times downright regressive. Unlike the federal excise tax, which is reserved for luxury items, the state sales tax is levied on items bought disproportionately by lower income residents. For those who save portions of their income—presumably the wealthier save more—it is not a tax on that aspect of their earnings at all. And it is the sales tax, not the more progressive income tax, that state and local governments favor as a source of revenue. Not only did states depend on the sales tax for 40% of their revenues in 1973, but local governments turned to this tax for 6.4%. By comparison, the income tax, which raises 42% of federal revenue, accounted for only 16% of state revenue and a puny 3% of local revenue. Moreover, the few local income taxes that are levied do not usually have the same progressive features characteristic of the federal income tax.

Instead, it is the "general practice" with respect to an income tax "to follow the flat rate approach" (Advisory Commission on Intergovernmental Relations, 1974).

One need not posit any local business elite to account for this propensity of local governments to favor these more regressive taxes. The constraints on policy highlighted by the unitary model are by themselves a sufficient explanation. The more starkly the *ability-to-pay* principle governs local tax policy, the greater the disjunction between taxes levied and benefits received, and the greater the negative impact that revenue policy has on the economic well-being of the community. On the other hand, proportional or, preferably, somewhat regressive local taxes come closer to approximating the benefit principle, the principle which, if applied, best strengthens the local economy.

Finally, it is evident that localities have become increasingly dependent on intergovernmental transfers from the state and federal government. As can be seen in Table 2, the percentage of local revenues coming in intergovernmental transfers increased from 26.1% in 1957 to 37.1% in 1973. Of course, localities have an interest in transferring the responsibility for taxation to higher levels of government. To the extent that local government activities can be subsidized by grants coming from resources external to the community, the local public sector contributes to economic growth. And, as a result, local governments compete with one another for as many state and federal resources as they can obtain. But the increasing shift in support for local services from locally generated revenues to revenues generated at the state and national level cannot be attributed simply to the local interest in getting others to foot their bill. That has always been present. Instead, the increasing role of intergovernmental transfers is a concomitant of the increasing redistributive role that local governments are now expected to play. But that requires that we

Table 2 Local Revenues from Intergovernmental Transfers and from own Resources 1957, 1962, 1967 and 1973[*]

Revenues	1957	1962	1967	1973
		(per cent)		
Local resources	73.9	73.0	68.8	62.9
Intergovernmental transfers	26.1	27.0	31.3	37.1
Total (%)	100.0	100.0	100.0	100.0
Total ($m)	28,896	43,278	64,608	129,082

[*]Sources: as for Table 1.

examine the range of activities and functions for which local governments are financially responsible.

EXPENDITURE POLICIES OF NATIONAL, STATE, AND LOCAL GOVERNMENTS

THREE POLICY ARENAS

Just as revenue-raising policies can be contrasted by the extent to which they follow the ability-to-pay as distinct from the benefits-received principle, so expenditure policies can be contrasted according to whether they are designed to provide services to residents consistent with the principle that distributes benefits in accordance with taxes paid or according to some perceived need for governmental assistance. Following this distinction, three kinds of public policies can be distinguished—redistributive, allocational, and developmental (cf. Lowi, 1964; Musgrave, 1959). Expenditures for redistributive policies allocate resources to individuals and groups in the population in reverse proportion to their contributions in taxes. The beneficiaries of the policies are seldom synonymous with those paying for them. A substantial income transfer—in money or in kind—occurs as a result of the governmental expenditure. The pure case is welfare assistance to the nontaxpayer. Expenditures for developmental policies have the polar opposite qualities. Those who benefit from the policy pay for their full cost. Members of the community who derive no benefits pay no charges, and those who do pay charges receive benefits fully commensurate with the charges paid. Indeed, since they prefer the service to the charges paid, there is a net gain for the community. As a result, these programs conserve and maintain the community's economic productivity. A third set of policies falls roughly in the middle. They are designed neither for developmental nor redistributive purposes but simply to provide a variety of benefits and services for the community, taken as a whole. Since taxes fall on community residents unequally, and since the services are valued unequally, the marginal benefit/tax ratio to the average taxpayer is less than 1:0. But, on the other hand, the policies have a considerably higher benefit/tax ratio than the redistributive policies designed to aid those paying few or no taxes. These may be called *allocational* policies.

Government programs are not nicely classified according to these distinctions, and therefore any attempt to apply the classification will necessarily be less precise than one would like. However, the categories by which governmental expenditures are classified by the U.S. Census provide a breakdown which permits some reasonable approximations of the pure distinctions I have outlined. The most obvious examples of redistributive policies are welfare, social security and other forms of social insurance, health and hospital care, and housing. In general, there is at best only a loose correspondence between the individuals who pay for these services and the individuals who receive them.

In the United States, developmental policies are most difficult to discern. Most types of services where beneficiaries can be readily identified and charged accordingly are handled by the private market. But some types of government policies seem comparable to private investments where it is expected that customers purchase sufficient amounts of a good to cover the costs incurred in producing it. The most obvious examples are governmental efforts to improve the transportation and communication systems of the society. In many of these cases, the direct consumers of these services pay charges covering their costs. Gasoline taxes and automobile and truck licences cover the costs of highway building. Management of the national forests is paid for by the charges imposed on farmers, campers and lumber companies. Yet the correspondence between benefits and costs is never exact. The closest one comes are judgments by government officials that the program pays for itself. The community as a whole—and local government in particular—would be less well off economically and financially without the program.

Finally, allocational policies are those which are neither calculated to bring an economic benefit to the community nor provide assistance to the needy. The housekeeping services of local government are the best example. All members of the community benefit from the most valued aspects of police and fire protection and from systematic, community-wide collection of garbage and refuse. These services preclude catastrophic conflagrations, wholesale violations of persons and property, community epidemics, and the use of public spaces as dumps and junkyards. The value each individual places on these services may vary, but all receive important benefits. Moreover, it is likely that these services are particularly appreciated by those taxpayers who possess more valued resources and who therefore pay more in taxes.

POLICY ARENAS AND LEVELS OF GOVERNMENT

Different types of public policies are likely to become the functional responsibility of different levels of government (Oates, 1972). Allocation is the function that local governments can perform more effectively than central governments. Decentralization allows for a closer match between the supply of public services and their variable demand. Citizens migrate to those communities where the allocation best matches their demand curve. Redistribution, on the other hand, is a national function. The interest of the local government in the community's economic prosperity, and its permeability by external forces, precludes achievement of this function. The more a local community engages in redistribution, the more the marginal benefit/tax ratio for the average taxpayer declines, and the more the local economy suffers. Finally, developmental policies will be shared among levels of government, depending on the size of their ripple effects or externalities. Efforts to stabilize the economy through fiscal and monetary policies is a national prerogative. Should a local community attempt to perform this activity, any positive effects its actions have would be quickly dispersed into the larger environment, while the interest on debts incurred would remain a burden the community itself must carry. But other developmental policies may have more specifically local consequences, and in these cases local governments are able to commit their own resources. Building highways and distributing utility services are obvious examples. Developmental policies are thus a responsibility shared among all levels of government. The level of government that assumes responsibility for a particular type of developmental policy depends on the extent of the ripple effects.

Given these considerations, I hypothesize that allocational policies are primarily the responsibility of local governments, while redistributive policies are primarily the responsibility of national governments. The state can be expected to have policy responsibilities midway between. Developmental policies are the shared responsibility of all levels of government.

The pattern of financial responsibility for government policies, as presented in Table 3, is generally consistent with these hypotheses. Redistributive policies have been the fiscal responsibility of the federal government. Of its domestic budget, 47% was allocated for redistributive purposes even at the beginning of the 1960s and, after the Great Society programs, this increased to over 55%. By contrast, the percentage of local revenues used for redistributive policies was only 12.9% in 1962. It is significant that even after the civil rights movement and its supposed impact on local service-delivery systems (Piven, 1976), increased over the next decade by less than 1%. The role of the state stands midway between that of the national and local governments. It has contributed somewhat less than 35% of its budget to redistributive programs.

Table 4 provides an alternative way of analyzing the division of fiscal responsibility among the various levels of government. Here the data are percentaged across the rows rather than down the columns. Instead of obtaining the percentage of each level of government's total resources

(text continued on page 166)

Table 3 Percentage Distribution Among Functions of Direct and Intergovernmental Expenditures by Local, State and Federal Governments from their own Fiscal Resources, 1962, 1967 and 1973

Function	Local Government[1]			State Government[2]			Federal Government[3] (domestic only)		
	1962	1967	1973	1962	1967	1973	1962	1967	1973
	(Percentage of total expenditures by each level of government)								
Redistributive									
Welfare[4]	2.5	2.5	2.0	6.2	6.4	11.2	11.2	11.9	12.6
Hospitals and health[5]	6.1	6.7	8.6	7.4	7.2	6.2	3.3	3.7	3.5
Housing[6]	2.4	1.5	.9	.2	.2	.4	1.5	1.9	3.4
Social insurance[7]	1.9	2.2	2.3	14.4	9.4	17.0	29.7	34.0	35.6
Subtotal	12.9	12.9	13.8	28.2	23.2	34.8	46.7	51.5	55.1
Allocation									
Housekeeping[8]	26.8	26.4	28.5	12.4	12.9	8.4	4.6	4.5	3.8
Developmental									
Utilities[9]	13.2	13.1	11.1	–	–	–	–	–	–
Postal[10]	–	–	–	–	–	–	7.0	7.2	5.1
Transportation[11]	8.1	6.6	5.7	17.8	16.0	11.3	6.2	5.8	4.2
Natural resources[12]	1.1	1.1	0.7	2.9	3.5	2.3	19.3	9.9	7.8
Subtotal	22.4	20.8	17.5	20.7	19.5	13.6	32.5	22.9	17.1
Interest[13]	4.1	4.4	5.6	2.2	2.3	2.7	12.3	12.1	9.9
Education[14]	33.4	35.2	34.2	33.6	39.5	38.4	3.2	7.2	8.2
Other[15]	.4	.3	.4	3.0	2.6	2.2	.8	1.8	5.8
Total (%)	100.0	100.0	100.0	100.1	100.0	100.1	100.1	100.0	99.9
Total ($m)	33,591	45,853	77,886	29,356	45,288	89,504	58,960	86,852	186,172

SOURCE: Appendix A, which presents the sources from which the above table was prepared, can be found on pages 281 to 314 of the July 1979 issue of the *British Journal of Political Science*. Those unable to obtain a copy of the issue may request reprints from Professor Paul Peterson, Department of Political Science, University of Chicago, Chicago, Illinois 60637.

Table 4 Percentage Distribution Among Governments of Direct and Intergovernmental Expenditures by Local, State and Federal Governments from their own Fiscal Resources, by Function, 1962, 1967 and 1973*

Function	Local Government			State Government			Federal Government			Total		
	1962	1967	1973	1962	1967	1973	1962	1967	1973	1962	1967	1973
	(Percentage of expenditures for each function by all governments)											
Redistributive												
Welfare	8.5	7.8	4.3	18.4	20.1	28.7	73.1	72.1	67.2	100.0	100.0	100.2
Hospitals and health	33.2	32.2	35.4	35.2	34.0	29.6	31.6	33.8	35.0	100.0	100.0	100.0
Housing	46.7	29.3	9.7	2.5	3.8	4.5	50.7	66.9	84.8	99.9	100.0	100.0
Social insurance	2.9	2.9	2.2	18.9	12.3	18.2	78.1	84.8	79.6	99.9	100.0	100.0
Subtotal	10.8	9.7	7.4	20.6	17.2	21.5	68.6	73.2	71.1	100.0	100.0	100.1
Allocational												
Housekeeping	58.7	55.4	60.2	23.7	26.6	20.4	17.5	17.8	19.4	99.9	99.8	100.0
Developmental												
Postal	–	–	–	–	–	–	100.0	100.0	100.0	100.0	100.0	100.0
Utilities	100.0	100.0	100.0	–	–	–	–	–	–	–	–	–
Transportation	23.3	19.7	20.1	45.1	47.3	45.0	31.6	33.0	34.9	100.0	100.0	100.0
Natural resources	3.0	4.7	3.3	6.7	14.9	12.0	90.3	80.4	84.7	100.0	100.0	100.0
Subtotal	23.0	24.9	23.8	18.5	23.1	21.0	58.5	52.0	55.2	100.0	100.0	100.0
Interest	14.9	14.8	17.2	6.9	7.6	9.6	78.2	77.6	73.2	100.0	100.0	100.0
Education	48.9	40.0	34.9	43.0	44.4	45.0	8.1	15.6	20.0	100.0	100.0	99.9
Other	8.6	5.4	2.2	60.1	41.1	15.3	31.3	53.5	82.5	100.0	100.0	100.0

*See notes to Table 3.

devoted to a governmental activity, Table 4 provides the percentage of all expenditures devoted to a particular activity contributed by each level of government. Presented in this way, the figures are even more dramatic. Not only was the local contribution to redistribution scarcely more than 10% in 1962 but also it has declined since that time. On the other hand, the federal role is once again shown to be especially significant. If the political pressures for federalizing welfare policy and health care are any sign, this pattern is likely to continue. As the United States continues to become an increasingly integrated political economy, the redistributive function must become an almost exclusively federal prerogative.

The allocative function is just as clearly the domain of local governments. The delivery of housekeeping services that all members of the community depend upon are both delivered *and financed* locally. As can be seen in Table 3, over 28% of local government revenues were devoted to this purpose in 1973. The state plays a supporting role, but the proportion of its revenues devoted to this purpose is less than half that of the local governments. And the federal government is hardly involved at all.[4]

The developmental function is shared more or less equally among the three levels of government, all of whom have allocated about 20% of their revenues for these activities. The role of the federal government in promoting economic productivity is larger than these figures suggest, once its interest payments on the national debt are taken into account. Since these are in large measure due to the federal government's responsibility for managing the national economy through its fiscal policies, they can be considered to be a cost of carrying out its developmental function.[5] The bulk of local expenditures for developmental purposes are used to operate municipal utilities. Since customers pay for services received, costs and benefits are largely internalized. It is this type of developmental function that a local government can perform most easily.

I have classified education separately in Tables 3 and 4 because classification of this governmental function is particularly difficult. In a separate paper I show that the probable impact of government educational policies is slightly redistributive, but the redistributive impact seems to be much less than in the arenas of welfare, housing or health policy.[6] When one considers the allocation of responsibility among the various levels of government, it is quite consistent with a social impact that is neither strictly allocational nor highly distributive. On the one side, local governments contribute substantial portions of their resources to the financing of local schools. In 1973, 34% of all local government expenditures were for educational purposes, a level of local commitment that does not seem feasible if education were a highly redistributive public policy (see Table

3). On the other side, there have been long-term pressures for increased state and federal support for schooling and, indeed, the percentage of the federal domestic budget devoted to education increased from 3.2% to 8.2% in the decade between 1962 and 1973. When one examines the data percentaged across the columns in Table 4, the increasing federal role is all the more apparent. Whereas local governments paid for nearly one-half of the public cost of education in 1962, by 1973 their contribution declined to little more than a third. In the meantime, the federal share increased from 8% to 20%. It is worth noting that this change in the financing of education occurred precisely at the time when redistributive pressures in the educational sector were most intense.

The increasing role of the federal government in education has been exercised largely by means of a system of intergovernmental transfers. And it is not only in the field of education that intergovernmental transfers have been a concomitant of redistributive policy making. In Table 5, the distribution by function of intergovernmental revenues from the federal

Table 5 Intergovernmental Expenditures by State and Federal Governments, by Function, 1962, 1967 and 1973*

| | Intergovernmental Expenditure (per cent) | | | | | |
| | State Government | | | Federal Government | | |
Function	1962	1967	1973	1962	1967	1973
Redistributive						
Welfare	16.3	15.2	18.4	31.6	28.2	29.0
Hospitals and health	1.8	1.6	2.1	2.2	2.7	4.2
Housing	.3	.4	.4	4.1	4.5	5.1
Social insurance	–	–	–	6.0	3.8	1.9
Subtotal	18.4	17.2	20.9	43.9	39.1	40.2
Allocation						
Housekeeping	–	–	–	.9	.9	2.1
Developmental						
Transportation	12.2	9.9	7.4	36.3	27.4	13.2
Natural resources	.2	.2	.2	1.8	1.6	1.6
Subtotal	12.4	10.1	7.6	38.1	29.0	14.8
Education	59.4	62.2	57.1	15.1	26.1	20.8
Other and undesignated	9.7	10.6	14.4	2.0	4.9	22.0
Total	99.9	100.0	100.0	100.0	100.0	99.9
Dollars (millions)	10,906	19,056	40,822	7,735	15,027	41,666

*See notes to Table 3.

and state governments to lower governmental levels is reported. The states allocate most of their intergovernmental moneys for educational purposes. But the primary role of the federal government has been to finance the redistributive expenditures of states and localities. Even in 1973, after the establishment of a revenue-sharing programme by the Nixon administration, 40% of intergovernmental revenues received by states and localities were specifically designated for a redistributive function. The increase in undesignated revenues in that year came largely at the expense of funds for productive and for educational purposes, not as a substitute for redistributive activities.

DETERMINANTS OF STATE AND LOCAL EXPENDITURES

These distinctions among developmental, allocational, and redistributive policies are not only useful for distinguishing among the programs likely to be funded by varying levels of government. In this section I shall show that they also help account for the factors that determine variations in expenditure levels among state and local government units. In general, three variables can be expected to influence the level at which local (and, to a lesser extent, state) governments provide any particular public service—fiscal capacity, economic demand, and the cost of supplying the service.

THREE POLICY ARENAS AND EXPENDITURE PATTERNS

These three variables have varying relationships with the level of expenditures, depending on the type of public policy being provided (see Table 6). In the case of redistributive policies, the relationship between fiscal capacity and expenditure levels is high. Because the beneficiaries of the policy are different from the taxpayers, the benefit/tax ratio for the average tax payer is particularly low. Any increase in the tax rate for redistributive services is likely to have particularly harmful economic consequences. Consequently, tax rates financing redistributive policies must be much the same,[7] and variations in fiscal capacity will thus determine much of the variation in expenditure. Measures of the supposed need for redistributive policies, on the other hand, will be weakly correlated with expenditures. Because the need for redistributive policies is unlikely to be felt by taxpaying residents of the community, there is no way for the need to become translated into effective demand. Similarly, one does not hypothesize a strong relationship between the cost of

Table 6   Types of Public Policy and Determinants of Local
Government Expenditure: Hypothesized Relationships

| | Determinants of Expenditure | | | |
Type of Policy	Fiscal Capacity	Demand	Supply	'Need'
Redistributive	High	–	Low	Low or negative
Allocational	Moderate	Moderate	Moderate	–
Developmental	Low	High	Moderate	–

supplying a service and expenditure levels. Because the benefit/tax ratio is low, redistributive policies are the one type of local government service for which price elasticity of demand is probably equal to 1:0. As costs of the service increase, the supply of the service will decrease by a comparable amount so that overall expenditures remain the same.

Exactly opposite patterns of correlation are expected in the case of developmental policies. Because the marginal benefit/tax ratio for these services is high, and the perceived benefits may even exceed costs, fiscal capability is not likely to have a significant effect on expenditure levels. Measures of need, on the other hand, will be strongly correlated, because need will reflect itself in economic demand for the policy. And supply variables can also be expected to affect expenditures, because the price elasticity of demand for the service is likely to be less than 1:0.

Allocational policies fall somewhere in between. Because the benefit/tax ratio is less than 1:0, fiscal capability will affect the level at which services are provided. On the other hand, the benefit/tax ratio is not as low in the case of redistributive policies, and therefore indicators of economic demand and the cost of supplying the service also affect expenditure levels.

AN EMPIRICAL TEST

After this section of the article had been drafted, I tested these propositions relating fiscal capacity, economic demand, and the cost of supplying government services to the three different types of policies. Although the unitary model is more applicable to local than to state governments, the test was conducted on the aggregated policies of state and local governments for all 50 states. Problems of identifying comparable units of analysis at the local level are so severe that the expenditures of state and local governments, taken together, provide the best available dependent variables.[8]

State and locally financed expenditures and three financially significant welfare policies provided measures of redistributive, allocational, and developmental policies. Expenditures on welfare and health and hospitals, together with the average payments to recipients of old age assistance, aid to dependent children, and to the unemployed, provided six measures of redistributive policy. Police and fire expenditures yielded information on allocational policies. The best quantitative measure of developmental policies consisted of expenditures on streets and highways. I also obtained per-capita expenditures on education.

Eight independent variables were selected to identify the relative importance of fiscal capacity, demand-supply factors, and noneconomic needs. The two indicators of the fiscal capacity of state and local governments were median family income and its per-capita property value. Three measures of urbanization—the percentage living in metropolitan areas, density, and percent employed in nonagricultural occupations—provided indicators of variation in the economic demand for, and the cost of, supplying several of the dependent variables. Because urbanization is correlated with wage rates and the price of many materials, urbanization may be accepted as a proxy for variations in the cost of supplying government services. At the same time, they reflect changes in the economic demand for allocative policies, such as police and fire protection. Urbanization is also negatively associated with the economic demand for roads and highways. Besides these three measures of urbanization, a more direct indicator of the cost of supplying government services was included—the average wage paid in the manufacturing sector. Finally, two indicators of need unable to reflect itself in economic demand were included—per cent with low incomes and the percentage black. A full description of all the independent and dependent variables is given in Peterson (1979c: Appendix B).

The simple correlations between these eight independent variables and each of the nine public policies are presented in Table 7. Although the pattern of correlation is generally consistent with the hypotheses, simple correlations can be misleading. Apparently strong relationships may turn out to be spurious when controls are introduced; apparently weak relationships may become stronger once impeding variables are removed. At the same time, the inclusion of highly correlated independent variables in a regression analysis creates other problems of interpretation. After numerous analyses, in which I sought to minimize these contrasting but equally exasperating problems, I discovered that almost as much of the variance in the public policies could be explained by just three variables—income, metropolitan population, and percentage black—as by regressions including

Table 7 Simple Correlations between Public Policies and Fiscal Capacity, Demand/Supply and 'Need'

| | Determinants of Expenditure[14] | | | | | | | |
| | Fiscal Capacity | | Demand/Supply | | | | 'Need' but no Demand | |
Type of Policy	Income[15]	Property Values[16]	Density[12]	Metropolitan Population[18]	Non-agricultural Employment[19]	Wages[20]	Poverty[21]	Black[22]
Redistributive								
Old age assistance[1]	.50	.44	.12	.20	.32	.26	-.41	-.25
Aid to dependent children[2]	.71	.59	.45	.26	.45	.37	-.76	-.57
Unemployment benefits[3]	.81	.74	.46	.53	.58	.47	-.70	-.33
Welfare expenditure[4,5]	.59	.58	.53	.47	.56	.22	-.50	-.28
Hospitals and health[8,9]	.33	.47	.16	.33	.42	.17	-.14	.19
Education[6,7]	.74	.54	.11	.22	.35	.70	-.66	-.46
Allocational								
Police[10]	.70	.73	.37	.60	.65	.39	-.50	-.11
Fire[11]	.69	.73	.55	.64	.71	.28	-.56	-.20
Developmental								
Highways[12,13]	.12	.06	-.35	-.58	-.25	.38	-.15	-.44

SOURCE: Appendix B, which presents the sources from which the above table was prepared, can be found on pages 281 to 314 of the July 1979 issue of the *British Journal of Political Science*. Those unable to obtain a copy of the issue may request reprints from Professor Paul Peterson, Department of Political Science, University of Chicago, Chicago, Illinois 60637.

twice that number. Since the three variables provided one indicator of each of the three theoretically significant concepts that had been elaborated, the simple regression presented in Table 8 proved to be the best test of the hypotheses.

In Table 8 it becomes even more apparent how important fiscal capacity is for determining redistributive policies. The level of old age assistance, the amount of aid to dependent children, and the level of unemployment benefits are all heavily dependent on the fiscal resources of state and local governments. To a lesser extent, overall expenditures on welfare and on health and hospitals are also dependent on the fiscal resources of the jurisdiction. Educational policies, too, are a function of the state's income level. Even though education is a less redistributive policy, it is heavily financed by local governments and therefore seems especially sensitive to fiscal factors.

It is equally important to note the variables with which redistributive policies are unrelated. Although blacks are one of the most needy groups in the American population, for most redistributive policies there is a negative relationship between their percentage of a state's population and the level of benefits received. Also the result does not change when the percentage of low-income people living in the state is substituted for the per cent black. As can be seen in Table 7, both the presence of blacks and the presence of poverty are negatively related to redistributive expenditures. The only exception to this pattern is the case of health and hospital expenditures, where there is a hint that black need for hospital care actually increases expenditures for the service. The peculiar mechanisms by which this need becomes and effective determinant of locally financed public health care seem worthy of specialized attention. On the other side, note that even when a state's fiscal resources are controlled, as in the regression analysis in Table 8, the presence of blacks dampens the amount of support for dependent children.

Allocative policies were, as predicted, responsive to both fiscal capacity and demand/supply factors. In the case of fire expenditures the two seemed roughly equal in importance. On the other hand, police expenditures seemed somewhat more responsive to fiscal capacity than to demand/supply factors. Perhaps by 1970 local authorities were beginning to believe that marginal increments in police expenditures yield relatively small marginal benefits to average taxpayers, and therefore more is paid for these services only if fiscal capacity is ample.

Developmental policies proved to be very strongly related to demand/supply factors in just the way that had been anticipated. The more rural the state, the more it spends on highways. Given the greater importance of

Table 8 Income, Metropolitan Population, and Per Cent Black as Determinants of Three Types of Public Policy (Standardized Beta Coefficients)

| | Determinants of Expenditure | | | |
| | Fiscal Capacity | Demand/Supply | 'Need but no demand | |
Type of Policy	Income	Metropolitan Population	Black	Multiple R
Redistributive				
Old age assistance	.58†	-.14	-.01	.51
Aid to dependent children	.63†	-.07	-.32†	.78
Unemployment benefits	.71†	.12	-.07	.81
Welfare expenditures	.35*	.29*	-.18	.63
Hospitals and health	.48†	-.00	.38†	.48
Education	.88†	-.29*	-.09	.79
Allocational				
Police	.59†	.24*	.08	.74
Fire	.42†	.40†	-.10	.75
Developmental				
Highways	.67†	-.97†	-.06	.81

*t statistic significant at .05 level.
†t statistic significant at .01 level.

173

highways for the economy of the rural state, such policies are certainly sensible. Yet the strong responsiveness of this developmental policy to the needs of the rural economy contrasts sharply with the impotence of need as a determinant of redistributive policy. On the other hand, my hypotheses had not anticipated the relatively smaller but nonetheless strong relationship between fiscal capacity and highway expenditure.

Skeptics may may raise three objections to these findings: (1) the separate effects of economic demand for services and the cost of supplying them have not been analyzed; (2) the relationship among the variables may change once the impact of federal assistance is taken into account; and (3) the findings may be heavily influenced by the presence of southern states in the sample of 50 states. All three possible criticisms gain little support from additional data analysis.[9]

First, consider Table 9 which makes an attempt at separating out the effects of the economic demand for services and the cost of supplying them. Income remains the indicator of fiscal capacity and in Table 9 metropolitan population is treated as an indicator of positive demand for educational and allocational services and of negative demand for highway expenditures. I also include hourly earnings in manufacturing as a plausible indicator of the cost of supplying allocational, developmental, and educational services. The findings confirm the initial propositions in almost all details. Redistributive policies are strictly a function of fiscal capacity; the other variables have little effect. As might be expected, educational policies are influenced both by fiscal capacity and by the cost of supplying this labor-intensive service. Relationships between allocational policies and the independent variables are also much as hypothesized. They are influenced by all three factors: fiscal capacity, demand, and, in the case of fire services, by the cost of supply. Finally, highway expenditures, the one example of a developmental policy, are most heavily influenced by the higher demand for the services in rural areas, but it is quite consistent with my expectations that they are also influenced by cost factors. The one unanticipated finding is that highway expenditures are also a function of fiscal capacity.

Next consider the impact of federal aid on locally financed expenditures. In doing so, remember that the dependent variable includes only those expenditures not directly financed by federal grants-in-aid. Table 10 nonetheless shows that federal aid is strongly associated with welfare and highway expenditures locally. The causal direction of this relationship is not easily discerned. On the one hand, the availability of federal assistance may encourage local spending on these programs. On the other hand, matching formulae produce increased federal commitments whenever local

(text continued on page 177)

Table 9 Income, Metropolitan Population and Wages as Determinants of Public Policy (Standardized Beta Coefficients)

| | | *Determinants of Expenditure* | | |
| | *Fiscal Capacity* | *Demand/Supply* | | |
Type of Policy	*Income*	*Metropolitan Population*	*Wages*	*Multiple R*
Redistributive				
Old age assistance	.71†	-.18	-.16	.52
Aid to dependent children	1.04†	-.30†	-.24*	.76
Unemployment benefits	.82	.06	-.08	.81
Welfare expenditures	.69†	.13	-.27*	.64
Hospitals and health	.25	.20	-.04	.37
Education	.71†	-.28†	.30†	.82
Allocational				
Police	.57†	.28*	-.05	.74
Fire	.67†	.30†	-.23*	.77
Developmental				
Highways	.47†	-.93†	.31†	.84

*t statistic significant at .05 level.
†t statistic significant at .01 level.

175

Table 10 Federal Aid and Local Expenditure (Standardized Beta Coefficients)

| | | Determinants of Expenditure | | | |
| | | Fiscal Capacity | Demand/Supply | 'Need' but no demand | |
Type of Policy	Federal Aid	Income	Metropolitan Population	Black	Multiple R
Redistributive					
Welfare	.67†	.62†	.02	-.08	.89
Hospitals and health	-.06	.47†	.03	.38†	.49
Education	.19*	.88†	-.37†	-.14	.81
Allocational					
Police	.15	.54†	.33*	.08	.76
Fire	.12	.38†	.47†	-.10	.76
Developmental					
Highways	.65†	.34†	-.47†	.02	.94

*t statistic significant at .05 level.
†t statistic significant at .01 level.

contributions increase. In any case, these correlations are not my primary consideration; wheat is relevant to the hypothesis being tested is whether federal aid changes the relationships between expenditures and the fiscal capacity, demand, and supply factors. Table 10 reveals that the federal impact on these relationships is minimal. Fiscal capacity remains the primary determinant of redistributive expenditures; demand/supply variables remain the most important determinant of developmental expenditures; and allocational policies remain affected by both fiscal capacity and demand/supply factors. Except for health policy, the needs of minorities have no significant effect on expenditure levels.

Finally, the pattern of relationships changes only slightly when the states of the Confederacy are deleted from the analysis. I do not know any particularly good reason for deleting the South from the analysis; it is part of the market economy of the United States and is subject to the same external pressures as any other region. Cultural differences are not so great that entirely different patterns of interaction among variables are to be expected. But for those who insist that interstate comparisons take into account the distinctiveness of the South, Table 11 reports the findings only for the other 39 states.

SUMMARY AND IMPLICATIONS

This article has advanced a unitary model of policy making to supplement bargaining models that have been previously used to interpret the politics of local taxation and expenditure and the study of local politics more generally. This model assumes that the local government system seeks to maximize the economic productivity of the local community and that all policies are selected with this overriding goal in mind. In pursuit of this goal, local governments, to the extent possible, raise revenues according to the benefits-received principle rather than the ability-to-pay principle and, where this is not possible, they tax those resources that can only be transported elsewhere at considerable expense.

Local governments also prefer to spend moneys on those services for which beneficiaries overlap taxpayers. Three types of public policies can thus be distinguished: redistributive, allocational, and developmental. Redistributive policies, whose primary beneficiaries are nontaxpayers, are seldom financed by local governments from their own resources. Instead, local governments spend most moneys on either developmental policies, which contribute to the local economy, or on allocational policies, which are desired more or less equally by all members of the community and which, in the aggregate, have only a marginal, negative effect on the local

Table 11 Income, Metropolitan Population, Non-agricultural Employment and Percent Black as Determinants of Public Policy, Non-South Only (Standardized Beta Coefficients)

| | Fiscal Capacity | Determinants of Expenditure | | | Multiple R |
| | | Demand/Supply | | 'Need' but no demand | |
Type of Policy	Income	Metropolitan Population	Non-agricultural	Black	
Redistributive					
Old age assistance	.54†	-.17	.09	-.14	.52
Aid to dependent children	.58†	-.01	.01	-.25	.59
Unemployment benefits	.61†	.29	-.07	-.08	.76
Welfare expenditures	.13	.28	.32	-.21	.62
Hospitals and health	.98†	-.18	.39*	.18	.55
Education	.98†	-.28	-.32*	.04	.70
Allocational					
Police	.39*	.13	.24	.09	.72
Fire	.17	.31*	.42†	-.17	.76
Developmental					
Highways	.72†	†1.04†	-.10	-.01	.84

*t statistic significant at .05 level.
†t statistic significant at .01 level.

economy. Determinants of the level of government spending vary by these three policy arenas. Expenditures for redistributive purposes vary with the fiscal capacity of the local community, because these services can be supported only by a tax rate which is no higher than the tax rate for such purposes in competing communities. Expenditures for developmental purposes vary with the economic demand for the policy, because the local community, whatever its fiscal resources, has an incentive to make the investment whenever a reasonable economic return is likely. Expenditures for allocational policies, whose characteristics fall midway between developmental and redistributive policies, are influenced by both fiscal capacity and demand/supply factors.

These findings have implications for the study of local politics and policy formation.[10] In many studies of urban politics, it has been assumed that findings from the local level can be generalized to the nation as a whole. But, given the quite different function that local governments perform in the national political system, their political processes are likely to be substantially different. For one thing, redistributive questions are unlikely to become local political issues. Some scholars have suggested that this is due to a power elite or to some hidden force which is preventing such issues from becoming manifest (Bachrach and Baratz, 1962; Hunter, 1953). Others have suggested that conservative business interests are particularly powerful in the small constituency politics of the local community (McConnel, 1966). But, if my analysis is correct, it is more likely that redistributive issues are not raised locally because a wide variety of political groups active in local politics implicitly appreciate the impracticality of locally financed redistribution (Peterson, 1979b).

NOTES

1. My approach is quite different. From the perspective of the unitary model, political variables are assumed to be unimportant. State and local units of government are presumed to be unitary systems that rationally respond to environmental conditions with policies that maximize their economic well-being. To test the model the relative importance of various environmental variables is examined; political variables are left out of the equation altogether. Therefore, it is appropriate to use findings from research that has solved the unit-of-analysis problem by aggregating the combined expenditures of state and local governments at the state level. I discuss these methodological issues in greater detail in Peterson (1978).

2. Just how inefficient this can be is demonstrated by a comparison of the relative costs of public and private garbage collection in New York City. Even though

the conditions for collection are more or less the same, the costs of public collection are double those in the private sector (see Savas, 1974).

3. Even this may not be the correct way of making the point unless one takes into account both direct and indirect contributions to tax coffers. A local firm may be exempt from any direct local taxes, but it may nonetheless be important to the local economy and thus indirectly a most important taxpayer. Were it to leave the community, the fiscal resources of the area would be adversely affected.

4. I have included general control expenditures among the housekeeping services of government, and it is this that accounts for the 3.8% of federal expenditures on allocational activities.

5. State and local government deficit spending does not have the countercyclical effects that federal deficits are expected to have (see Hansen and Perloff, 1944; Rafuse, 1965; Sharp, 1965). Consequently, it is not appropriate to classify local interest payments as expenditures for developmental policies unless the project that the debt financed paid for itself.

6. I have discussed this problem more fully in Peterson (1979a).

7. Thus, variations among states in expenditures as a percentage of state income is much less than variation in expenditures uncontrolled for income differences. In 1973, for example, state and local moneys spent on public services as a percentage of the personal income earned by state residents varied only modestly. The coefficient of variation was .12. By contrast, the coefficient of variation for expenditure per capita (uncontrolled for income differences) was a substantial .36. When federal aid was included, this coefficient declined only slightly to .32 (data computed from Maxwell and Aronson (1977).

8. A discussion of methodological problems can be found in Peterson (1978).

9. The hypotheses are also supported by many other studies of expenditure policies. Although these studies have been cast within other conceptual frameworks, their specific findings, when placed within the framework of the unitary model, yield patterns of correlation similar to those reported here. Space precludes presentation of this supporting evidence; see Peterson (1978, forthcoming).

10. I explore the many implications of these and other findings generated by the unitary model in Peterson (forthcoming).

REFERENCES

Advisory Commission on Intergovernmental Relations (1974) Local Revenue Diversification: Incomes, Sales Tax and User Charges. Washington, DC: Government Printing Office.

AGGER, R., D. GOLDRICH and B. SWANSON (1964) The Rulers and the Ruled. New York: John Wiley.

ALLISON, G. (1971) Essence of Decision: Explaining the Cuban Missile Crisis. Boston: Little, Brown.

BABCOCK, R. F. (1966) The Zoning Game. Madison: University of Wisconsin Press.

BACHRACH, P. and M. S. BARATZ (1962) "Two faces of power." American Political Science Review 56: 947-952.

BANFIELD, E. (1961) Political Influence. New York: Macmillan.

BRAZER, H. S. (1959) City Expenditures in the United States Occasional Papers 66. New York: National Bureau of Economic Research.

CEBULA, R. J. (1974) "Local government policies and migration: an analysis for SMSAs in the United States." Public Choice 19: 85-94.

CLARK, T. N. (1968) "Community structure, decision making, budget expenditures, and urban renewal in 51 American cities." American Sociological Review 33: 576-593.

DAHL, R. (1961) Who Governs? New Haven, CT: Yale University Press.

DYE, T. (1966) Politics, Economics and the Public Policy: Policy Outcomes in the American States. Chicago: Rand McNally.

FABRICANT, S. (1952) The Trend of Government Activity in the United States Since 1900 Occasional Papers 66. New York: National Bureau of Economic Research.

HANSEN, A. H. and H. S. PERLOFF (1944) State and Local Finance in the National Economy. New York: Norton.

HUNTER, F. (1953) Community Power Structure. Chapel Hill: University of North Carolina Press.

KING, A. T. (1977) "Estimating property tax capitalization: a critical comment." Journal of Political Economy 85: 425-431.

LINEBERRY, R. and E. P. FOWLER (1967) "Reformism and public policies in American cities." American Political Science Review 61: 701-716.

LOWI, T. (1964) "American business, public policy, case studies and political theory." World Politics 16: 677-715.

MAXWELL, J. A. and R. ARONSON (1977) Financing State and Local Governments. Washington, DC: Brookings Institution.

McCONNELL, G. (1966) Private Power and American Democracy. New York: Alfred A. Knopf.

McDOUGALL, G. S. (1976) "Local public goods and residential property values: some insights and extensions." National Tax Journal 29: 436-447.

MELTSNER, A. J. (1971) The Politics of City Revenue. Berkeley: University of California Press.

MILLS, E. S. and W. E. OATES [eds.] (1975) Fiscal Zoning and Land Use Controls. Lexington, MA: D. C. Heath.

MUSGRAVE, R. A. (1959) The Theory of Public Finance. New York: McGraw-Hill.

NETZER, D. (1966) Economics of the Property Tax. Washington, DC: Brookings Institution.

OATES, W. E. (1973) "Effects of property taxes and local public spending on property values: a reply and further results." Journal of Political Economy 81: 1004-1008.

——— (1969) "The effects of property taxes and local public spending on property values: an empirical study of tax capitalization of the tiebout hypothesis." Journal of Political Economy 77: 957-971.

——— (1972) Fiscal Federalism. New York: Harcourt Brace Jovanovich.

PETERSON, P. E. (forthcoming) City Limits. Chicago: University of Chicago Press.

——— (1979a) "Developmental versus redistributive policies in central city and suburban schools." Presented at the meeting of the American Educational Research Association, San Francisco.

——— (1979b) "Redistributive policies and patterns of citizen participation in local politics," in L. G. Sharpe (ed.) Decentralist Trends in Western Democracies. Beverly Hills, CA: Sage.

––– (1979c) "A unitary model of local taxation and expenditure policies in the United States." British Journal of Political Science 9: 281-314.

––– (1978) "The politics of taxation and expenditure: a unitary approach." Presented at the meeting of the American Political Science Association, New York City.

––– (1976) School Politics Chicago Style. Chicago: University of Chicago Press.

PIVEN, F. (1976) "The urban fiscal crisis," in S. D. and P. Peterson (eds.) Urban Politics and Public Policy. New York: Praeger.

POLLAKOWSKI, H. O. (1973) "The effects of property taxes and local public spending on property values: a comment and further results." Journal of Political Economy 81: 994-1003.

RAFUSE, R. W., Jr. (1965) "Cyclical behavior of state-local finances," in R. A. Musgrave (ed.) Essays in Fiscal Federalism. Washington, DC: Brookings Institution.

ROSEN, H. S. and D. J. Fullerton (1977) "A note on local tax rates, public benefit levels and property values." Journal of Political Economy 85: 433-440.

SAVAS, E. S. (1974) "Municipal monopolies versus competition in delivering urban services," in W. D. Hawley and D. Rogers (eds.) Improving the Quality of Urban Management. Beverly Hills, CA: Sage.

SHARP, A. M. (1965) "The behavior of selected state and local government fiscal variables during the phases of the cycles, 1949-1961." Proceedings of the National Tax Association: 599-613.

TIEBOUT, C. M. (1956) "A pure theory of local government." Journal of Political Economy 64: 416-424.

U.S. Department of Commerce, Bureau of the Census (1976) "Local government finances in selected metropolitan areas and large counties: 1974-75."

WEBER, M. (1958) "Class, status, and power," in H. H. Gerth and C. W. Mills (eds.) From Max Weber. New York: Oxford University Press.

WEICHER, J. C. (1970) "Determinants of central city expenditures–some overlooked factors and problems." National Tax Journal 43: 379-396.

6

POLITICAL THEORY AND TRANSFORMATIONS
IN URBAN BUDGETARY ARENAS:
The Case of New York City

STEPHEN M. DAVID

PAUL KANTOR

Fordham University

POLITICAL THEORY AND POLICY FORMATION

Although the study of public policy formation has mushroomed to a point where the state of the art is at an all-time high, we are witnessing a familiar predicament. Theoretical innovation has tended to be one of piecemeal breakthrough, focusing on particular sets of variables while neglecting the larger phenomena to which these parts are related. Environmental, decisional, and policy output theories constitute three such innovative currents. Yet, because all of these are essentially segmental theoretical attempts to deal with policy formation, they are unable to adequately explain how changes in policy-making processes occur. Such a result is illustrated by the case of urban budgetary politics which contemporary

AUTHORS' NOTE: We wish to acknowledge the financial assistance of the Fordham University Research Council in preparing this article. We wish to thank Vincent Brevetti for his efforts as a research assistant and Mark Ritze who provided invaluable editorial assistance.

theory interprets as a relatively static aspect of local governance. Drawing upon the case of New York City since 1945, we argue that major transformations in the city's budgetary arena are evident; further, these changes can be explained by examining systematic interrelationships among the city's economic environment, decisional processes, and budgetary outputs.

While theories of policy formation all recognize certain systemic characteristics of government at the highest levels of analysis, each has, in fact, been more concerned with demonstrating the political relevance of isolated sets of social, economic, and institutional variables (Easton, 1953). One major consequence of such analysis is that policy-making theory has not developed much capability for explaining how changes in the political order occur, i.e., substantive alterations in the ways public policies are formulated and in the output responses of government. Environmental theory is one such case (Hofferbert, 1974; Dye, 1966, 1969, 1972; Hofferbert and Sharkansky, 1969; Lineberry and Fowler, 1967; Sharkansky, 1967, 1968, 1969; Cnudde and McCrone, 1969). Environmental theory assumes that the authoritative activities of decision makers tend to be responsive to the influence of largely impersonal social and economic forces. Relying heavily on aggregate data analysis, these theorists have focused on measuring and evaluating socioeconomic inputs in the political process because their studies have revealed that differences in political structures appear to have a very limited impact on the pattern of governmental outputs (Dawson and Robinson, 1963). Given the demonstrated significance of contextual variables, environmental theory posits that policy making is typically a "transactional" phenomenon, i.e., it involves subtle social and economic relationships which go beyond any single issue or decision.

However, the environmental model is incapable of explaining the possible sources of political change. By seeking to identify only simple statistical associations between socioeconomic variables and policy outputs at a point in time, patterns of socioeconomic development and their causes are excluded from the theoretical framework. In particular, one source of developmental change—the impact of policy outputs on society—are ignored. This is so because the environmental approach is essentially unidirectional; it posits that the environment supposedly explains policy, neglecting to identify feedback effects on society which result from the decisions of public authorities (Ranney, 1968). Consequently, more recent scholars seeking to understand the political economy of urban government have generally ignored the framework employed by environmental theorists since it is a limited tool for explaining patterns of socioeconomic development (Walton, 1976).

Further, by characterizing political changes solely as changes in governmental outputs, environmental theory neglects transformations in the governmental process by which outputs are formulated. Typically, the political system is treated in a formalistic fashion, as though it were a sort of black box through which outputs are expected to flow in direct response to contextual pressures. It would seem to matter a great deal if rioting and disorder, business elites, or lobbies are necessary to produce particular outputs in certain governmental systems, yet changes in the way issues are determined (apart from what is determined) are not accounted for in the environmental model (Coulter, 1970).

In contrast, decisional theorists do deal with how policies are formulated. Truman (1951), Dahl (1961), Dror (1968), Allison (1971), and many others stress the idea of policy making as a decisional process, i.e., the interaction of socially microscopic phenomena encompassing interpersonal relations, groups, and other aggregates. Larger macroscopic elements, such as environmental and institutional forces which impinge on individual behavior are treated in micropolitical terms. Thus, rules of the game, political norms, and legislative bodies are considered to be specialized processes in themselves. Consequently, the major unit of analysis is considered to be the decision, a kind of "resultant" of interaction among the microelements in the political process.

Despite the supposed surface realism of decisional theory, it is also difficult to use this form of analysis to explain transformations in the policy-making order. Decisional theorists have assumed that the mechanism for political change exists within each decisional process; the explanation for change lies in an understanding of the intricacies of the process. For example, change occurs in a pluralist system when previously apathetic groups decide to involve themselves in an issue of consequence to them. This notion of political change is open to the same criticism as was made with respect to the environmental theorists. Like their environmental counterparts, decisional analysis does not explain what causes the developments in the decision process which lead to new patterns of policy formation and governmental outputs. Additionally, the assumption that decisional processes are the source of all change has been challenged by environmentalists who see their set of variables as primary causal factors.

The major reason for this theoretical limitation is that decision theory cannot specify the conditions or circumstances under which transformations in the decisional process take place. Socioeconomic constraints imposed by the environment on the political order are largely impersonal and, as such, they are not easily aggregated in microscopic terms and expressed as individual decisional units. Consequently, they are reduced to mere "residuals" at the periphery of analysis. By the same token, the impact of policy outputs as a source of change is also obscured in decisional theory because "policy" is considered to be essentially indistinguishable from "decision" (Lowi, n.d.). Or, as Fror suggests, policy is considered "the direct output of public policy making" (1968: 35), i.e., it is synonymous with process. By treating all decisions as though they were alike (and their content as politically irrelevant) and reducing environmental variables to "residuals," decision theory fails to deal with the question of political change.

On the other hand, output theorists have attempted to link decisional processes with different types of policy outputs. Lowi (1964a), Wildavsky (1964, 1976), Froman (1968), Smith (1968-69), and others suggest that the impact of particular policies tends to be associated with distinctive forms of decision making. Again, however, we are confronted with a theoretical approach which fails to specify the conditions which lead to changes in the independent variable and also neglects the possibility that environmental factors may be an important source for change. For example, Lowi (1964a) suggests that distributive issues facilitate logrolling decisional processes, regulatory outputs evoke patterns of group competition, while redistributive policies tend to impact on social classes, mobilizing elite-oriented decision making. The difficulty in using Lowi's scheme to explain changes in policy formation arises from the fact that he, like other output theorists, regards the type of output as the determinant of political change.

Lowi, himself, recognizes the possibility that environmental factors may be a prime source of change in the impact of a particular output, but he does not incorporate this into his scheme of analysis. For instance, he notes that up to the 1930s, tariff battles were essentially logrolling activities centered in congressional committees. But by the 1960s, the tariff arena lost much of its distributive character and underwent a transition to a regulatory policy which involved wider congressional participation and group competition. As Lowi admits, the reasons for this change were essentially environmental: "the tariff, especially following World War II and our assumption of international leadership, became a means of regulating the domestic economy for international purposes" (1964a; 699).

In essence, contemporary policy theory has difficulty explaining political change because it tends to segment critical sets of political variables which in reality are linked. Environment, decisional, and output variables are important dimensions of policy formation and changes in public policy making can, in theory, be initiated from any one or combination of these sources.

POLITICAL THEORY AND CITY BUDGETING

To the extent that segmental policy analysis neglects to integrate the interrelationships among key sets of variables, some areas of local government activity may appear more static and unchanging than they are. Just such an instance is the case of city budgetary politics which contemporary theory tends to regard as one of the more stable, routinized, and predictable aspects of local governance. Environmental theorists suggest that this is so because city budget makers are highly dependent upon more or less given economic conditions, particularly the level of wealth within their jurisdictions and state laws which forbid operating deficits and restrict tax powers. Because any attempt at budgetary manipulation must be filtered through a severe revenue constraint which budget officials cannot hope to control, environmentalists have concluded that city budget decisions are mainly responsive to environmental pressures (Sharkansky, 1969; Brazer, 1959).

Decisional and output theorists see in local budget decision making few opportunities for discretionary choice. As a result, most of their conclusions are remarkably similar to those of the environmental analysts. Studies of local budgetary decision making picture a highly stable process in which participants follow decision rules which are internalized, insulated from outside pressures, and seldom subject to much alteration (Crecine, 1969; Wildavsky, 1976; Meltsner, 1971; Anton, 1964). Wildavsky (1976), whose work is primarily that of an output theorist, stresses that the very nature of dealing with budget decisions leads to the adoption of stable political relationships. Because it is not possible to calculate all spending options, practitioners must, in the end, utilize various heuristic aids to calculation. Last year's budget is more or less accepted as a base for the present year, expectations of justice require a "fair share" for nearly all petitioners while the routinization of these kinds of political relationships leads to relatively fixed cutting and spending roles among key participants. As a result, budgeting in cities, as in virtually all other governmental contexts, can be expected to take on fairly stable incremental decisional and output patterns.

Wildavsky does not completely ignore the impact of environmental influences on this general pattern for he does recognize that the discretionary choices open to budget authorities can vary, particularly in reference to the wealth and predictability of the budgetary context.[1] Consequently, Wildavsky considers American cities to be differentiated mainly by the absence of much budgetary discretion because of their typically "poor and certain" fiscal environment:

> Few strategic choices are available to municipal officials because spending always leans right up against the politically feasible or constitutionally permissible rate of taxation. Little attention goes to alternative allocation of resources because there are so few resources to allocate. . . . Rather than using the budget process for purposes of steering, that is, to determine new directions for city operations, budgeting becomes largely a maintenance activity [1976: 132].

That is, city budgeting "is insulated from the [political] environment" (Wildavsky, 1976: 116), distinguished mostly by its routine, predictable, and bureaucratic character.

POLITICAL THEORY, CITY BUDGETING, AND CHANGE: TOWARD AN INTEGRATIVE APPROACH

While such an interpretation of city budgeting may be an accurate one in certain instances, we would argue that it is not likely to be so in all cases because critical interrelationships among environmental, decisional, and output variables are left so unexplored. While we cannot attempt a comprehensive analysis of the systematic interaction of these variables at a high level of abstraction, we are able to take a more modest step: to reconcile and integrate existing theoretical formulations in an attempt to explain major transformations in the budgetary politics of one American city over the span of several decades.

As Lowi (1964a) has rightly contended, the types of political relationships in a policy-making order are shaped to a large degree by the expectations of participants—by what they hope to achieve or get from political authorities. If this is so, then what are the major determinants of actor expectations? Lowi argues that it is sufficient to focus on actor expectations regarding the "type of policy at stake" (1964a: 688) because experiences with past policies tend to color expectations concerning the consequences of new, but similar, policy endeavors. In order to promote their interests successfully, participants cannot utilize decision-making strategies and political institutions in random ways; rather, they must take into account the anticipated outcome the policy is likely to have on the community based on past results with similar types of policies. Thus, the type of policy is an important determinant of the relatively stable political relationships, or arenas, which emerge at least in the short run in reference to particular areas of government decision.

However, actor expectations are unlikely to be determined solely by the type of policy at stake because changes in the environmental and decisional context of government can alter the impact or "outcome" of particular public policies, in turn affecting actor expectations. That is, the type of policy at stake can serve as an important "cue" in structuring the policy process only in the short run (Kantor, 1976). In the *long run*, however, changes in actor expectations are likely to occur if the environmental or decisional contexts of public policy change. The case of New York City suggests that the most important long-run determinants of actor expectations derive from (1) changing assessments of the city's competitive economic position vis-à-vis other cities and (2) changing political demands among those participants who decide the allocation of scarce budgetary resources. Interrelationships among these policy output, environmental, and decisional variables are systematic enough to prompt at least three different arenas of budgetary politics as actor expectations change.

INCREMENTAL BUDGETING

Certain economic and political conditions facilitate the routinization of budget politics to a point where political actors expect to utilize the budget largely for maintenance activities, much as Wildavsky has described. Among the most crucial long-run conditions for this pattern have been urban economic expansion accompanied by political quiescence. During the late 19th century and for years after, today's older urban centers achieved a preeminent economic position as they steadily attracted wealth and people in a period of rapid economic growth. The city constituted an essential growth point of industrialization where the forces of production could be efficiently organized to take advantage of mechanization, technological change, and economies of scale in production. With its vast accumulation of industrial wealth, a skilled labor force, massive transportation and port facilities, and valuable real estate, the burgeoning central city won tremendous political independence and came to dominate the surrounding rural and suburban hinterland.[2]

Such massive and steady urban economic growth had at least two important political ramifications for city fiscal decisions. First, given the dominant economic position of the central city, the ease with which annexations ,could be undertaken, and the steady inward flow of wealth, the financial viability of the metropolis could be taken for granted; local officials could turn inward and view most fiscal decisions in terms of piecemeal concerns and particularistic goals. Although this pattern was probably carried to its extreme during the era of the political machine (Mandelbaum, 1965); Merton, 1968), such expectations could dominate city budgetary politics as long as leaders felt they could ignore the city's ecological context.

Second, sustained economic growth could function to minimize the importance of status conflicts—particularly social class conflicts—in the political process. City growth provided increasing amounts of revenue which could be distributed to service-demanding groups within the city, enabling conflicts over status to remain latent or at least minimized by adept city leaders. Lower status groups who entered the political process could expect to steadily accumulate favors, jobs, and other rewards from political party leaders who had the means of co-opting potentially hostile groups (Lowi, 1964b).

So long as political demands can be accommodated within the resources of an expanding public sector, budgetary politics is likely to be dominated by essentially incrementalist expectations along the lines of what Lowi (1964a) has termed "distributive politics." Participants are likely to be small groups promoting highly particularized interests and sharing the expectation that growing budgets can be easily disaggregated and dispensed on a piecemeal bases. Logrolling, shifting alliances, and segmental and specialized arenas become the basic characteristics of decision making as the availability of these high divisible outputs encourages independent political activity.

Since there is a fairly widespread consensus among political actors concerning the basic pattern of public resource distribution, there are likely to be few incentives for making major departures in public expenditure patterns. To do so would disrupt the stable coalitions of supporters which already exist. For this reason, the purpose of the budget will tend to be one of system maintenance and will function to control the city's service-demanding interests for this objective. It is precisely this kind of context which facilitates the routinization of budgetary decision making and the elaboration of stable budgetary rules such as Wildavsky has described. In essence, city growth accompanied by relative political quiescence among budgetary actors facilitates highly limited expectations about the purposes and function of the city budget; over time, these expectations and political relations become stable enough to produce predictable, incremental patterns of budget outputs.

PLURALIST BUDGETING

In a time of city expansion, the largess available to public authorities occasioned by a favorable economic environment *can be* a powerful mechanism for co-opting potentially hostile service-demanding groups and maintaining highly individualized patterns of budgetary politics. But even under growth conditions, there are economic and political changes which can disrupt budgetary incrementalism if the expectations upon which it is based are no longer widely shared.

The post-World War II central city encountered such changes. The city increasingly declined in importance as a manufacturing and industrial center while undergoing a massive demographic shift in the social character of its population. At the same time, its dominant political institution—the machine—declined while the union movement achieved increasing gains among city employees. Not unexpectedly, these changes resulted in the emergence of group coalitions based on shared interests which challenged existing patterns of public resource distribution. In this case, political authorities, finding their bases of support shaken or uncertain, are likely to abandon many past budgetary commitments in order to use the budget as a means of distributing rewards in ways that knit together new supportive alliances.

Given the coalition-building function of the budget in this context, it is unlikely that budgetary outputs can remain very incremental in any strict sense. The instability occasioned by this sort of political transformation is likely to have a shattering impact on previously inviolate budgetary constraints. In particular, the size of the budget is unlikely to remain geared to past revenue constraints because political leaders tend to see the advantages of bargaining out conflicts of interest in terms of material benefits. As Clark and Wilson have suggested, differing interests are more easily reconciled if they can be framed in terms of material rather than nonmaterial benefits, for the former "are readily divisible and the propriety of compromising dollar benefits is widely accepted" (1961: 141). The only limitation is that contending groups often compete for the same pool of resources; however, by increasing revenues, the budget can more successfully be used to reconcile group conflicts. Thus, the orthodox order of budgetary calculation—determining available revenue and then fulfilling priority commitments—is likely to be reversed. Instead, the dominant fiscal constraint is more likely to be one of meeting expenditure demands of key supporters and then redefining the revenue constraint in light of political commitments.

To the extent that this pattern materializes, it is less likely that budgetary decision making will proceed in as incremental a fashion as when the budget had mainly a maintenance function. Consequently, logrolling within the constraints of elaborate rules and routines is likely to be abandoned in favor of a game of pluralist bargaining; public officials will seek to influence budgetary decisions in order to produce new supportive followings. Budget outcomes are most likely to be a result of building winning coalitions comprised of shared political interests.

ELITE BUDGETING

A declining city economy is likely to create conditions which lead to changed actor expectations about the impact of budgetary decisions.[3] In a declining city, participants in the budget process cannot ignore the importance of the city as a collective social unit which must optimize its revenue base if it is to stem deterioration and minimize social disruption. As Hirschman (1970) observes, the dominant issue in a declining organization in which consumers are sovereign is the future of the collectivity— whether to voice the demand for reform and regeneration or to simply exit and relocate elsewhere.

The pressures of urban deterioration encourage cities to approximate the behavior of a firm in a competitive market which seeks to optimize its competitive position. The provision of public goods in local government is different from that in national government. As Tiebout (1968) has suggested, in the latter case the preferences of the consumer voter are simply given in local government, however, the consumer voter can move to the community which best satisfies his set of preferences for public goods and amenities. Tiebout's notion of public goods optimization may only be a crude approximation of the real local government world, but in a declining city the kinds of competitive pressures suggested by this model become abundantly evident. Prosperity diminishes with the outward flight of industry, disinvestment in the aging public infrastructures, abandonment of commercial and residential neighborhoods, and with the dissipation of the city's skilled labor force; the city's competitive position vis-à-vis the suburban fringe, other cities in the region, and nation becomes apparent. Consequently, budgetary calculations among participants are more likely to take into account the notion of the city as a interdependent social unit which must maximize its revenue base in order to stem decline and attract new sources of wealth.[4]

Such a change in political calculations necessarily transforms the politics of the budgetary process toward one based more on centralized political coordination of the city than on particularistic competition by group interests. First, more centralized political coordination of city budgetary operations is likely because the city's declining competitive position imposes severe fiscal constrains on all participants, diminishing opportunities for budget compromises based on satisfying the organizational maintenance needs of particular groups. The need to achieve certain city-wide fiscal objectives cannot be totally ignored even by the most powerful particularistic interests in the city budgetary system without suffering costs in the long run.

Second, greater political coordination of the budgetary process emerges because of the new political and economic dependency relationships which accompany city decline. Economic decay at the local government level tends to bring about greater dependency on external political actors who are able to directly or indirectly influence the competitive position of the city and minimize the disruptive consequences of declining revenues. State and federal officeholders as well as potential investors are in such a position and are liable to impose city-wide budgetary objectives in exchange for their financial assistance. This type of dependency puts a premium on the city's ability to close ranks in order to compensate for a weak bargaining position, to press for greater assistance, and to implement budget strategies imposed by those outside of the city.

Finally, pressure for more centralized coordination is likely to arise from the inability of coalition building to resolve conflicts over the issues of redistribution which dominate politics in a declining city. Attempts to improve the city's competitive status are likely to entail the redistribution of social and economic burdens among the city's revenue producers and service users (Cox, 1973; Harvey, 1973). For example, business groups which have a major stake in protecting their immovable investments in the central business district are likely to have different interests in city survival than ghetto residents who are more dependent on the municipal payroll. Cuts in major services are unlikely to affect both of these groups equally. These kinds of conflicts between the city's service users and revenue producers produce a struggle over the budget which essentially involves only two sides and focuses on intense disagreement over social and political status. As such, budget decisions are difficult to bargain out and are likely to require a more hierarchical pattern than coalition building.

In essence, political coordination in a declining city springs from pressures to simultaneously impose city-wide objectives, deal with the city's dependency status, and resolve status group conflicts in the political process. All this transforms the budget into a means of city-wide economic planning and is likely to mobilize those elites which Mills (1956) has described in another context as owning "command post" positions in major executive institutions. That is, it mobilizes those elites which share access to sources of executive power and authority which are capable of coordinating the city as a collective social structure. Almost invariably this would include banking, real estate, and other business elites which share what Mills calls a "coincidence of objective interests" and which are capable of uniting to defend them. Budgetary decision making becomes largely removed from the so-called middle levels of power to places where those in political and economic command posts set the agendas.

Thus, at least three different city budgetary arenas can emerge over time as actor expectations about the function and impact of the budget are altered. At particular points in time the budget may be perceived as a means of maintaining the political status quo, building new political coalitions, or as an instrument of city economic planning. These expectations about budgetary outputs are in turn related to transformations in the city's economic environment and its political system. Consequently, incrementalist, pluralist, and centralist patterns of political behavior are likely to characterize city budgeting under given circumstances (see Table 1).

POLITICAL CHANGE IN NEW YORK CITY BUDGET POLITICS

In order to illustrate this analysis, we undertook a longitudinal survey of budgetary politics in New York City. By exploring the period from 1945 to the mid-1970s, each of the three political patterns is evident in the budgetary politics of the city; more important, the transition from one budgetary pattern to another is explained by demonstrating the systematic relationships among budget outputs, economic environment, and political demands of the city's decision makers.

INCREMENTAL BUDGET POLITICS 1945-1962

During the 17 years following World War II, the expectations of participants in New York's budgetary arena were influenced by (1) stable and continuous growth in the city's economy and (2) relative political quiescence in its political system. Relatively free of exogenous concerns, (3) the function of the city's budget was regarded as primarily one of maintaining the existing coalition of participants in the city's budget process. Consequently, (4) the decisional arena was remarkably similar to Wildavsky's characterization of budget politics in the typical American city—stable budgetary roles, widespread acceptance of prevailing revenue constraints, and incremental expenditure patterns were the norm.

Table 1 Environmental, Decisional, and Policy Variables in Three Budgetary Arenas

Type of Arena	Budget Outputs			Decisional Patterns			Environment
	Political Function	Expenditure Pattern	Dominant Fiscal Calculus	Political Relationships	Mode of Conflict Resolution	Unit of Representation	
Incrementalist	maintain political supporters	incremental, stable patterns of distribution	available revenue	stable, "rulebound"	diffuse, logrolling, "accommodation"	organization, agency	economic stability, growth
Pluralist	build political support	non-incremental, instable pattern of distribution	expenditure demands	unstable, based on "shared group interests"	competitive group bargaining	group coalition	economic stability, growth
Elitist	impose economic plan	disjointed, redistributive	city revenue base	stable, based on "coincidence of executive interests"	hierarchy, elite coordination	status group (class, race, etc.)	economic decline

ECONOMIC GROWTH AND THE BUDGET

Although New York City was experiencing many patterns of economic change which were replicated in other central cities during the post war period, the external economic dangers posed by the growth of suburbia appeared far less threatening. Confidence in the continued growth and stability of the city's economy was expressed by both political and academic observers alike. "Because of its size and diversity," noted Horton in describing this period, "the city's economy seemed the prototype of mature urban economies ... posessing a 'ratchet-like' capacity that enabled them to avoid the vicissitudes of the business cycle and continue to grow at steady if not spectacular rates" (1977: 10).

Such expectations of economic vitality were hardly unfounded, for New York's economy presented a mixed, but relatively stable picture. Changes in the level and composition of employment are generally regarded as one of the best indicators of city economic health as well as a major link between changes in economic activity and tax revenue (Bahl et al., 1974). In line with national patterns, New York City experienced a decline of nearly 190,000 manufacturing jobs between 1952 and 1964 (Tobier, 1970) as the automobile and truck freed manufacturing from dependence on rail and water transportation, resulting in great industrial dispersal. Nonetheless, the city economy was holding its own because the development of New York as a corporate headquarters city provided it with the hedge it needed to balance the loss of manufacturing. The city gained over 225,000 jobs in white collar occupations from 1952 to 1964, primarily outside of the public sector (Tobier, 1970). New York's function as a headquarters city insured the presence of important growth industries, particularly services, finance, and communications, which placed New York in a decidedly advantageous position in comparison with most American central cities.

POLITICAL QUIESCENCE

Writing of New York City politics during this period, Sayre and Kaufman (1960) noted the contest of "service-demanding" and "money provider" forces in the city's political affairs. But these authors were quick to point out that these "two camps" were not stable alliances because most participants were constantly shifting from one camp to another in efforts to promote their particularistic interests on given issues. So-called service-demanding groups, such as city employees, were particularly fractionated. As a result of reform victories over the regular Democratic organization and, later, winning the right to organize and bargain collectively, public employee unions rapidly gained political power in the city. While this newfound power soon brought organized bureaucracies some influence over the city's employment practices, they encountered major difficulties seeking to determine salaries and wages. Lack of unity in the union movement and resistance by tax conscious defenders of a tight budget who did not otherwise strongly oppose other personnel aims of the bureaucracies invariably limited union power (Sayre and Kaufman, 1960).

Lack of a stable alliance among city employees was replicated by the city's minority community which, despite their growing number during this period, had yet to enter the local political system to make major demands. Neither the newer residents of the city nor interests affected by their growing presence put much pressure on local officials to initiate many new funding patterns. For example, the number of welfare recipients (Aid to Dependent Children and Aid to Families with Dependent Children) increased by only 100,000 between 1954 and 1962 (Research Department, Community Council of Greater New York, Bureau of Statistical Services, 1963) despite the enormous migration of poor nonwhite groups into the city since the end of the war. In contrast, it took only three years after 1962 for the welfare rolls to gain another 100,000 (New York City Council on Education, 1976). Similarly, there were relatively few demands for more law enforcement personnel during this period of quiescence because, according to official crime reports, New York City had yet to experience large increases in street crime. For instance, in 1952 there were some 8,000 offenses in two major street crimes involving "strangers," aggravated assault and robbery; 10 years later, the number of robberies had declined by 2,000 while assaults numbered only some 12,000. In contrast, in 1972 the number of reported robberies increased by 1,300% to 78,000 and assaults totaled 37,000 (U.S. Department of Justice, Federal Bureau of Investigation, 1973).

The downtown business community and the city's lower middle class, particularly Catholic homeowners, were major money provider interests during this period. Yet these groups often located themselves in the camp of the service-demanding forces, especially when organized business promoted development programs to aid the city's economic base or when property owner groups sought neighborhood improvements. Their promotion of such particularistic demands and the tenuousness of their coalitions failed to differentiate them from service-demanding groups. It is only in their general opposition to revenue increases that one can describe this alliance as having a degree of stability and shared interests lacking in the other interests in the city's political system.

INCREMENTAL BUDGET DECISIONS

This pattern of political quiescence and fragmented demands was in turn reflected in the process of budgetary decision making. During the entire 17-year period a unique New York City institution, the Board of Estimate, held a commanding position within the city government with respect to budgetary and financial decisions (Sayre and Kaufman, 1960). In general, board decision making displayed a remarkable stability and continuity in a process which Schick has described as "encumbered by past decisions and commitments and with procedures which are slow to change" (1974: 67). The dominant alliance within the board comprised the comptroller and the five borough presidents whose combined voting power limited mayoral influence and almost invariably dampened attempts to increase spending for new programs or services. The prevailing bargains were most often struck by these six officials in a continuous logrolling process which largely resulted in incremental budget increases designed to keep pace with inflation (Sayre and Kaufman, 1960).

The comptroller, who drew much of his support from the real estate and banking groups in the city, sought to insure that the budget remained within prevailing revenue constraints by seeking to block sympathetic mayoral responses to his service-demanding constituencies (Sayre and Kaufman, 1960). The borough presidents sensed their common cause to protect the special interests of their boroughs, to contend with growing union power, and to survive the city-wide decline in the fortunes of the regular Democratic party organization. Consequently, they joined with the comptroller in an effort to maintain existing public expenditure patterns and placate city employees (Sayre and Kaufman, 1960. In short, the dominant coalition on the board used the budget to maintain support from both the revenue-producing interests in the city and the city's civil servants. To the first group the board placed limits on the growth of the city's budget; for city employees, the board sought to allocate budgetary increases for improvement in their income and working conditions rather than in the direction of new programs. The support of both sets of interests was maintained by allocating budgetary gains largely to existing personnel.

INCREMENTAL OUTPUTS

The board perceived that they were elected more on their ability to keep city expenditures under control than on their managerial perform-ance, i.e., promoting service delivery and launching new programs. Conse-quently, board members adopted a budget strategy which minimized the risk of disturbing the existing political consensus over city expenditures and provided maximum control over city spending. The result was a very stable, seemingly rule-bound decisional process which facilitated an incremental pattern of budget outputs during the entire period under review (Schick, 1974).

First, the risk of disrupting the consensus among budgetary participants was minimized by depoliticizing the question of revenue availability. Rather than bargaining out this issue on any continual bases, the board simply regarded existing revenue constraints as the inviolate, given bases for making spending calculations. Since the growth of the city's economy was providing increasing amounts of revenue year after year, the board could make incremental adjustments in spending without opening up the revenue side of city fiscal policy.[5] Consequently, growth in the city's budget and the sources of city revenue remained remarkably stable from the late 1940s to the early 1960s. From fiscal 1949 to fiscal 1962, the average annual expenditure increase was 6.5%, with the increases during these years ranging from 3.6% to 8.8% (Schick, 1974). The three major revenue sources for the city—real estate taxes, other local taxes, and intergovernmental aid—exhibited similar consistent patterns. The relative importance of each of these revenue sources changed very little. The real estate tax, reflecting the continued high value of city land, remained the largest of the three sources of income. It provided, on an average, almost half of the total expense budget revenues.[6]

Second, the board concerned itself more with exercising tight controls on how money was spent than on program management. The board was able to dominate budgetary decision making due to its pivotal role in the administration of the budget. Even after the budget was formally approved, the board frequently acted to modify it throughout the course of the fiscal year. Working closely with its "trusted agent," the Bureau of the Budget, the board imposed various procedures which provided tight control over expenditures (Sayre and Kaufman, 1960).

Overall board and budget bureau control over expenditures was facilitated by the use of a line-item budget, in which every object of expenditure is fitted into a specific line. As a result, there were countless unavoidable transfers of funds from line to line during the course of a year which required board approval (generally after recommendation by the budget bureau). Further, the budget bureau utilized other procedures for keeping abreast of all details of expenditure. For example, the permission of the bureau was required before any city agency could fill a vacant position—even if the position had been authorized and the appropriations duly made. In addition, all equipment proposals and contracts for work which exceeded $2,500 had to be approved by the bureau. Last, the bureau utilized an "accrual" system—agencies were forced to save a certain percentage of their budget by not filling vacancies in their department or postponing promotions—whereby expenditures could be checked in anticipation of revenue shortages (Robertson and Vecchio, 1975).

To summarize, New York City's budgetary politics during this period took on the characteristics of a locality experiencing economic growth and political stability. The growing availability of resources and the limited claims emanating from service-demanding groups enabled public authorities to deal with these demands when they were still formulated in particularistic terms. The absence of stable coalitions sharing broader concerns enabled the Board of Estimate and the Bureau of the Budget to dominate the arena in a decision process which emphasized predictability, incrementalism, and expenditure control. Budget politics largely reinforced the status quo as city fiscal leaders "muddled through" by juggling lines and funds.

PLURALIST BUDGET POLITICS 1963-1974.

In the 11 years after 1963, a transformation of the city's political system induced major changes in the expectations of budgetary participants. The consensus underlying the postwar system was shattered by politicization among the city's minorities and public employees. Advancing less particularlistic public expenditure claims, these two sets of actors forced a restructuring of the budgetary arena. Able to rely on continuing economic growth during most of this period, the city's political leaders used its monetary largess to reestablish a supportive coalition within the city. The budgetary arena changed dramatically as open, pluralistic bargaining replaced rule-bound activities and incremental behavior. Budget outputs reflected these changes as expenditures became nonincremental and the revenue constraint was abandoned in favor of seeking new revenue sources to meet the demands of the new claimants. In essence, (1) budget outputs, (2) economic growth, and (3) new political demands accompanied the transformation of (4) budgetary decision making along more pluralistic lines.

NONINCREMENTAL BUDGET OUTPUTS

Whereas budget outputs in the previous period were characterized by slow incremental expenditure growth within existing revenue constraints, the decade after 1963 shared none of these patterns. From almost any perspective, New York City budgets exhibited nonincremental features which mirrored major changes in city budgeting. First, the growth in the size of the budget was unparalleled. For example, from 1966 to 1971, operating expenditures increased at an average annual rate of 16.5%; during the previous period, the annual expenditure growth rate was 8.9% (Schick, 1974). The developing inflation which began in the late 1960s hardly explains this phenomenal expenditure growth since the increased rate of expenditure was seven times the rise of the consumer price index for New York City during most of the years of this period (Bernstein, 1969). In effect, this unprecedented growth signaled that the budget no longer simply embodied the continuance of previous city programs with additional outlays reflecting inflation and incremental increases.

Second, nonincremental patterns of allocating budgetary resources to various claimants became a key feature of budget politics. As Figure 1 suggests, after 1962-1963 the budgets of various departments no longer evidenced very predictable growth patterns. For three major city services— fire, police, and education—it is clear that the Board of Estimate's treatment of each (as expressed in simple percentage changes in annual budget allotments) shows notable continuity prior to 1962 for there is relatively little divergence in the pattern of resource allocation among the three. After that year, however, considerable divergence and discontinuity in the funding patterns among these services became the norm, indicating decline in incremental budget responses.

The singling out of particular groups of claimants for favored treatment by city authorities is evident during the whole of this period. As we document more fully below, city employees and the minority community were major beneficiaries of change in the budgetary system. Both the growth in the number of city employees and the increases in personnel costs were greater than during the first postwar period. City employment grew at 5.5%—twice the rate of the 1950s—while personnel costs, including fringe benefits and pensions, also rose rapidly (Bahl et al., 1974). Much of this employment growth initially reflected both the new public sector jobs that were made available to minorities and the increased personnel costs that went to compensating the providers of municipal services for the new demands placed upon them. However, as tighter budgets were imposed during the later years of this period—Lindsay's last two years and Beame's first (1974)—the city's civil servants did not suffer a similar decline in their accumulation of benefits. Indeed, controlling for inflation, compensation for most city employees increased more rapidly in the 1970-1975 period than in the 1965-1970 period (Horton, 1977). The decline in expenditure growth was primarily born by minority interests partly because federal and

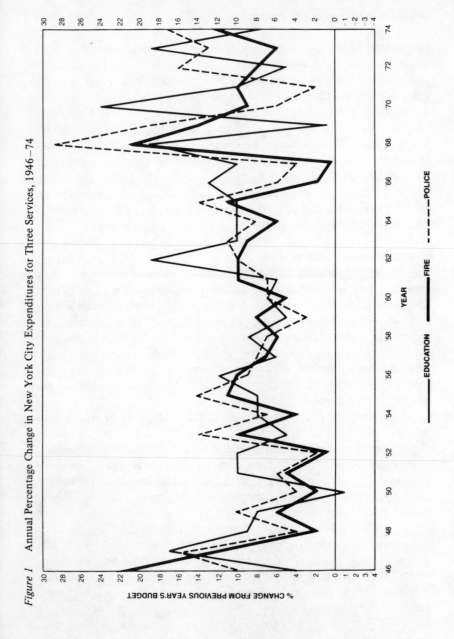

Figure 1   Annual Percentage Change in New York City Expenditures for Three Services, 1946–74

202

local expenditures for this constituency declined during the early 1970s and by a decrease in public services in general (Horton, 1977; Shefter, 1977).

Third, the revenue constraint which authorities previously considered sacrosanct was largely abandoned as a control on budgetary growth after 1962. In fact, budget growth outstriped revenues so much that by the end of the 1965-1975 decade, a deficit of more than $3 billion had accumulated. In order to finance the massive growth in city spending, city officials tapped revenue sources which previously were regarded as relatively fixed.

All three major sources of finance—intergovernmental aid, local nonproperty taxes, and real estate taxes—were extensively altered in order to fund this expenditure growth. An enormous increase in state and federal aid took place mainly as a result of new programs and increased usage of existing programs in the area of social welfare (Bahl et al., 1974). At the same time, the city effected major changes in the local taxes it imposed, gaining yields from nonproperty taxes and charges faster than those from real estate taxes. The net result was a significant restructuring of the budget's financial base. For example, in fiscal year 1958-1959 the city received 47% of its revenues from the real estate tax, 30% from other local taxes, and 23% from intergovernmental aid. A decade later, 29% of the city's revenue came from the real estate tax, the same percent from other local taxes and charges, and 42% from intergovernmental aid (Bernstein, 1969).

While the proportion of revenue raised locally declined in comparison with federal and state assistance, this should not obscure the very large increase in revenue from local sources. In the decade between fiscal years 1958-1959 and 1968-1969, the revenues from the city's own sources more than doubled, going from $1.6 billion to $3.5 billion. This income growth was due to significant changes in both the city's nonproperty taxes and, to a lesser extent, its real estate taxes. Changes in the city's nonproperty taxes were major and included for the first time the imposition of an income tax on residents and nonresidents. In addition, a more lucrative business income tax replaced the general business tax, the city sales tax increased by 1%, while yields from the stock transfer tax were shifted from the state to the city. At the same time, the real estate tax furnished additional yields as a result of changes in the administration of the tax and increased assessed valuation of local properties. As a result of these modifications in city taxes, revenue yields rose faster than the growth in personal income of city residents (Bernstein, 1969).

Finally, city officials departed from the revenue constraint in order to balance the city's budget by yet another method, namely, the issuance of short-term revenue and tax anticipation notes to cover deficits in the expense budget. These short-term notes were issued to "roll over" deficits which had not been covered by revenue collections. This practice of rolling over deficits to the subsequent fiscal year began with Mayor Wagner's last budget and was continued throughout the remainder of the period, allowing city officials to technically comply with the charter requirements of a balanced budget.

ECONOMIC GROWTH AND POLITICAL INSTABILITY

The pattern of nonincremental expenditure growth and the abandonment of well established revenue constraints mirrored changed expectations about the functions of city budgeting. But it is difficult to explain these outputs only in terms of developments in the city's economy, for the 1960s in fact witnessed few changes in the city's postwar pattern of relatively stable growth.

As in the previous period, New York continued to be the nation's major business headquarters city and enjoyed a total gain of over 200,000 new jobs. This new increase again resulted from growth in white collar occupations, particularly services, which outweighed losses in the manufacturing sector (Bahl et al., 1974). Though there was a substantial growth in government jobs, especially at the local level, the relative sizes of the private and public employment sectors changed only marginally; the private sector's share of the total employment market fell from 88% to 85% (Bahl et al., 1974). As detailed below, the recession which began in 1969 precipitated a sharp reversal in this trend of continued net employment growth and eventually came to threaten the relative stability of the city's economy. But continuing overall expansion characterized New York City's economy during the period as a whole.

Consequently, the presence of modest, but relatively stable growth at least provided public officials with the *option* of seeking additional revenue to finance new programs; in particular, continued economic growth afforded the *possibility* of altering the tax structure in favor of taxes with greater income elasticity (nonproperty taxes) and, perhaps, generated the expectation that future growth would facilitate repayment of the enormous deficits incurred during this period. Nonetheless, the essential continuity of New York City's economic patterns since the 1940s suggests that economic factors alone cannot explain the extraordinary transformation of budget outputs after 1962.

Events in the larger political system appear to be much more crucial for such a dramatic change. As a result of events at the national and local

level, the previously quiescent minority community became highly politicized and for the first time sought to become a major contender in the
city's political system. Their bid for power during this period has been
extensively documented elsewhere, but its impact on the city's budget
during the early Lindsay years clearly reflects this change. From 1966 to
1971, the three municipal programs with the largest rate of increase were
higher education (251%), welfare (225%), and hospitals (123%; Shefter,
1977). The open admissions program, aimed directly at the city's minorities and ethnics, accounts for the extraordinary increase in the higher
education budget while nonwhites make up most of the clients for the
other two programs.

The emergence of the minority community as a major new participant
in the budgetary arena was matched by the city's public servants. While
authorized to bargain collectively since 1958, the city employee unions
did not begin to utilize this weapon to obtain liberal settlements until the
Lindsay administration. Confronted by a mayor who sought to diminish
their power, the civil service unions successfully fought his attempts to
mobilize public opinion, to stand fast against strikes, and, in one instance,
to call for the use of the national guard. The city employee unions became
a united force and by 1969, when Lindsay needed assistance in his
reelection campaign, they secured very generous contract settlements. In
that year the unions representing the big traditional city departments—
Police, Fire, Sanitation, and Education—obtained major increases for their
members.

The impact of these two groups of claimants was such that the basic
pattern of political reckoning in the city's budgetary affairs changed—
expectations of a stable budgetary coalition could no longer be maintained. The demands on the budget could not be accommodated by
particularistic responses since neither established revenue constraints nor
past patterns of resource allocation were accepted by major participants in
the budgetary process. On the one hand, the mayor was caught between
demands of the minority community for a major expansion of public
services and jobs and the power of service providers whose cooperation he
needed. On the other hand, the consensus among revenue-producing
groups which was based on holding down taxes and city expenditures was
shaken by the social disorder which seemed to accompany the militancy of
minorities and unions in the city's political affairs. Consequently, the
pressures for utilizing the budgetary arena as a venue for bargaining out
the differences among all these contenders became irresistible. By expanding the pool of scarce resources, abandoning past constraints, and opening

up budget decisions in order to facilitate bargaining among these groups, officials could work toward building a new stable budgetary coalition.

PLURALIST DECISION MAKING

These shifts in city budgeting brought about a system of decision making which centered upon the mayor who played a major role in using the city's money to deal with the management of group conflict. By virtue of the charter revision in 1963, the crucial power to modify the budget was transferred from the Board of Estimate to the mayor. The most important of the charter changes provided that the authority to transfer funds within an agency belonged to the particular agency head, subject to the authority of the mayor who could withdraw its authority and retain it for himself. Generally, the mayor reserved this power to himself throughout the period (Schick, 1974). In addition, the charter provided that the mayor could transfer unassigned appropriations—considerable sums which amounted to over $900 million or over 8% of the 1974-1975 budget—to any agency.[7]

Under pressure from their service-demanding constituencies, Mayors Wagner and Lindsay used their newly gained authority to transform the process of budgetary decision making by separating decisions which involved mandated or recurring expenditures from those associated with new programs. The latter decisions were made by City Hall during the course of the year; the budget was then modified to reflect the fiscal implications of the decisions. This change essentially reversed the order of budgetary calculation of the earlier postwar period. As Schick described it, "the city would launch and adjust programs at any time during the year when the opportunity arose, not when the budget process called for program decisions" (1974: 67-68).

This change in budgetary decision making was of course reflected in many policy areas. While the regular budget process became the vehicle for financing recurring and mandated expenditures in such areas as social welfare and education, innovative programs initiated by new federal and state moneys generated a host of budget modifications during the year as the mayor embarked on new policies. When collective bargaining agreements were reached with public employee unions, the mayor used budget modifications, unallocated moneys, and accruals to finance the agreements. In short, City Hall managed to "divorce policy from budgeting" (Schick, 1974).

This transformation was accomplished after attempts to reorganize the Bureau of the Budget and make it more a responsive agent of the mayor had failed. When Mayor Lindsay took office he sought to make the bureau less a prisoner of its past practices and more responsive to a broader, more innovative policy perspective. The encrusted examiners in the bureau had sole responsibility for preparing and administering the expense budget. To counter the bureau's commitment to the procedures of the past, Lindsay authorized the hiring of professional managerial personnel who would staff a new unit in the bureau—a Program, Planning and Analysis Unit. This unit was to involve itself with management and policy issues of every agency on a systematic bases, enabling it to oversee the day-to-day budgetary decisions made by the examiners.

While the size of the unit grew until 1970, it never did have much of an impact on budgetary decisions. The veteran bureau examiners successfully resisted the intrusion of the planning unit and retained their influence within the bureau for administering the expense budget (Harris, 1974). As a result, the mayor simply utilized a different decisional process for budgetary matters involving policy initiatives.

Thus, the city's environment, decisional processes, and budgetary outputs were interrelated in a new way after 1962: New York's budget politics exhibited the characteristics of a locality using its growing revenue base to deal with disruptions in its political system. As the budget became the central instrument of city leaders for resolving growing political conflicts, incremental and particularistic modes of budgeting were abandoned in favor of openly competitive bargaining. Consequently, previously inviolate revenue constraints, rule-bound procedures, and well-established patterns of public resource distribution no longer were key features of New York City's budget politics. In a pattern of unparalleled expenditure growth, the city's budget initially reflected large increments for its minority community and later for its city employees.

ELITE BUDGET POLITICS 1975-1978

The persistence of the race issue and growing union power into the 1970s might well have prompted continuing pluralist conflict over the budget for many years in New York City. Alternatively, given the historical adaptability of the city's political system, a new consensus about public expenditure could have emerged eventually, making possible a return to some form of incrementalist budget politics similar to New York's postwar pattern. However, neither of these patterns materialized because expectations of economic decline became apparent. In a context of economic decline, city budgetary politics took into account the need to utilize public resources in order to optimize the city's revenue base and competitive position. Consequently, environmental, decisional, and policy output variables became interrelated in a distinctively different way in the city's budgetary politics.

Declining revenue availability imposed fiscal constraints on all participants, created new political dependency relationships for the city, and prompted efforts to improve the city's competitive position vis-à-vis other urban economies. Consequently, (1) economic decline in New York City became associated with (2) a hierarchical decisional process which emphasized political coordination of the city's fiscal affairs by elites who (3) perceived the function of city budgeting as a form of economic planning. The emphasis on planning and coordination did not, however, produce a convergence of interests among the various participants. While financial and corporate elites in the city attempted to achieve planning objectives through retrenchment and austerity budgets, other participants sought to shift these burdens and to promote alternative programs. These groups, constrained by their inferior bargaining position in such a "coordinated" system, were limited in their access to the budgetary arena.

ECONOMIC DECLINE

The recession that began in 1969 precipitated a sharp reversal in New York City's economic fortunes (Newfield and Dubrul, 1977; Ferretti, 1976). Between 1969 and 1972, the city lost 250,000 jobs, reflecting an employment decline not only in manufacturing but also an unprecedented loss of jobs in nonmanufacturing sectors. Despite the fact that New York City had long been spared the spectre of central city economic decline by virtue of its corporate headquarters function, there was no reversal of the city's adverse economic trends. During the 1970s the city's revenue base deteriorated more rapidly as the number of jobs in the private sector declined from 3,182,000 in 1970 to 2,877,700 by 1974 (Congressional Budget Office, 1976).

As described above, the initial response of the city's officials to these trends of deterioration was to place controls on spending for local services and diminish the moneys available to the minority community. Still, budgetary expenditures continued to exceed available revenues for a number of reasons (Congressional Budget Office, 1976). Inflation kept driving up costs despite local attempts to stabilize its bundle of services. The city's expenditures for retirement benefits which were negotiated during the previous decade rose from $364 million in 1965 to $1.12 billion in 1974. The city's borrowing practices were proving to be highly costly; in 1965 the city's debt service payments had been $470 million but by 1974 had risen to $1.27 billion. Most important, the new participants who had gained entrance to the city's political system during the Lindsay reign—the public employee unions and minorities—were not expelled. Their claims continued to receive recognition during Lindsay's last years and by his successor, Abe Beame.

PLURALIST STALEMATE AND ELITE DECISIONS

The city's deteriorating fiscal condition did not go unnoticed by its major creditors. In March 1974 the minutes of Chase Manhattan's municipal credit review committee concluded that "we view the city as being saddled with fundamentally adverse financial trends. . . . In view of this assessment, our judgment is that the portfolio's New York City bond holdings are somewhat heavier than desirable" (Newfield and Dubrul, 1977: 37). Since anticipated growth in the city's revenue base was now dismissed as unlikely, only an absolute but orderly cut in city expenditures could offer much chance of repayment of the enormous credit extended to the city, reassure suspicious investors, and make the city more competitive in attracting or retaining businesses and people. Since the recession forecast for 1974 had already begun, only fairly prompt, timely responses to the deteriorating fiscal situation would have proved sufficient.

Working within the constraints of the city's pluralist political system, however, city political leaders were unable to make appropriate responses; the latter seemed incapable of planning a recovery strategy or making significant expenditure cuts. The city continued borrowing at even higher levels. In the July 1974 Beame budget, over $700 million of expense items, such as textbooks and salaries, were put into the capital budget. A new agency—the Reserve Stabilization Corporation—was created to borrow $520 million, a further $280 million was raised by borrowing from union pension funds and changing the sewer collection dates, and, finally, the budget was brought into balance by predicting a decrease in the number of welfare recipients at a time of rising unemployment. Later, the mayor and comptroller publicly disagreed over whether the deficit in the year's expense budget was $430 million or $650 million (it later turned out to be $3.3 billion). By January 1975 when crisis was imminent and Mayor Beame sought to reassure the financial community by firing 12,000 employees, the New York *Times* ("Layoffs ordered by Beame are not taking place," 1975) revealed that only 1,700 employees were actually let go because the city was merely switching people from one budget line to another.

The point is not that New York simply had poor leadership talent in the midst of a crisis, but rather that its leaders were in no position to make the kind of budgetary decisions appropriate to New York's deteriorating condition. They lacked what Mills (1956) has termed a "coincidence of objective interests" in the city as a collectivity; that is, they lacked the access to positions of control for imposing city-wide coordination and gaining support from appropriate constituencies. If Mayor Beame had difficulties firing a few thousand employees, the idea of abandoning nearly all past budgetary calculations, reevaluating the entire expenditure budget in a process of political triage, and taking such unpopular decisions as ending a generations-old policy of free tuition at the city's university was clearly outside of his political thinking.

In the face of this pluralist stalemate, the large New York commercial banks and later other banks across the country intervened by precipitating the fiscal crisis.[8] On May 22, 1974 Chase Manhattan quietly sold off 134,000 shares of its New York City securities and was followed by other commercial banks which all together dumped approximately $2.3 billion of their city holdings between the summer of 1974 and the spring of 1975; in March 1975 the market for New York City securities collapsed, leading to the state legislature's intervention, the creation of the Municipal Assistance Corporation (MAC), and, later, the Emergency Financial Control Board (EFCB).

ELITE BUDGETING AND POLITICAL COORDINATION

Since the fiscal crisis, the real locus of power in the budgetary process has shifted to financial and business elites who virtually set up and then came to dominate the emergency boards.[9] Under these new fiscal leaders, the whole purpose of the budgetary process has changed to one of political coordination and economic planning in an effort to stem further deterioration of the city's economic base. The primary beneficiaries of the pluralist system—the public employee unions and the minority community— have been unable to compete in this new political process because they lack equivalent positions of power.

In fact, these two groups have been the primary targets of the city's financial and corporate elite. The unions have been compelled to accept large layoffs and a wage freeze and have been forced to invest some $3.7 billion of their pension funds in New York City and MAC bonds (this compares with much smaller amounts invested by the city's major financial institutions since the fiscal crisis). This latter development has had the impact of moderating municipal employee wage demands and essentially making the strike threat a useless weapon. Almost one-third of the retirement funds of municipal unions is now invested in city-related debt.[10] With the pensions of current and retired city employees now heavily invested in the city, it is hardly likely that the municipal unions will seek payroll gains which might threaten city bankruptcy.

It was the threat of municipal bankruptcy which forced the unions into this inferior position. Under bankruptcy, a court-appointed receiver would have full authority over union contracts and pension benefits; bankruptcy would mean the end of collective bargaining. As a result, union leaders have not only accepted the demands of the financial elite, but have also taken on the task of persuading their membership to accept the decline in their status.

The city's minority community has suffered under budgetary retrenchment even more than have municipal employees. With their low turnout at the polls and relatively weak organizational base, it has not been difficult for budgetary elites to impose their demands upon the minority groups in New York. As Boast's (1978) analysis of city budget cuts between 1975 and 1978 has revealed, the city has managed to cut the budgets of human service programs—such as compensatory higher education, addiction services, and youth services—at a much higher rate than the budgets of housekeeping and traditional service programs. Moreover, as last hired among city personnel, blacks and Puerto Ricans have borne the brunt of the layoffs.

The case which best illustrates the pivotal role of the city's budgetary elite in political coordination and economic planning is its decision to avoid default and bankruptcy. This, more than any other experience since the fiscal crisis, revealed the ability of the city's business elite to use its commanding positions of power and access in the new budget politics.

In the context of economic decline, political power accrues to those who can transform the budget into an instrument of political coordination which can materially affect the city's competitive position in relation to other cities; that is, those who gain power are most likely to do so by virtue of their ability to *simultaneously* manage the city's increasing political dependency, resolve conflicts over redistribution, and impose city-wide objectives on all participants. The city's business elite showed itself to be a major power broker in all these respects as the fiscal crisis continued during the summer of 1975 and the city was faced with the possibility of bankruptcy.

Despite the efforts of MAC, the inability of the city to market its securities soon became evident and in July MAC representatives concluded in their minutes that any action by the mayor "would be viewed as having no credibility (Newfield and Dubrul, 1977: 185). It was implicitly assumed from the beginning that the primary goal should be one of avoiding default, but it was only in MAC's July 17 meeting that the detailed requirements of such a strategy were formally discussed (Newfield and Dubrul, 1977). The obstacles were indeed formidable. First, in addition to fairly prompt aid from the Republican-dominated state legislature, long-term assistance, hopefully in the form of security guarantees from the federal government, was regarded as a top priority. Pressure from city officials for such a federal response had started long before, but had been rejected out of hand by a very unsympathetic Ford administration. In fact, after a May 13 meeting Mayor Beame and Governor Carey had with President Ford, Vice President Rockefeller, Treasury Secretary Simon, and others, the federal position had become rigid. Simon, in a detailed press announcement following that meeting, virtually committed the administration to not aiding New York City even if it defaulted. Default, Simon concluded, would occasion but a "moderate, short-lived disruption" ("Effects on national economy of New York City default negligible says Simon," 1975).

Second, MAC concluded that in order to avoid default, a dramatic and substantial austerity program, including a means of long-term monitoring of such a program, was essential. Though such a program was not laid out in detail, its key components were identified and debated. The status group character of the debate within MAC is revealed by the fact that the implementation of nearly any one of its proposals would constitute major policy departures that imposed clear burdens on have-not groups, particularly minorities. Rather than attempting such alternatives as a restructuring of the city's debt or raising the commercial real estate tax, the austerity agenda included a wage freeze for city workers, across-the-board service cuts, thousands of layoffs, raising the transit fare by 40% or more, and the end of free tuition at the City University of New York.

Clearly, both strategies had to be coordinated simultaneously. Federal support would not be forthcoming without implementation of an austerity program; by the same token, an economizing program without outside support was insufficient. But the city's financial elite managed both horns of the dilemma. On one hand, every austerity proposal discussed at MAC's July meeting was eventually implemented, including the creation of the EFCB as a fiscal monitoring agency that would develop longer range austerity programs for the city. Further, union pension funds were forced to absorb several billion dollars in city securities.

On the other hand, during the autumn of 1975 the banking community became virtually united in demanding some form of federal intervention. In October the three major New York commercial banks—Citibank, Rockefeller's Chase Manhattan, and Morgan Guaranty Trust—jointly informed the Senate Banking Committee that they attributed the recent decline in the value of the dollar in foreign currency markets to concern over the impact of a New York City default (Tolchin, 1975). By November, Arthur Burns, the Federal Researve Chairman, implicitly came out in favor of aid to New York City while President Ford remained adamantly opposed. Two months later, after the President changed his position under tremendous pressure from the banking community and agreed to make seasonal loans available to the city, the Federal Reserve issued a report which suggested that 954 banks in 33 states actually held $6.491 billion in securities issued by city and state agencies in New York; if they defaulted, 234 banks in 29 states would probably have lost half of their capital and 718 banks in 33 states would have seen between 20% and 50% of their holdings wiped out ("Federal reserve reports widespread impact of New York City default," 1976).

Since 1975 budgetary decisions have continued expenditure contraction, reduced agency budgets that are "most expendable and least productive of future private sector economic growth"[11] are given priority to protecting the powerful political position of the city's investment community. At the same time, the financial community has moved to set the rules governing the city's future fiscal course. The latter have had all of their New York City notes and bonds paid off or refinanced and, most important, in 1978 won federal guarantees for all future financing of the city. In contrast, city officials and other participants have been forced to accept the continuation of the EFCB and the elimination of borrowing for operating expenses four years earlier than was agreed in the city's initial recovery program, increasing pressure to make further cuts in so-called expendable budgets.

CONCLUSION: POLITICAL CHANGE, CITY BUDGETING, AND POLITICAL THEORY.

As the emergency nature of the fiscal crisis fades, it seems unlikely that the new political forces unleashed by it will disappear. New York remains a city in decline and must now compete harder than ever to survive in an era which seems to offer so many advantages to growth centers in the South, the West, and the suburban fringes. It may be that the politics of elite fiscal planning will evolve in a more telescoped pattern in declining older cities of the Northeast and Midwest than was the case in New York City. As other urban governments try to achieve competitive advantages for declining economies, the trend toward business coordination of city fiscal affairs may well be duplicated.

However, our framework for explaining political change in city budgetary politics also suggests that there is another path of political development which declining urban political systems like New York may follow. As our above analysis suggests, actor expectations about the city's economic prospects and the consensual or conflictual structure of political demands are crucial variables for understanding the historical emergence of incrementalist, pluralist, and elite budgetary systems. As Table 2 illustrates, each pattern of policy making is associated with different combinations of these economic and political variables; however, New York City has somehow managed to avoid the kind of political order which could emerge in the fourth cell. Despite the fact that the city has moved from periods of economic growth to times of revenue scarcity and political leaders have witnesses years of consensus as well as conflict, budget politics has not yet entered a period of scarcity accompanied by intense conflict.

In the 1960s the response of city officials to political instability and conflict was one of abandoning incrementalist budgeting and utilizing the city's growing economic base to deal with threats to the city's social order by inflating governmental expenditure in a pluralist budgetary arena. But such a response is no longer very likely in an era of retrenchment and centralized planning by elites for the purpose of redeveloping the private economic sector of the city. The key question for the future of urban budgetary politics is what kind of political order is likely to emerge if and

Table 2 Economic Conditions, Political
Demands, and Types of Budgetary
Arenas

	Political Demands	
	Consensual	Conflictual
Growth	Incremental Budgeting	Pluralist Budgeting
Economic Conditions		
	Elite Budgeting	?
Decline		

when New York or other declining cities must again contend with conflicts similar to those of the 1960s? Such a prospect is not at all remote given that city politics under conditions of decline has relegated minorities, public employees, and others to inferior positions and has put political power in the hands of elites whose interests are often opposed to these groups. Political instability and declining material resources could lead to a governmental order in which the unavailability of supposedly slack resources leaves few other options than the use of more coercive techniques for obtaining social control over a hostile citizenry. This threat to democratic urban politics is the danger of a fiscal crisis characterized by conflict amid scarcity.

Theories of policy formation have failed to address such issues. Instead, extant environmental, decisional, and output theories tend to segment the politics of public policy in such a way that critical interrelationships among sets of variables are ignored. Analysis of change in political orders is relegated to a secondary concern of political theory. While we are not able to offer a more comprehensive theory of policy change at a high level of analysis, we do suggest that existing theoretical approaches can be reconciled and integrated to identify systematic interrelationships in one policy area—city budgetary politics.

By doing so in the case of New York City our longitudinal analysis has suggested the possibility of explaining major transformations in the city's budgetary politics and probing future paths of political change. Rather than an area of policy characterized by routine, political stability and insulation from broader political forces, we uncovered three major systems of budgetary politics since 1945. In each of these, the expectations of political actors reflected systematic changes in the functions of city budget outputs, the city's ecological context, and the politics of decisions. While the type of policy was an important short-run determinant of political expectations, over time the character of political demands and economic constraints were particularly important.

Segmental approaches were inadequate for explaining the changing political patterns we managed to identify in New York's budgetary politics. Environmental theory would not have predicted the expansion of the budget which occurred in New York during the 1960s or would it have been sensitive to the transformation of the city's political system during this period or in the fiscal crisis that followed. Indeed, it would seem to have suggested "automatic" responsiveness to the city's declining economy in the 1970s. Decisional theorists had even less to offer in the way of addressing the matter of change in the budgetary process. Changes from logrolling among particularistic interests to decision making by group competition and, later, by more hierarchical processes often resulted from sources outside of the decisional process itself. Finally, output theory which contends that the "type of policy" determines the pattern of responses in the political order neglected the fact that the function and impact of budgetary outputs can change over time. Studies of other policy areas in other settings will very likely suggest other dynamic relationships among environmental, decisional, and output variables. However, theories of policy formation must become more integrative than they have in the past in order to discover new dynamic relationships.

NOTES

1. Yet, even this does not really qualify Wildavsky's assessment of the budgetary process as one based on relatively stable and incremental calculations, for this pattern is considered to be more or less inherent in the nature of governmental budgeting regardless of variations in the governmental environment. Even underdeveloped countries, which own a "poor and uncertain" fiscal environment, maintain an essentially incremental decisional process by using "repetitive budgeting" as a technique for dealing with environmental uncertainties.

2. This fact was well appreciated by observers of these new urban developments. Marx and Engels saw in city growth a process of expropriation of the countryside, an interpretation which seems confirmed by the continual annexation of suburban fringes and the persistent town and country antagonism in the course of central city growth (Harvey, 1973). Similarly, the overpowering influence of the city over the hinterland was stressed by the Chicago school of urbanism which saw city growth extending out in concentric zones from the dominant central core in Chicago and believed that this pattern was typical of all industrial cities. So powerful was the central city that Burgess (1967) observed that changes in land use and technology in the core city forced all other zones outward, producing patterns of succession and change. Although the Chicago pattern of concentric rings was later shown by other urban scholars to be far from universal, the interdependent spatial character of urban areas expressed in physical features, a notion which Park and his colleagues stressed, has been widely accepted (Thomlinson, 1969; Downs, 1973).

3. We are particularly indebted to Paul E. Peterson (1976) who has called our attention to some of the developments we discuss.

4. Nation states struggling for power and wealth in the international order have been considered to behave along the lines we are suggesting in the case of cities (see Allison, 1971). As we argue below, however, the highly coordinated intercity competition stressed by our framework of analysis does not assume the unified pursuit of supposedly rational interests, a point suggested by Allison.

5. The best known management study of the city government during this period was the one done by the Mayor's Committee on Management Survey. It concluded that increases in the city budget were due to inflation rather than "an excessively

high standard of municipal living" (The Mayor's Committee on Management Survey, 1953). For its detailed analysis of the city's financial and budgetary practices, see Mayor's Committee on Management Survey (1953: ch. 7).

6. New York City's property tax has two components: a constitutionally limited rate for current expense budget purposes and an unlimited rate for capital budget items. Real estate taxes for the expense budget are limited by the State Constitution to an amount equal to 2.5% of the five-year average of the full valuation of real property in the city, plus whatever amount is necessary to pay the debt service. As a result of this peculiar property tax situation, the city, in time, began to utilize the capital budget for items that more properly belonged in the expense budget (Netzer, 1967).

7. Moreover, while modifications of the budget which involved interagency transfers or increased total expenditures formally required approval by the Board of Estimate and the City Council, this requirement in fact had little impact on mayoral control of the modification process. This limitation did not apply to funds received from the federal or state government, and other charter provisions enabled the mayor to avoid the two local bodies if he so desired (Robertson and Vecchio, 1975).

8. During the preceding decade, the banks had accepted two of the major strategies used by city officials to avoid a balanced budget—the placement of operating budget expenses into the capital budget and overestimating revenues—thereby necessitating the issuance of short-term debt instruments to cover the deficit. Despite the unorthodox nature of these techniques and the large city debt burden they helped create, the municipal bond market continuously purchased New York City securities.

9. Of the nine original members of MAC, five were chosen by the governor and four by the mayor; all but one of these appointees had banking or brokerage connections. The MAC was to convert the city's $3 billion in short-term debt into long-term bonds. It also was empowered to audit the city's budget for 10 years. The EFCB, created three months after MAC, included Governor Carey, Mayor Beame, State Controller Levitt, City Controller Golden, and three business members—the President of Colt Industries; an Assistant to the President of ITT; and Felix Rohatyn, the investment banker who chaired MAC. In addition, EFCB met regularly with a Financial Community Liaison Group which comprised the city's major banking and investment houses, particularly the top executives of Citibank, Chase Manhattan, Morgan Guaranty Trust, Solomon Brothers, Lehman Brothers, Merrill Lynch, and Metropolitan Life. The EFCB's powers were extensive. It was charged with administering the city's finances, including the preparation of a three-year financial plan, producing a balanced budget by 1978, reorganizing the city's budgetary practices, preparing revenue and expenditure estimates, approving all city borrowing, disbursements, and reviewing contract agreements. The EFCB's powers extended to even the city's semiindependent agencies.

10. On June 30, 1975, the five main employee pension funds had only 4.4% of their assets invested in city securities. Three years later, 31.9% of their assets were invested in city and MAC debt (Boast, 1978).

11. From 1975 to 1977, the average annual growth of expenses financed by city tax-levy dollars has been 7.7%; it had been 15% in the 1970-1975 period (Boast, 1978).

REFERENCES

ALLISON, G. T. (1971) Essence of Decision. Boston: Little, Brown.

ANTON, T. J. (1964) Budgeting in Three Illinois Cities. Urbana, IL: Institute of Government and Public Affairs.

BAHL, R. W., A. K. CAMPBELL, and D. GREYTAK (1974) Taxes, Expenditures, and the Economic Base: Case Study of New York City. New York: Praeger.

BERNSTEIN, D. (1969) "Financing the city government," pp. 75-89 in R. H. Connery and D. Caraley (eds.), Governing the City: Challenges and Options for New York: New York: Praeger.

BOAST, T. (1978) "Coping with capital: strategies for budgetary retrenchment in New York City." Presented at the meeting of the American Political Science Association, New York.

BRAZER, E. (1959) City Expenditures in the United States. New York: National Bureau of Economic Research.

BURGESS, E. W. (1967) "The growth of a city," ch. 2 in R. Park et al. (eds.), The City. Chicago: University of Chicago Press.

CLARK, P. B. and J. Q. WILSON (1961) "Incentive systems: a theory of organizations." Administrative Science Quarterly 6: 129-166.

CNUDDE, C. F. and D. J. McCRONE (1969) "Party competition and welfare policies in the American states." American Political Science Review 63: 858-886.

Congressional Budget Office (1976) "The causes of New York City's fiscal crisis." Political Science Quarterly 90 (winter): 659-674.

COULTER, P. B. (1970) "Comparative community politics and public policy." Polity 3 (fall): 22-43.

COX, K. R. (1973) Conflict, Power and Politics in the City. New York: McGraw-Hill.

CRECINE, J. P. (1969) Governmental Problem Solving: A Computer Simulation of Municipal Budgeting. Chicago: Rand McNally.

DAHL, R. A. (1961) Who Governs? New Haven, CT: Yale University Press.

——— and C. E. LINDBLOOM (1953) Politics, Economics and Welfare. New York: Harper & Row.

DAWSON, R. E. and J. A. ROBINSON (1963) "Interparty competition, economic variables, and welfare policies in the American states." Journal of Politics 25: 265-289.

DOWNS, A. (1973) Opening Up the Suburbs. New Haven, CT: Yale University Press.

DROR, Y. (1968) Public Policy Making Reexamined. Scranton, PA: Chandler.

DYE, T. R. (1972) Understanding Public Policy. Englewood Cliffs, NJ: Prentice-Hall.

——— (1969) Politics in States and Communities. Englewood Cliffs, NJ: Prentice-Hall.

——— (1966) Politics, Economics and the Public. Chicago: Rand McNally.

EASTON, D. (1953) The Political System. New York: Knopf.

"Effects on national economy of New York City default negligible says Simon" (1975) New York Times (May 16): 1.

"Federal reserve reports widespread impact of New York City default" (1976) New York Times (January 11): 1.

FERRETTI, F. (1976) The Year the Big Apple Went Bust. New York: Putnam.

FROMAN, L. A. (1968) "The categorization of policy contents," ch. 3 in A. Ranney (ed.), Political Science and Public Policy. Chicago: Markham.

HARRIS, M. (1974) "Budget bureau in a budget crisis." New York Affairs 2(2): 22-37.

HARVEY, D. (1973) Social Justice and the City. London: Edward Arnold.

HIRSCHMAN, A. O. (1970) Exit, Voice and Loyalty. Cambridge, MA: Harvard University Press.

HOFFERBERT, R. I. (1974) The Study of Public Policy. Indianapolis: Bobbs-Merrill.

——— and I. SHARKANSKY (1969) "Dimensions of state politics, economics and public policy." American Political Science Review 63: 867-880.

HORTON, R. D. (1977) "Sayre and Kaufman revisited: New York City government in the post-1965 period." Presented at the meeting of the American Political Science Association, Washington, D.C.

KANTOR, P. (1976) "Elites, pluralists and policy arenas in London: toward a comparative theory of city policy formation." British Journal of Political Science 6: 311-334.

"Layoffs ordered by Beame are not taking place" (1975) New York *Times* (February 2: IV, 1.

LINEBERRY, R. L. and E. P. FOWLER (1967) "Reformism and public policies in American cities." American Political Science Review 61: 701-716.

LOWI, T. J. (1964a) "American business, public policy case studies and political theory." World Politics 16: 677-715.

——— (1964b). At the Pleasure of the Mayor. New York: Macmillan.

——— (n.d.) "Decision making vs. policy making: toward an antidote for technocracy." (mimeo)

MANDELBAUM, S. (1965) Boss Tweed's New York. New York: John Wiley.

Mayor's Committee on Management Survey (1953) Modern Management for the City of New York (vol. 1). New York: Author.

MELTSNER, A. J. (1971) The Politics of City Revenue. Berkeley: University of California Press.

MERTON, R. K. (1968) "The latent functions of the machine," pp. 223-233 in E. Banfield (ed.), Urban Government. New York: Macmillan.

MILLS, C. W. (1956) The Power Elite. New York: Oxford University Press.

NETZER, D. (1967) "New York City's finances," pp. 372-383 in W. Kroeger and J. G. Longworth (eds.), Perspectives in Pragmatism: New York City Government in Transition. New York: AM-PM.

NEWFIELD, J. and P. DUBRUL (1977) The Abuse of Power. New York: Viking.

New York City Council on Education (1976) 1976-77 Fact Book on the New York Metropolitan Region. New York: Pace University.

PETERSON, P. E. (1976) School Politics: Chicago Style. Chicago: University of Chicago Press.

RANNEY, A. (1968) "The study of policy content: a framework for choice," pp. 3-22 in A. Ranney (ed.), Political Science and Public Policy. Chicago: Markham.

Research Department, Community Council of Greater New York, Bureau of Statistical Services (1963) Social Welfare and Health Expenditures and Their Financing. New York: Author.

ROBERTSON, A. F., Jr. and L. A. VECCHIO (1975) "A legal history of expense budgeting in New York City." Fordham Urban Law Journal 4(fall): 1-37.

SAYRE, W. and H. KAUFMAN (1960) Governing New York City: Politics in the Metropolis. New York: Russell Sage.

SCHICK, A. (1974) Central Budget Issues under the New York City Charter. Report prepared for the State Charter Revision Commission for New York City. New York: State Charter Revision Commission.

SHARKANSKY, I. (1969) The Politics of Taxing and Spending. Indianapolis: Bobbs-Merrill

——— (1968) Spending in the American Status. Chicago: Rand McNally.

——— (1967) "Economic and political correlates of state government expenditures." Midwest Journal of Political Science 11: 173-192.

SHEFTER, M. (1977) "New York City's fiscal crisis: the politics of inflation and retrenchment." Public Interest 48(summer): 98-127.

SMITH, T. A. (1968-69) "Toward a comparative theory of the policy process." Comparative Politics 1: 498-515.

THOMLINSON, R. (1969) Urban Structure: The Social and Spatial Character of Cities. New York: Random House.

TIEBOUT, C. M. (1968) "A pure theory of local expenditures," pp. 355-366 in S. Greer et al. (eds.), The New Urbanization. New York: St. Martin's.

TOBIER, E. (1970) "Economic development strategy for the city," pp. 27-84 in L. C. Smith and A.M.H. Walch (eds.), Agenda for a City: Issues Confronting New York. Beverly Hills, CA: Sage.

TOLCHIN, M. (1975) "Top bankers say default can hurt world markets." New York Times (October 19): 1.

TRUMAN, D. B. (1951) The Governmental Process. New York: Knopf.

U.S. Department of Justice, Federal Bureau of Investigation (1973) Crime in the United States: Uniform Crime Reports for the U.S. Washington, DC: Author.

WALTON, J. (1976) "Political economy of world urban systems: directions for comparative research," pp. 301-314 in J. Walton and L. H. Masotti (eds.), The City in Comparative Perspective. New York: John Wiley.

WILDAVSKY, A. (1976) Budgeting. Boston: Little, Brown.

——— (1964) The Politics of the Budgetary Process. Boston: Little, Brown.

7

TOWARD A VIABLE URBAN FUTURE
IN A SOCIETY OF LIMITS:
Possibilities, Policies, and Politics

LOUIS H. MASOTTI

Northwestern University

The possibilities for urban viability explored here grow out of an increasing disenchantment with the effectiveness of present policies and programs aimed at urban areas, their populations, and the quality of life. It has been contended for a number of years that the urban policies of both public and private institutions were becoming, or had become, counterproductive, alienating, dependency-producing, and disenabling. If there is to be a viable urban future—one that functions relatively effectively and efficiently in terms of the quality of lives people live—existing policies and the institutions, public and private, which produce them need to be reevaluated, options explored, and major adjustments made.

California's Proposition 13 has now become a household word in America, and "Jarvising" has been added to the list of politicized verbs. While Proposition 13 was doubtless a significant event in contemporary domestic history, and Howard Jarvis may go down in history as the Ralph Nader of the taxpaying public, I submit that the panoply of processes and

AUTHOR'S NOTE: *A revised version of this article appeared in* Fiscal Retrenchment and Urban Policy *(Volume 17, Urban Affairs Annual Reviews) John P. Blair and David Nachmias, eds. (Beverly Hills, CA: Sage, 1979).*

events which have led to the current set of critical tensions between the ruled and rulers in our society is considerably broader than that and, indeed, much more fundamental. It is those phenomena which are examined here in the search for alternative approaches to a viable urban future.

PRESENT POLICIES AND THEIR LIMITATIONS

Despite some rhetoric to the contrary, urban policy in America, by and large, has been designed to be therapeutic, i.e., to treat the symptoms of the urban malaise rather than to uncover its fundamental causes and engage in preventive action. It is clear that, since the rediscovery of the urban crisis in the early 1960s, the approach has been to develop more programs, create more bureaucracy, and spend more money in an effort to stem the tide of urban decay; and most of this behavior was a political response to pressure from the cities and their advocates. For the most part the result of all this activity has been to develop a programmatic, bureaucratic, institutionalized failure. In general, the cities and their residents are less well off than they were before the flurry of urban policies. Those policies have been ineffective and inefficient in pursuit of their ostensible goals—the improvement of the quality of urban lives and the support of cities as economic entities. Our urban policies, which currently use terminology such as "targeting and tailoring" ofr "distressed cities," operate primarily as a maintenance function. They are designed to prevent things from getting worse rather than to help things get better. Urban policies tend to be dependency-producing for urban populations, and for cities vis-a-vis the federal agencies. Such dependency significantly reduce the possibilities for the emergence of either effective, self-sustaining citizens or viable cities. This condition, it has become clear, is unacceptable to the recipients of urban assistance, to its target population, and to its critics, but for different reasons. The recipients are dismayed that extant policies are not effective in terms of their purposes, while the critics tend to emphasize programmatic inefficiency. Both are correct.

In short, there seems to be ample evidence that current treatment-maintenance-dependency policies and programs are not working. Let me cite some evidence from three critical urban policy areas—health, education, and security. We have dramatically increased our commitment to medicine and simultaneously decreased the quality of health (measured by morbidity and mortality rates); we have increased our budgets for police (professionalization, new equipment, and technologies) in return for a growing crime rate and a greater perceived sense of insecurity; and in education, we have focused resources on school facilities and elegant curricula and have seen dramatic decreases in the quality of education (measured by scores on standardized tests). In addition, it is clear that other institutions in our urban society charged with responsibility for a variety of needed functions are failing to perform them effectively—the jails, the mental health institutions, the child welfare system, and gerontological programs.

More important, however, as we look toward the future, it does not seem likely that an approach to the urban condition which has operated in an era of expansion focused on *increases* in budgets, personnel, and institutions can function effectively as we become increasingly a "society of limits." The environmentalists and the Arab nations have demonstrated that there are limits on our natural resources; and Californians have dramatically indicated the probabilities of significant decreases in public financial resources available in the future for urban, as well as other, problems.

It is imperative for us also to understand the current limits of our institutional imagination and thus the possibilities for developing effective policies, and even less the probabilities of implementing them. Institutions with an urban orientation—both public and private, both national and local—engage in self-perpetuation and self-maintenance despite the emergence of such accountability-encouraging techniques as sunshine and sunset laws and zero-based budgeting. Institutional bureaucrats have been able to circumvent such efforts at accountability by assigning to themselves the roles of need definition and client identification. In addition, institutional bureaucrats have been effectively protected either by civil service programs which sanction incompetence more often than imagination, or by public service unions which give the impression that they exist to stifle the productivity of their members.

Thus, the very institutions, professionals, and bureaucrats which under present urban policy are charged with alleviating or mitigating urban problems, or at a minimum, with the maintenance of the status quo have become counterproductive, inefficient, ineffective, and very expensive; in short, they have become more disabling than enabling.

At the same time, public awareness of such inefficiency and ineffectiveness has led (1) to increased alienation from both governments and their programs, (2) to a reduced level of tolerance for incompetence and inefficiency, and (3) to increased demands for more accountability, productivity, and a higher quality of service. Encouraged by continued rampant inflation, which reduces their purchasing power and the quality of their lives, the middle class has joined the more disadvantaged in protesting the shortcomings and failures of governments. The level of government they can do most about—local government—is feeling the brunt of this disaffection, although its effects are now being felt in the statehouses, the White House, and on Capitol Hill. The basic demand is for more service and fewer taxes, which clearly sets the stage for major political conflicts and the potential for significant political realignments. We are used to getting less for more in this nation; it will be more than a little interesting to see how we handle demands that there be more for less.

RESETTING THE CIVIC AGENDA

In order to explore the possibility of a viable urban future in America, it becomes necessary to clarify or redefine the goals of an acceptable or desirable urban condition. In general, this involves improving the quality of life, developing appropriate procedural arrangements for effective citizen participation, and fostering a meaningful sense of community. More specifically, I would contend that a viable urban future requires policies which promote vital communities of healthy, educated, employed, and decently housed citizens secure in person and property, with reasonable opportunities to participate effectively in the governing process, and with reasonable expectations that both public and private sector policy makers and bureaucrats will function under fundamental rules of equity and justice. The possibility of achieving such goals, given our failures to date and the impending imposition of new limits on resources, is a considerable challenge to our conceptual ingenuity and our sense of commitment. The problems we confront as we go about resetting the civic agenda include reconceptualization of the urban problem, imaginative use of increasingly limited resources, appropriate procedures to ensure effectiveness, and ongoing evaluation of both intended and unintended consequences.

Clearly, more of what we have done in the past is an inadequate way to approach the future. It becomes necessary to explore options and alternatives in policy and procedure for the potential achievement of the stated goals. This process includes at a minimum:

(1) an evaluation of the appropriate allocation of functions in contemporary urban society
(2) the functional "capture" of current trends, movements, experiments, moods, and themes which might be put to positive use in an effort to enable and empower individuals, groups, neighborhoods, and cities to increase the probabilities of a viable urban future in an era of resource limitation.

The necessity for asking some tough questions and finding appropriate answers to them is obvious. It is imperative that we begin to think about policies that are both different and more effective. If we are agreed, at least in general, that it is the quality of life that individuals lead in their local communities that is or should be our primary concern, and that it has been our inability or unwillingness to organize ourselves effectively, to design imaginative policies, and utilize *all appropriate resources creatively* in an effort to move toward a condition of citizen and community well being, our choices are three:

(1) to *capitulate,* leaving the cities to atrophy and become "sandboxes" or "reservations" for the disadvantaged and have-nots, which is clearly unacceptable

(2) to continue our *present policies and procedures* which have led to dependency and have proven so ineffective in a period of growth as to project increased levels of failure in a society of limits

(3) to express our dissatisfaction with the current urban condition and, rather than wringing our hands in despair, to set about the task of *reconceptualization, reorganization,* and *recommitment* to the most effective use of the vast personal, community, and governmental resources available to us.

The real contemporary challenge to the cities, their leaders, and their citizens is to design imaginative policies which use scarce resources more creatively and thus energetically pursue policies which do more with less.

This pursuit requires significant adjustments and alterations (1) in the definition of our urban problems, (2) in the allocation of authority, responsibility, and accountability, and (3) in the evaluation of policy success and failure. The federalization and centralization of government and the concentration of corporate economic power has resulted more often than not in the stifling of imagination, the restricting of policy, and the growth of institutional dependency and counterproductive bureaucratization. Increasingly the measure of success have become the bottom line and/or the size and the complexity of the institutions to which they are assigned, rather than the consequences and impacts which dollars, programs, technology, and organization have on the problem addressed. We have become enamored of programs more than productivity and of institutions more than impact. Our policies too often are structure oriented rather than solution oriented. Our priorities have been misplaced and must be replaced with those more attuned to the real needs of real people in real communities.

We must decentralize, deinstitutionalize, and deregulate where and when it can be demonstrated that such actions will accrue to the benefit of citizens, clients, students, patients, and consumers in particular, as well as to cities in general. Schools which do not or cannot educate, medical facilities which are iatrogenic rather than health-giving, welfare systems which blame the victims rather than enhance their opportunities, and police departments which are unable to keep secure people and their property must be reorganized in ways which will improve the quality of individual and community life.

In a society of limits we must begin the process of "enabling" and "empowering" individuals, neighborhoods, communities, and organizations to help themselves by facilitating the flow of private capital and public funds and professional/technical assistance where such resources will improve the quality of life through the active participation of those affected. There is some evidence to indicate that such programs already in force are not only more policy-effective but also more efficient in the utilization of scarce resources, particularly where labor intensity and preventive behavior displaces fiscal intensity and treatment. In short, decreasing institutional/bureaucratic dependency and encouraging the building of capacities at the local level might well move us in the direction of both program effectiveness and cost efficiency at precisely the time when each is being defined as a significant issue. I would argue that the key question is not *who* makes social policy or *where* it is made but what difference the policy makes in the lives of those it is intended to help and on the life of the community itself. By questioning current assumptions about the determinants of the quality of life in this society it becomes possible to identify those interventions—public and private, institutional and individual, short and long range, small and large scale, professional and voluntary—which are judged most likely to make a difference, to pursue those policies purposefully, and to evaluate their effects. In this process it is important to identify the most appropriate role (1) for governmental institutions by level and policy area and (2) for the private sector whether it be corporation, financial institution, service organization, neighborhood, family, or the individual.

The potential success of such an approach to urban policy in an era of limits will be based on our capacity to identify *real problems,* rather than bureaucratic and professional definitions of problems, and to design intervention strategies which employ the most effective and imaginative combination of public and private resources in terms of the needs of those to be served and of the community of which they are a part. In order to do this, it will be necessary to take advantage of existing and emerging tendencies designed to overcome dependency and to make the most effective use of existing resources, opportunities, and procedures.

Illich, for example, has argued convincingly against counterproductive technology and for the deinstitutionalization of education and criticized the medical industry as a "nemesis." The disabling and repressive effects of professionalism have been argued persuasively by Freidson (1970) and McKnight (1976). In the serviced society which we have become (more than two-thirds of us now derive our income by delivering services), there is a dilemma in the growth of the service economy. In order to serve one another we need more clients who need help or clients who need more help. In a society served by professionals and bureaucrats, people are increasingly defined as lacking, disabled, or deficient. There is a need for need and professionals are entrusted with the responsibility for defining that need which is in turn self-serving, dependency producing, and costly. A growing serviced society depends on more people who can be defined as problems rather than as productive participants. A professionally dominated society/economy thrives on the increase in the deficiencies of the population rather than on its potential to develop a capacity for well-being. Even the consumer/voter revolt, symbolized recently by Proposition 13, does not address itself to the issue of professional dominance and client dependency. It is more an expression of alienation and disaffection for the cost effectiveness of products, services, and programs. In effect we are hearing the protests of the beleaguered middle class who want reliable products and accountable public officials.

There are, however, some indications of capacity building, enablement, and empowerment which portend the possibility of viable cities and populations. Berger and Neuhaus (1977) offer moral, political, and practical reasons for supporting and enhancing "mediating structures"—neighborhoods, family, church, and voluntary organizations—as effective bridges between individuals and societal megastructures. They argue forcefully that such mediating structures be protected and fostered by public policy as essential ingredients for capacity building and, therefore, for effective democratic procedures. But they also submit that such structures can be utilized effectively by public policy makers to realize social goals. The mediating structures are, in fact, an argument for dissembling large-scale public and private power and resources for more effective and efficient use.

Others, including Schumacher (1973), have made a case for redesigning tools and technology for more effective utilization at the community, familial, and individual level. The so-called appropriate technology approach insists that economies of scale are not always economic and very often are counterproductive. The Center for Neighborhood Technology was recently established in Chicago to act as a clearinghouse for new ideas in utilizing technology to enhance family, neighborhood, and community well-being. Following its theme, that "if your only tool is a hammer, all problems look like nails," the center makes a concerted effort to identify the diversity of technological innovations available, such as cost-efficient household solar energy and rooftop hydroponic greenhouses to improve the supply of inexpensive fresh vegetables in a lower class black neighborhood. Other appropriate technologists in the Chicago area have argued forcefully that the $7.9 billion Deep Tunnel Project of the Metropolitan Sanitary District (the largest public works project in the history of the United States) is not only outrageously expensive but also when finished is not likely to reduce the flooding problems for which it is designed; they argue instead for the development of water retention devices located locally with a provision for recycling on site.

Appropriate technology is only one of several facets of the new interest which has emerged focusing on neighborhood viability. The National Commission on Neighborhoods is at least symbolically significant in this regard, although the dramatic increases in neighborhood revitalization throughout the country are much more important. Neighborhoods are being upgraded in many cities because of newly available mortgage money resulting from successful anti-redlining legislation, and by the rehabilitation and redevelopment which is brought on by "regentrification" (especially in cities such as Baltimore, Washington, D.C., and San Francisco). Neighborhood revitalization is a good example of the combined effects of resident politicization and effective regulation by appropriate governmental agencies (anti-redlining). Since people live in neighborhoods and not in cities, the renaissance of those neighborhoods bodes well for urban viability.

Another area of low-cost/high-effectiveness activity which reduces dependency on professionals and bureaucrats is the so-called self-help phenomenon which has grown simultaneously with the disaffection with human service bureaucracies. By forming groups with members who share similar problems, i.e., through mutual assistance, the self-help groups have achieved considerable success across a wide variety of purposes—from the venerable Alcoholics Anonymous to organizations for child-beating parents, the overweight, the divorced, parents of twins, cancer patients, and an endless variety of physical, mental, and emotionally distressed persons. Current estimates indicate that there are more than one-half million self-help groups in the United States comprising more than 15 million members. These groups are characteristically developed outside of established institutions by persons sharing a characteristic or a problem who have agreed to take responsibilities for themselves and to help others do the same. Self-help is for the most part a nonprofessional, nonbureaucratic, grass-roots response to the increasing inefficiency of our complex, technological society.

Renewed interest in mediating structures, appropriate technology, neighborhoodism, and self-help groups results, in part at least, because of dissatisfaction with the options and, in part, because there are no options. Such activity is an expression of antiinstitutionalism, antibureaucracy, and antiprofessionalism and constitutes a sort of service populism which has significant impact at the personal and small-scale organizational level. The critical question may be whether these small-scale, cost-efficient, high-efficacy efforts at providing advice, aid, and service to millions of people can be and should be a substitute for, or a complement to, existing large-scale bureaucratic, social, and human service programs in both the public and private sectors. Such activities seem to fill the vacuum created by the limits and failures of established bureaucracies and that may, in fact, be their strength. It does seem somehow inappropriate to try to transform highly successful small-scale programs into organized service delivery programs; perhaps they work best because they operate on the basis of felt need and outside the established bureaucracy. It is tempting to suggest that, since such programs seem to have real potential for effectiveness, they be substituted for existing, inefficient programs in the public sector. But because it is clear that such programs work because they are not bureaucratic, institutionalizing them would merely undermine them rather than transform them into large-scale policies and programs.

What is suggested, however, and possible is a careful reconsideration of how private interests and purposes can be used in the public interest. Governments will have to begin to think more seriously about using their authority to regulate and to use tax expenditures (subsidies, loans, credits) rather than spending reduced public dollars on maintenance and income services and on incentive-reducing capital grants. Governments must increasingly use their authority to provide incentives for the private sector, including groups and individuals, to do things in their own best interest, which are also in the public interest. In Chicago recently, the city was able to loosen the mortgage money market considerably and to provide an incentive for home buying for middle-class families by authorizing $100 million in municipal bonds to be used by financial institutions as subsidies in reducing home mortage rates from 10% to 8%. Chicago's financial institutions were more than happy to comply, it cost the city nothing, and it has created a significant increase in housing investment in the city at precisely the time when high mortgage interest rates were stifling the market.

Schultze (1977) argues for taxation rather than regulation on the grounds that regulations bureaucratize and require expensive implementation and enforcement procedures. Tax incentives on the other hand tend to be more effective because they reduce profits for noncompliance. Taxation, however, requires a better understanding of the process dynamics, plans for the long range, and a well-grounded set of public policy goals.

THE IMPLICATIONS OF URBAN ALTERNATIVES:
POLITICAL, SOCIAL, AND ECONOMIC

All policies have costs and benefits. I am concerned here with those associated with thinking small, creatively, and effectively. The implication for shifting urban policy in the direction of the private sector including at least the following: the possibilities for new political coalitions, the impact on political forms and processes, the practicality of disaggregating responsibility for the quality of urban life, and the problem of maintaining our commitment to the disadvantaged.

One of the most interesting possibilities suggested by the urban policy options suggested above includes the potential for a liberal/conservative coalition. Liberals interested in more effective urban policy, neoconservatives concerned with more efficient policy, and classical conservatives who want ideological purity might find some agreement if effective policies can be identified which reduce both the role of government and the expenditure of public dollars. Whether such coalitions come to pass depends on how well the policies are articulated and the nature of their nuances.

The policy options I have been discussing involve a decentralization of responsibility and control. This may involve the decline of order and accountability in the world of public policy. Public officials, unsure of their role in a public/private partnership, may resort increasingly to buck-passing techniques such as the referendum. There are real questions associated with a shift from indirect citizen participation through elected officials and the kind of town meeting democracy which Proposition 13 and the recent Cleveland mayoral recall election portend. Complex social legislation may be more difficult than the populists would have us believe, since direct democracy removes the possibility of compromise and bargaining during the policy process and places the responsibility for deciding the problem of interpretation and implementation in the hands of the very bureaucrats at whom referenda and initiatives are directed. One of the more interesting side shows following the passage of Proposition 13 is the kind of "we'll show you" revenge evidenced among some California public agencies which were potentially damaged by the loss of tax revenue. Under the circumstances, elected officials may be forced to demonstrate their capacity to lead and act responsibly in the public interest.

There are also some doubts about the potential for a disaggregated responsibility for social policy in the cities. The rich have always been able to buy the services they need and do not necessarily rely on public providers. The poor, for the most part, have been unable to provide their own services; they tend to lack adequate knowledge of the system and adequate technological skills. The middle class, which has indicated the strongest interest in self-help and reduced public service as a trade-off for lower taxes, may very soon tire of "doing it themselves" as the romance wears off and the drudgery sets in. For example, how many of us want to, can, or will sweep our own streets, dispose of our own garbage, supplement a reduced school curriculum, or participate in a neighborhood security watch. The substitution of labor intensity for fiscal expense quickly becomes inconvenient for a society spoiled by service and socialized to expect it. Acceptance of a process of *lowered* expectations rather than rising ones will not come easily, if at all. The heralded Chinese model of cooperative self-help is a function of intensive socialization, peer group pressure, and government sanction; it is an act of political, economic, and social will for which I suspect the American urban middle class is not yet ready.

Perhaps the most serious implication of social service disaggregation and self-help concerns the dynamics of maintaining our commitment to the disadvantaged. Most of the social spending or maintenance policies of the government have been directed at the poor, and in many cases it is precisely those programs which are the target of tax resistance and revolt. Initiatives such as Proposition 13 rely on majority disaffection rather than on minority need. Issues of equity, compensatory assistance, and need are not taken into account in most populist techniques. In a short time we have moved from a concern for service equity as articulated in the *Rodriquez* and *Serrano* cases to a service equivalent of the *Bakke* case. Policy options which simply give vent to the felt need for reduced taxation rather than to the more effective delivery of service to all urban residents in need may be judged not only a failure but also a disaster. The middle class may need and get tax reductions or stabilization through its political clout, but there must be some assurances that the poor and disadvantaged will be adequately protected and serviced and, if possible, enabled to develop the capacity to do things for themselves in the same way that the middle class has been.

CONCLUSIONS: RISKS AND PAYOFFS

If indeed we have approached an era of limits and if there is some potential for viability despite those limits, it would appear that we have three options:

(1) we can do fewer of those things which we have done
(2) we can do less of the same things or
(3) we can do the same things differently including the transfer or sharing of responsibility for all or some of them.

It does not seem to me that there are any other options. Which of these options is embraced or which combination of them is devised is indeed a political question with serious implications for the future viability of cities, neighborhoods, and populations. An effective set of imaginative urban policies which decreases dependency, increases a sense of community, and develops the potential of citizens and their communities would be welcome indeed. However, the path toward urban viability involving the use of human energy and private capital is not clearly charted. I have long thought that the impending era of limits was a cloud with a silver lining, one which would cause us—indeed, force us—to reconceptualize our problems and solutions in some more meaningful and effective way. I hope that I have not been too optimistic.

REFERENCES

BEAL, F. (1978) "Helping cities help themselves: American urban problems and prospects." Presented at "The Conservative Approach to Inner City Problems," A Conference for Those Concerned with the Problems Facing our Inner City Areas, Birmingham, England.

BERGER, P. L. and R. J. NEUHAUS (1977) To Empower People: The Role of Mediating Structures in Public Policy. Washington, DC: American Enterprise Institute for Public Policy Research.

CARTER, J. (1978) "New partnership to conserve America's communities." (President Carter's urban policy statement, March 27.)

FREIDSON, E. (1970) Professional Dominance: The Social Structure of Medical Care. Chicago: AVC.

GORDON, A., M. BUSH, J. McKNIGHT, L. GELBERD, T. DEWAR, K. FAGAN, and A. McCAREINS (1974) Beyond Need: Toward a Serviced Society. Evanston, IL: Center for Urban Affairs, Northwestern University.

GORDON, A., M. T. GORDON, and R. LeBAILLEY (1976) "Beyond need: examples in dependency and neglect." Presented at the meeting of the American Sociological Association, New York.

HAIDER, D. (1978a) "Urban policy options: where we have been, what we have learned, and where can we go?" Background Paper prepared for a Conference on Viable Urban Futures, April 1978, Center for Urban Affairs, Northwestern University.

——— (1978b) "Viable urban futures: a proposal for a national conference and publications." Evanston, IL: Center for Urban Affairs, Northwestern University.

ILLICH, I. et al. (1977) Disabling Professions. London: Marion Boyars.

——— (1975) Medical Nemesis. London: Calder and Boyars.

——— (1973) Tools for Conviviality. New York: Harper & Row.

KHARASCH, R. N. (1973) The Institutional Imperative: How to Understand the United States Government and Other Bulky Objects. New York: Charterhouse Books.

LONG, N. (1971) "The city as reservation." Public Interest 25(fall).

MASOTTI, L. H. (1977) "Social policy in America: the need for reassessment." Evanston, IL: Center for Urban Affairs, Northwestern University.

McKNIGHT, J. (1976) "Professionalized service and disabling help." Presented at the First Annual Symposium on Bioethics of the Clinical Research Institute of Montreal.

MOLOTCH, H. (1979) "Capital and neighborhood in the United States: some conceptual links." Urban Affairs Quarterly 14: 289-312.

MORRIS, R. S. (1978) Bum Rap on America's Cities: The Real Causes of Urban Decay. Englewood Cliffs, NJ: Prentice-Hall.

Office of Planning and Research, State of California (1978) "An urban strategy for California." Sacramento, CA: Author.

OLSON, M. (1965) The Logic of Collective Action: Public Goods and the Theory of Groups. Cambridge, MA: Harvard University Press.

——— and H. H. LANDSBERG [eds.] (1973) The No-Growth Society. New York: Norton.

SCHULTZE, C. L. (1977) The Public Use of Private Interest. Washington, DC: Brookings Institution.

SCHUMACHER, E. F. (1973) Small Is Beautiful: Economics as if People Mattered. New York: Harper & Row.

STERNLIEB, G. (1971) "The city as sandbox." Public Interest 25(fall).

——— and J. W. HUGHES (1978) Revitalizing the Northeast: Prelude to an Agenda. New Brunswick, NJ: Center for Urban Policy Research.

"Toward a more effective approach to urban problems: definition, analysis, intervention, and evaluation." (1973) Evanston, IL: Center for Urban Affairs, Northwestern University.

WALSH, A. H. (1978) The Public's Business: The Politics and Practices of Government Corporations. Cambridge, MA: MIT Press.

PART IV

DISTRIBUTION OF BENEFITS

8

DISTRIBUTION OF SERVICES:
Studying the Products of
Urban Policy Making

RICHARD C. RICH

Virginia Polytechnic Institute and State University

> The city has been under seige, both by those within and those
> without to live up to an equality norm in the treatment of its
> inhabitants [Long, 1972: 36].

Neither the "fiscal crisis" nor our new "age-of-limits" mentality has
diminished the importance of distributive issues in urban politics. They
have, if anything, heightened their importance. Local fiscal austerity raises
the issue of how burdens, both in terms of taxes and in terms of service
cut backs, are to be distributed and makes the contest to determine who
gets what from local government a more serious matter than it might have
been in an era of expanding budgets when a wider range of needs could be
met. This new focus of urban politics makes it increasingly urgent that we
be able to accurately measure public service distributions and understand
their implications, for we can expect in the 1980s to see a resurgence of
the trends of the 1960s toward legal and political challenges to municipal
service distributions which turn on questions of equity.[1]

Social science has made valuable strides in describing and understanding
service distributions. In this chapter I will review the research on service
distributions, argue that it has slighted major issues in ways that severely

restrict our capacity to assess the social significance of service delivery patterns, and suggest some new directions for the study of local service distributions.

Public services have traditionally been evaluated against standards of efficiency, effectiveness, equity, and responsiveness. In much of the literature on local services, there is an unarticulated presumption that equity is a stepchild in this quartet; a supposed luxury to be pursued if we have sufficient resources left after meeting the so-called important goals. Fiscal distress would seem to demand an even greater attention to efficiency and effectiveness, but it is crucial to recognize that the four criteria are intimately bound. Certainly it is clear that equitably distributed services which are inefficient and ineffective are little benefit to anyone. It should be equally clear, however, that assiduous pursuit of equity and responsiveness, while potentially at odds with narrowly defined efficiency and effectiveness, can contribute to local governments' effectiveness and efficiency, broadly conceived in terms of the allocation of social resources in ways that maximize human potential and satisfaction.

My argument is simply that it continues to be important to evaluate public services against the standard of equity. Past work on service distributions is valuable for focusing on the equity criteria. It has, however, been weak in developing the link between equity and other goals. Much of this inquiry has been initiated through a desire to discover whether or not municipal services are delivered in a manner which violates constitutional or common law guarantees to equal protection of the laws by discriminating among class or racial groups within the city (Diamond et al., 1978). As a consequence of this concern, the research has characteristically sought systematic differences in services that cannot be justified on technical grounds and that *differentiate class and/or racial groupings* in the city (Merget and Wolff, 1976). It has concentrated on telling us (1) how services are distributed among class and racial groups and (2) what the reasons are for observed variations in service levels.

Examinations of the allocation of different types of services in different cities have not produced a simple, universal description of distributional patterns. While poor neighborhoods sometime suffer inadequate services and affluent communities sometime receive the best that cities have to offer, the opposite patterns are also present. Empirical patterns differ among both the cities that have been studied and the services examined within any given city.

Reports of these research efforts leave the overall impression that there is a good deal of equality in service distributions. Municipal services do not appear to be consistently manipulated by the affluent to the disadvantage of the poor. They also are not clearly redistributive instruments through which the government attempts to redress inequalities in private resources with public services for the less affluent. While systematic inequalities may exist in any particular research site, the literature suggests that factors other than class or race most often determine the distribution of municipal services.

The evidence accumulated includes both cases in which distributions favored middle- and upper-class groups and cases in which the poor received favored treatment. Whether we look at education (Katzman, 1968; Levy et al.), library services (Martin, 1969; Lineberry, 1977), police protection (National Advisory Commission on Civil Disorder, 1968; Weicher, 1971; Bloch, 1974), recreational facilities (Lyon, 1970; Gold, 1973), or other services such as street maintenance or sewers (Antunes and Plumlee, 1977; Boots et al., 1972; Levy et al., 1974; Lineberry, 1977), data can be found that show both patterned and unpatterned inequalities in the objectively measured distribution of services. This evidence provides no clear basis for either accepting or rejecting hypotheses about overall patterns in the distribution of public services or for assessing the performance of urban government in general with respect to the equitable provision of services.

Moving from supposedly objective data to reports of citizens' perceptions of interneighborhood service differentials reinforces the impression of rough equality across class and racial groups. An overwhelming majority of all citizens have reported feeling that services in their neighborhood were as good or better than those available in other neighborhoods of their cities (Aberbach and Walker, 1970; Fowler, 1974; Lovrich and Taylor, 1976; Schuman and Gruenberg, 1972).[2] While there are reasons for doubting the validity of citizens' perceptions as measures of actual interneighborhood service distributions (Stipak, 1979; Schuman and Gruenberg, 1972; Birgersson, 1977), this perceived equality provides little evidence that public service distributions contribute to the all-too-apparent inequalities of urban life.

Public services, because they must be paid for, impose burdens as well as bestow benefits. An adequate understanding of the equity of service distributions must include knowledge of the incidence of the burdens associated with whatever allocation of benefits is discovered. Efforts to provide such knowledge have resulted in contradictory evidence in much the same way that measurement of benefit distributions did. The property tax costs of public services have been found to be borne disproportionately by both the poor (Bish, 1976; Oldman and Aaron, 1969) and the affluent (Lineberry, 1977) in separate cities.[3]

Along with these efforts to describe the distribution of services and costs, there have been inquires into the sources of observed patterns. While efforts to account for service allocations by reference to overt political favoritism or racial discrimination have generally failed (Antunes and Plumlee, 1977; Lineberry, 1975), the evidence consistently points to the decision processes of service bureaucracies as crucial determinants of ultimate distrubitions (Antunes and Plumlee, 1977; Jonés, 1977; Levy et al., 1974; Lineberry, 1977; Mladenka, 1977). Agency personnel affect the allocation of resources among groups within the city both by creating and following generalized decision rules, and, as Lipsky (1976) has pointed out, by making on-the-spot choices about service performance. Factors such as the age, population density, architectural characteristics, and physical layout of neighborhoods may all affect the distribution of public services, but these factors' effects are mediated through the way in which municipal bureaucrats interpret their significance in the process of allocating resources. A neighborhood's supposedly greater need for services will result in more services only if bureaucrats take account of the factors creating that need in their distributional formulas.

Lineberry (1977) has argued that the influence of service personnel and the decision rules by which they operate is so great as to largely remove the allocation of public services from the control of even the strongest community elite or elected officials. If he is correct, the study of urban bureaucracy becomes more important for understanding the distribution of services than the study of local politics. If the patterns found in Detroit, Houston, Oakland, and San Antonio can be generalized, we might believe that the community power structure as traditionally defined is less important in determining the authoritative allocation of values through city government than is the organization of public service delivery systems.

This conclusion will not satisfy those who expect to see the inequalities of power that exist in the society used to control local policy outputs (Williams, 1971) or those who view municipal services as potentially redistributive mechanisms that can be managed through the political process to compensate for the inequalities created in the private sector (Miller and Roby, 1970; Harvey, 1973). Research to this point suggests that there is a rough equality (or at least an unpatterned inequality) of services among neighborhoods, but that equality is less the product of political choice than a result of decisions made by bureaucrats in an effort to simplify their tasks. This raises a question of what relationship such an unintentional equality can have to any more elaborate concept of equity in the allocation of public resources.

The image of rough equality in the treatment of racial and class groups by municipal government is also likely to seem counterintuitive to the lay observer familiar with the significant variation in the quality of life in different urban neighborhoods. Does past research present a full and accurate picture of municipal service delivery or are there limits to that research that should condition our interpretation of its findings? In the sections that follow I will suggest that past research in this field leads us to an image of municipal service delivery which is accurate in its detail, but most incomplete.

THE LIMITS OF PAST RESEARCH

Despite the highly diverse character of past research, it is possible to recognize four patterns in the foci and methods employed in most studies. These commonalities are important because they establish some of the limits of these studies' contribuiions to our knowledge and indicate more fruitful directions for future research.[4]

These similarities in past work include the following. First, research has concentrated on describing and explaining the distribution of services among geographic areas *within* jurisdictions, rather than examining differences in services *among* jurisdictions within metropolitan areas. Second, most studies have used measures of policy *outputs* with little attention to measures of the *outcomes* of service delivery. Third, prior research has employed *arbitrary definitions of neighborhoods* and has not explored the impact of residents' organized efforts on the quality or quantity of services found in different communities. Fourth, most previous research efforts have been based on *equality* of services as the standard against which to judge observed distributions, even though this standard implies a static state not characteristic of urban life.

Before exploring the question of how these characteristics have affected the contribution of past research to our understanding of service distributions, I should state the perspective from which I make this assessment. I assume that public services are the prizes of urban politics. The "game" is not played only to determine who will get available services but also to determine which services will be provided, what units of government will provide them, and who will bear their costs. The three latter conflicts are, in fact, more important to our understanding the socioeconomic impact of public services than is the conflict over the allocation of services within political jurisdictions. *The question of who benefits from public services is answered at least as much by decisions about what types of services will be*

provided as by decisions regarding the distribution of existing services.
This is because of the extent to which services are provided by both public
and private sources and because citizens' economic condition determines
their access to private services. Citizens in different socioeconomic circumstances simply require different service packages. Therefore, which groups
benefit from public services will be determined by what service packages
are offered, as well as by the geographic allocation of those services
(Neenan, 1972).

The relevance of this for the study of public services becomes evident
when we consider the interrelatedness of the criteria by which services are
judged. Studies of service *distributions* have been primarily concerned with
the equity criterion. If we define an equitable distribution as one which
leaves citizens in a more nearly equal circumstance after receiving the
service, it is clear that we cannot assess equity in service delivery without
considering the impact of those services on relevant social conditions. Yet,
when we ask about social impact we are asking about the effectiveness of
services and in a *broad* sense about the efficiency of resource allocation
and use. How have studies of service distributions contributed to our
knowledge of the answers to these questions?

THE PROBLEM OF JURISDICTIONAL BOUNDARIES

Past research concentrated on the analysis of differences among neighborhoods within single jurisdictions because legal guarantees of equal
protection apply only within, not between, jurisdictions.[5] While the focus
on intrajurisdictional inequalities is understandable, it imposes important
limitations on our understanding of the political significance of public
services. To look only within jurisdictions in any given metropolitan area is
to ignore some of the most crucial political processes in contemporary
urban America. Why? Neiman has stated the answer clearly:

> The central cities of metropolitan areas are becoming increasingly
> homogeneous, in marked contrast to the central city of the past,
> with its widely varying neighborhoods, each involving its own
> package of services and lifestyles. This diversity was rooted in the
> differential support of city government and other institutions,
> especially school districts, for different classes of individuals. The
> equal protection imperative of the courts and the equality rhetoric
> of federal policy, as well as the militance of disadvantaged groups,
> make it increasingly difficult for central city regimes to maintain the
> unequal distribution of advantages and disadvantages on a spatial
> basis. Hence, the metropolis has become *the functional and struc-*

tural equivalent of the older central city. The Metropolis today functions much as local areas have functioned traditionally, as regard the spatial distribution of races and classes, and the differential access to those things that all individuals tend to want, but which are scarce or would require much higher costs to provide to everyone, or would not be provided at all if everyone were allowed to freely compete for them [1975: 37].

Strategic use of the tools of municipal incorporation and land use planning have, to a significant extent, replaced competition for favors from city hall as a means of securing favorable service packages (Adrian, 1971; Hirsch, 1971; White, 1978b).[6]

A number of scholars have recently analyzed urban society as a setting for conflict over the allocation of values in which spatial location is a major strategic ploy (Cox, 1973; Harvey, 1973; Kaufman, 1974; Smith, 1974; Williams, 1971). Their work highlights the significance of legal arrangements which arm some citizens with weapons that can be used to obtain political advantages from spatial location that are far greater than their personal resources would allow under a system of private competition. Lax incorporation laws, increased use of special districts, the control of land uses by municipalities, stringent barriers to annexation, and federal tax policy and urban assistance and highway programs, coupled with advances in transportation, building, and communication technology have opened a much larger area to those pursuing locational strategies and ended the monopoly of central city regimes over service packages in post-World War II America (Long, 1972; Guest and Nelson, 1978; White, 1978a). More important, these developments have made it possible for citizens to enlist the power of government in their own search for desirable packages of taxes and services (Danielson, 1976; Downs, 1973; Gottdiener, 1977; Kassarda, 1972; Neiman, 1975).

If citizens do use the incorporation of suburban municipalities and the subsequent regulation of land use in those jurisdictions to isolate themselves from low-income groups and undesirable land uses in order to enjoy better services at lower tax costs, we should find significant differences in the quality of services among jurisdictions within urban areas, differences that are not explained by the preferences or the demographic composition of their populations. Indirect support for the argument that this locational strategy is being employed may be found in the consistent finding that jurisdictions with more middle-class populations provide a more limited range of public services and spend less on each service (except for schools) than less affluent jurisdictions (Brazer, 1964; Cox, 1973; Dye, 1970; Eulau and Eyestone, 1968; Kee, 1965; Masotti and Bowen, 1965).

The effective federalization of financing for some of the services which place the greatest fiscal pressure on central city governments has apparently reduced the concern for *metropolitan* service equity. Federal policies, however, have not been designed to reduce interjurisdictional inequalities. In fact, the present geopolitical organization of urban areas generally serves to reduce or redirect the redistributive impact of federal policies as affluent and poor jursidictions compete for funding (Nathan et al., 1977; Newton, 1975; Social Science Panel on the Significance of Community in the Metropolitan Environment, 1974; Captuto and Cole, 1974; Kassarda, 1972). To the extent that metropolitan populations are interdependent, it is appropriate to expand our concern for equity issues to the metropolitan area (williams, 1971, Harvey, 1973). From this perspective, the virtual federalization of public welfare has hardly resolved the equity issues associated with public services. Neiman argues that "the latent function of the metropolis, as an aggregate, macro-level entity, is to maintain and increase, through structure and policy, the unequal access of individuals to 'the good life'—through impediments to movement for one set of individuals and various subsidies for the pursuit of a locational strategy by other individuals" (1975: 37).

The above discussion has at least two implications for the study of service distributions. First, if we are to have a more comprehensive understanding of the political significance and sources of service patterns, we will have to expand our analyses to include interjurisdictional comparisons and investigations of the contribution of locational strategies to those distributions. Second, inquiry should be expanded to include examination of one important "service" that has not been part of past discussion of service distributions. This is the land use planning and regulation function. While it does not make sense to attempt to discover who is "receiving" this service and who is not (as we would with street lights, for example), it is important to study the access of different groups to the decision processes involved and the advantages conferred by planning and zoning. If some groups can structure their immediate community environment through zoning and land use regulations so that they are unaffected by the negative consequences of failing to provide adequate amounts of some public services, they can be content with a bureaucratically determined equality in the distribution of those services.

Zoning and land use planning processes are especially subject to influence by well-organized, affluent neighborhood associations which can muster the technical expertise necessary to effectively interact with municipal officials (Gottdiener, 1977; Nathan et al., 1977). In Indianapolis I found that several community associations had carefully directed the development of their areas and restricted the types of services that would be necessary to maintain desirable conditions there by taking an active part in land use planning and zoning. They also assured provision of some services in their neighborhoods by shaping planning decisions (Rich, 1978). If this pattern is widely reproduced in other cities, the capacity it affords the most politically active segment of the populace to circumvent the need for public services could explain much of the lack of political competition over service distributions found by other investigators.

THE QUESTION OF OUTCOMES

Prior research on urban service distributions has focused primarily on measures of policy outputs, not policy outcomes.[7] The outputs of local government may be conceptualized as the activity patterns of municipal personnel (Fisk and Winnie, 1974). The outcomes of such outputs or policies may be viewed as the effects specific governmental activities have on relevant social conditions (Ostrom, 1973). The building of a fire substation is an example of an output. A reduction in the loss from fire might be an associated outcome. Clearly, outputs do not always bear a direct relationship to outcomes. There are, however, grounds for discussing outputs as a surrogate for outcomes in terms of the adequacy or effectiveness of public services. If facilities and services (outputs) do not fulfill the purpose for which they were intended, they are ineffective.

The blame is not always with the city, of course. Increased police effort does not always reduce crime rates, and more teachers do not necessarily produce more learning. A great many factors beyond the control of service personnel can condition the results of governmental activity (Coulter et al., 1976). The important point here, however, is that given levels of output are more adequate to produce desired outcomes in some neighborhoods than others. A new park in a poor community may provide recreational opportunities for only a fraction of the local youth and thus contribute little to the reduction of traffic accidents caused by children playing in the street. The same park in a middle-class community with the same number of children, however, might prove quite adequate because of the availability of alternative, privately funded recreational opportunities in that area. Equal outputs in this case would produce very different outcomes because of the interaction of government activity with community resources.[8]

Because this is generally true, it is extremely difficult to discuss the equality of urban service distributions without consideration of outcomes. Is the purpose of city services to distribute contacts with municipal employees or is it to meet residents' service demands? If the purpose is to meet demands, then we must recognize that a given output may provide a highly unequal capacity for meeting different levels of need. Because the actual value of a service can be judged only by reference to measures of effectiveness, we cannot evaluate the equality of benefits from municipal services enjoyed by different groups unless we have outcome indicators. The question is not just "What does local government do for given groups?", but "How effective are local services in meeting the needs of different groups?"; "Are city services allocated in such a way as to produce approximate equality of outcomes?"

It is the lack of answers to the second pair of questions that leads to difficulties in trying to square the results of recent research with the casual observation that services in all cities are quite adequate (effective in maintaining or creating desirable conditions) in some neighborhoods but highly inadequate in others. Whereas effectiveness is a matter of *outcomes* produced by the relationship between community needs and available public services, equality has, to date, been assessed principally in terms of *outputs.*

There are, as Jones (1977) has argued, good reasons for studying output indicators. The systematic study of service levels need not be abandoned in search for quality-of-life indicators. We should, however, develop a capacity for assessing the effectiveness of the municipal services available to different groups and for relating outputs to outcomes if we are to have a more complete picture of equality in service delivery patterns. Indeed, the question of neighborhood needs is, as Thurow (1970) argues, logically prior to any question of distributional equity. We need to know what benefits we expect communities to receive from public services before we can evaluate the effectiveness of actual service delivery or assess the degree to which it is equitable.

An examination of city services in terms of their adequacy for meeting human needs for desirable community conditions should provide a new perspective on the significance of local politics vis-à-vis bureaucratic processes. The distribution of resources among geographic areas (an aspect of local services that seems to be in the control of the bureaucracy) will surely continue to be an important facet of equality of benefit. Outcome analysis, however, should sharpen our awareness of the crucial role played by *the allocation of resources among programs and the overall level of government spending* in determining the extent to which equality is achieved.

To the extent that the city concentrates on providing those services for which there are few private alternatives (street maintenance and lighting and water and sewer services provide examples), citizens will *tend* to benefit equally from government activity. To the extent that the city produces mostly those services for which there are readily available private alternatives (medical services and day-care facilities, for instance), the poor will be disproportionately served by government expenditure. This is because working class and poor citizens cannot generally afford to buy such services unless they are publicly subsidized. It is, therefore, common for middle- and upper-class persons to feel that they have an interest in (1) minimizing government's investment in services for which there are plentiful private alternatives and (2) individually purchasing the services for a price which they feel would be less than the taxes necessary to supply the service to both themselves and the less affluent.

Decisions about the range of government activity and the allocation of resources among services are made primarily in the local legislative body through its budgetary process. While often bureaucratically dominated and rule-driven, this is a supremely political activity; and it is probably here, rather than in the distribution of services among neighborhoods, that the highest stakes in urban politics are to be found. We should not be surprised, then, to find that local elites have little influence over the geographic distribution of services. Having set the rules of the game, they can leave the calling of plays to the bureaucratic referees.

Local elites have little reason to be disappointed at seeing a roughly equal distribution of limited services. Such a distribution poses no threat to the advantages they enjoy in the private sector. Lineberry (1977) has referred to the egalitarian distribution of public resources in the context of extremely unequal private resources as "the other face of service inequality." Social scientists will be able to contribute to the solution of the egalitarian problems of urban services only when they have a handle on outcome measures as well as output indicators. Only then can we both describe the degree of equality with which services are delivered and explain the social implications of maintaining a given distribution.

THE SIGNIFICANCE OF NEIGHBORHOODS

The third feature of past studies is actually two features that are so closely related that they are usefully considered together. These are the use of arbitrary definitions of neighborhoods and the exclusive focus on public employees as the producers of public services. The effects of these two choices on the results of past research merit discussion, because they are not as likely to be recognized as the implications of the limitations already considered and because controlling these effects would require significant modifications in the research designs employed to study service distributions.

Students of service distributions have generally used neighborhoods as their units of analysis. They ask how services were distributed among geographically defined groups, first, and investigate the distribution of services among social classes only to see if it accounts for observed differences among neighborhoods. These units of analysis have most commonly been identified by using census tracts or other essentially arbitrary boundaries. The spatial segregation of races and classes in our cities generally makes census tracts safe surrogates for neighborhoods because they are usually rather homogeneous in their socioeconomic make-up. We can therefore largely ignore the possibility that our failure to find significant, patterned inequalities in services is a result of the chance that our definition of neighborhoods lumps those who are advantaged and those who are disadvantaged into the same units for analysis. As long as the units are small enough, "mixed" neighborhoods should be rare.

This reasoning, however, overlooks the possibility that the crucial differences in communities with respect to their ability to secure service advantages may be between the organized and the unorganized. Citizens are not simply passive recipients of services. They can attempt to shape the services available to them both by influencing the decisions of bureaucrats and politicians and by taking direct action to augment services or increase their effectiveness (Rich, forthcoming; Washnis, 1976). The extent to which residents succeed in these efforts will depend to a considerable extent on the degree to which they are organized for collective action.

Some neighborhoods may be able to enjoy better services than similar communities in the same city simply because they are represented by active voluntary associations. This is true despite the findings that daily service delivery decisions are generally free from influence by citizens (Antunes and Mladenka, 1976; Jones, 1977). In Indianapolis, I found that while most service delivery decisions were made without citizen input, municipal agencies generally responded favorably when neighborhood demands were articulated by aggressive community organizations. It is precisely *because* most citizens acquiesce to service decisions that bureaucrats can sometimes respond to clearly stated neighborhood demands when they arise. Since public services are not an object of intense, overt political conflict, municipal personnel are often free to make allocative decisions on the "squeeky wheel" principle.

If limited budgets make service distribution a zero-sum game, effectively organized neighborhoods can gain a considerable advantage while imposing costs on other neighborhoods where much service delivery is based on responses to articulated demands. In Indianapolis some neighborhood organizations have secured a wide range of services for their communities (Rich, 1978), but similar evidence on the effectiveness of neighborhoods groups on service distributions in other cities is not available. If we are to have a full picture of the service distribution process, future research should include investigations of the differences among those neighborhoods with organizational representation and those without and should recognize that the boundaries of citizens' groups seldom correspond to census tracts.

In addition to examining the impact of community associations on public agencies' behavior, it would be useful to explore the direct contributions that such organizations make to service levels. Neighborhood residents can provide themselves with a number of public services through coordinated efforts. They can, for example, clean vacant lots, build park equipment, organize minitransit systems, purchase additional police protection, and provide day-care facilities through their own labors. Beyond efforts at supplementing public services by direct production, neighborhood associations can augment the effectiveness of public service by acting as "coproducers" (Rich, forthcoming). The quality of services available in a neighborhood often depends as much on residents' actions as on those of public employees.

The significance of this for the study of service distributions is twofold. First, community efforts may condition public service delivery patterns as bureaucrats are attracted to areas in which they receive greater cooperation or as they direct resources away from neighborhoods that "help themselves" and thereby reduce their need for outside services. Knowledge of neighborhood efforts may then contribute to explanations of observed service distributions. Second, and more important, is the fact that residents' collective efforts influence the effectiveness of public services. The activities of neighborhood associations can help determine what level of services will be needed to achieve a given state in different communities. Discovering either of these effects will require defining our units of analysis (neighborhoods) in ways which take their political organization into account.

This becomes especially significant if we are to examine equity issues from the standpoint of outcome analysis. One reason that equal service outputs may result in very different outcomes in different neighborhoods may be that some communities do more to make those services effective. Residents' ability to do so, in turn, generally depends on their material and organizational resources. Thus an equal distribution of outputs may support a very unequal and largely class-biased distribution of community conditions. It would be useful to understand this "second conversion process" in the service delivery system (the process by which communities utilize resources, including public inputs, to shape their environments) as well as the "first conversion process" by which public personnel turn resources into "services." This would serve not only to heighten our understanding of service impacts but also to inform the search for ways to make services more efficient and effective in anticipation of a day when tight budgets will force hard choices about government's support of the quality of life.

THE STANDARD OF EQUITY

The limitation in previous research which probably has the most far-reaching implications for interpretation of results and efforts to redirect inquiry is the almost exclusive focus on equality as the standard against which service distributions are judged. The focus is understandable given the legal context, but when we move away from relatively narrow questions of the equal protection clause, this emphasis provides us with little policy guidance and even less academic understanding of urban service delivery systems.

The concept of equity employed here is a rather simple one for which I will offer no elaborate justification. It stems from the idea that one of the more important purposes of government in contemporary Western societies is to offset the burdens imposed on some groups by the operation of the market economy so that a greater equality of "life chances" is achieved (Furness and Tildon, 1977). An equitable arrangement is then one which promotes greater (though not total) equality of condition. Services are *equally* distributed when everyone gets the same services. They are *equitably* distributed when citizens are in a *more nearly* equal life circumstance after receiving the services than before. This concept of equity is closely akin to the standard of "equal results" described in Levy et al. (1974). It opens the possibility that equity and equality may be incompatible.

The first failing of the equality standard relates to the prior discussion of outputs and outcomes as indicators of service quality. The provision of equal service outputs to groups of consumers who are in highly unequal circumstances may produce inequitable outcomes. This does not apply only to the differences among economic classes. Affluent neighborhoods may very well require a much higher level of some service than poor neighborhoods in order to achieve the same outcomes. Knowing the distributions of outputs, therefore, tells us little about the distribution of outcomes or about the equity of existing policy patterns.

Equal services may be inequitable services in another sense. Provision of an identical service in two neighborhoods can hardly be considered equitable if the residents of one area prize the service highly while those in the other feel no need for it and would prefer to see funds allocated to some other service. Just as equality of output does not measure *effectiveness,* so it does not measure the *responsiveness* of service delivery (the fit between the services provided and the services citizens desire). This is important because responsiveness can be crucial to equity. The link between equity and responsiveness arises from the fact that urban neighborhoods are not static. People move in and out of them. Residents' preferences and behaviors change. Facilities deteriorate. Service delivery efforts reduce some demands while creating others. This dynamic quality of neighborhoods dictates a dynamic concept of equity in urban service delivery because a service distribution which is satisfactory today can become patently inequitable tomorrow.

To the extent that achieving equity in service delivery depends not on applying a static rule such as equality but on responding to the changing needs of community residents, the institutional arrangements through which government responds to citizens' demands become a crucial variable in the study of public services. If equity cannot be guaranteed by reliance on fixed standards of service distribution, we are thrown back to attempting to achieve it through service delivery systems which are structured so as to allow diverse and changing demands to be translated into variations in services across time and space. Institutional arrangements which are biased against responsiveness to the interests of some groups and in favor of others work against achievement of dynamic equity.

The biases of contemporary urban governments have been well documented (Newton, 1975). These biases among class and racial groups in the city are serious barriers to equity. They may, however, be less significant than the pervasive bias against responsiveness to citizens in general. Increasingly, social scientists and citizens have questioned the capacity of urban government to recognize or respond to citizens' demands (Katznelson, 1976). If this is true, the inequities which exist in urban services may be largely products of the institutional arrangements through which service delivery is organized.

Such a conceptualization of the issue requires a shift of our criteria for judging service delivery from those that relate to the distribution of services to those that relate to the distribution of opportunities to influence service delivery. If we can assume that citizens will use their influence with government to secure those services which are most satisfying, we might expect equal access to the decision process to result in an equitable distribution of services. Of course we cannot make such an assumption because we can guarantee neither the quality nor the quantity of citizen participation in public decisions (Eulau and Prewitt, 1973). Under this condition even an allocative process which is equally responsive to all articulated demands may not produce an equitable distribution of services.

The most that can be expected is an institutional arrangement for service provision that is not "rigged" against the interests of any group and which provides equitable opportunities for influence. This suggests that a crucial criteria to be employed in judging urban service delivery systems is the degree to which they exhibit what Bish (1975) terms "institutional fairness." Equality of access to influence over decisions about public services is most likely to produce equitable service distributions where political units are organized so that the beneficiaries of a service are also those who determine the nature of that service. Equality of access is least likely to produce distributional equity in systems where control over services and control over their consumption is separated because such systems are generally biased against responsiveness to some groups (Long, 1972; Bish and Warren, 1972). In this situation, some groups will be able to control service decisions while others are consistently shut out; and service distributions will reflect the relative advantage granted to groups by the structure of service delivery institutions rather than any conscious effort to achieve equity.

Discussion of equality of opportunity for political participation encounters a problem which is closely analogous to that involved in assessing the equality of services. Some citizens are less able to take advantage of participatory structures than others because of educational, experiential, economic, and other disadvantages. Equal opportunities to participate will produce unequal rates of participation and amounts of influence across communities because of these disparities among citizens. Just as providing equal services to unequal neighborhoods can result in inequitable distributions of benefits, providing equal opportunities to influence policy decisions to unequal citizens results in an inequitable distribution of actual influence. While some communities can effectively use conventional channels of participation to shape policy outputs, others will need special mechanisms of direct involvement if their demands are to be effectively voiced. The United States has had a good deal of experience with community-based programs which build on this logic (Yin and Yates, 1974). In our search for solutions to the problems of equity in urban service delivery, we should neither neglect these experiences nor fail to consider the potential contributions of proposed structural reforms in service delivery systems (Rich, 1979b).

This line of argument suggests the importance of analysis of the institutional mechanisms through which service decisions are made. It directs our attention to the relationship between citizens and bureaucrats and to the capacity our political arrangements grant citizens for controlling the actions of public employees, as well as focusing on the differential access race, class, and geographic groups have to opportunities to secure responsive service delivery. Such analyses could produce policy recommendations that transcend efforts to enforce judicially articulated standards of equality in fluid urban settings to suggest ways of creating institutional arrangements that promote the achievement of dynamic equity by allowing all citizens to tailor services to meet the perceived needs of their neighborhoods (Rich, 1977).

CONCLUSION

I have argued that the study of urban service distributions would be improved by expanding the types of questions that are asked. Basically, I have suggested that inquiry might usefully take four new directions.

First, the development of politically fragmented "spread cities" demands that we gather evidence on the distribution of service packages among jurisdictions within metropolitan areas if we are to effectively address the larger questions of equity associated with local government activity. Understanding the differences that are found will require that we explore the role that the power of incorporation and land use controls play in shaping communities and conditioning their service needs and fiscal capacities. We will also have to seek information on citizens' service preferences and local conditions if we are to properly attribute service differences to different fiscal capacities. As part of this, we should recognize the crucial part that zoning and land use planning can play in determining the impact of given service patterns and creating opportunities for inequitable service distributions. The political processes that surround land use decisions, and especially the role of community associations in that process, should be targets of research.

Second, we should devote more energy to discovering the distribution of outcomes of service delivery policies among our cities' residents. This will require that we go beyond measuring service levels to measuring the effectiveness of those services in satisfying community demands and improving neighborhood conditions. In addition, it is important to understand how decisions about gross spending levels, the range of local government activity, and the allocation of funds among programs are related to observed distributions of outcomes.

Third, we need to investigate the distribution of services between those neighborhoods which are represented by community associations and those which are not. Understanding the impact of community associations requires attention to both the "second conversion process" through which residents' actions shape the effectiveness of public services and to the political influence of community groups in distributional decisions.

Fourth, it is necessary both to include criteria other than equality of services (such as efficiency, effectiveness, and responsiveness) in our research and to develop a more dynamic conceptualization of the equity issue than that implicit in the application of static equality criteria. This suggests the necessity of exploring the relationship between the institutional arrangements through which decisions about services are made and the impact of those services on community conditions. An appropriate criterion against which to judge these institutions is not the degree to which they produce equal service outputs for all communities but the degree to which they provide equitable opportunities for citizens to influence service delivery and shape services so that they are responsive to their demands.

These changes in research focus are compatible and several can be combined in any single research design. They will, however, require more wide-ranging and expensive methods of investigation. These will be justifiable only if the work produces information which provides an understanding of the dynamics by which public service distributions are produced and maintained and the significance of these patterns for urban life.

I would like to end on a note of caution. We should not overestimate the potential of public services as redistributive mechanisms. As long as services are locally financed and populations are socially segregated into different political units, public services can do little to remedy major inequalities. Bish (1976), in fact, has argued that attempts at service equalization in the context of a politically fragmented area and reliance on property taxation for funding might actually exasperate economic inequalities as improved services raise property values and impose heavier tax burdens on the poor.

The implication of this is that we should never make the error of examining urban politics in isolation from national politics. Many of the problems of inequality in services stem from the inequality of citizens.

These inequalities are not produced by local governments and cannot be altered by local policies alone. Local government may deal more or less equitably with economically unequal groups, but inequities would be more effectively attacked by national policies designed to reduce the inequalities of wealth and economic opportunity that leave citizens so differentially dependent on public services. State policies, however, can make a significant contribution by inhibiting the capacity of groups to isolate themselves from the costs of public services through the use of municipal boundaries and land use controls. Diamond et al. (1978) have suggested that Congress can take direct steps to encourage the states to insure a nondiscriminatory distribution of public services. Clearly, service inequities are so firmly institutionalized in the current geopolitical structure of our urban areas that they must be attacked on many fronts if they are to be remedied.

NOTES

1. Much of this legal activity is surveyed in Lineberry (1974).

2. One very important exception to this generalization is Black citizens' perceptions of public services. With respect to a number of services, Blacks tend to feel seriously discriminated against (Aberbach and Walker, 1970; Schuman and Gruenberg, 1972; Rossi et al., 1974; National Advisory Commission on Civil Disorders, 1968).

3. Since municipal services are often financed indirectly by state and federal tax efforts and by user charges, one cannot fully assess the distribution of service costs on the basis of an examination of property taxation alone.

4. The discussion that follows draws heavily on my former work (see, e.g., Rich, 1979a).

5. In the fields of education and land use regulation, recent court decisions have brought interjurisdictional differences under the coverage of the equal protection guarantee. This principle, however, has not been extended to other services which are less a state responsibility, and it has not been applied to aspects of education other than financing (Diamond et al., 1978).

6. Partial evidence of this shift is found in the degree to which research on service distributions has show the process of allocation within cities to be largely apolitical. For a summary, see Antunes and Mladenka (1976).

7. This is not because scholars have not recognized the need to develop and employ outcomes measures. A good deal of effort has been devoted to that task (Boots et al., 1972; Hatry, 1977; Schaenan, 1977). Those investigating the *distribution* of services have simply made less use of these measures than those interested in other performance indicators.

8. See, for instance, the decision in *Beal v. Lindsay* (468 F. 2d 287 2d Cir. 1972).

REFERENCES

ABERBACH, J. D. and J. L. WALKER (1970) "The attitudes of whites and blacks toward city services: implications for public policy," pp. 519-537 in J. P. Crecine (ed.), Financing the Metropolis. Beverly Hills, CA: Sage.

ADRIAN, C. R. (1971) "Metropology: folklore and field research," pp. 172-179 in M. N. Danielson (ed.), Metropolitan Politics. Boston: Little, Brown.

AUTUNES, G. E. and K. MLADENKA (1976) "The politics of local services and service distribution," pp. 37-60 in L. H. Masotti and Robert L. Lineberry (eds.), The New Urban Politics. Cambridge, MA: Ballinger.

ANTUNES, G. E. and K. MLADENKA (1976) "The politics of local services and service: ethnicity, socioeconomic status, and bureaucracy as determinants of the quality of neighborhood streets." Urban Affairs Quarterly 12: 312-332.

BABCOCK, R. F. and F. P. BOSSELMAN (1973) Exclusionary Zoning. New York: Praeger.

BENSON, C. S. and P. B. LUND (1969) Neighborhood Distribution of Local Public Services. Berkeley: Institute of Governmental Studies, University of California.

BIRGERSSON, B. O. (1977) "The service paradox: citizen assessment of urban services in 36 Swedish communes," pp. 243-267 in V. Ostrom and F. P. Bish (eds.), Comparing Urban Service Delivery Systems. Beverly Hills, CA: Sage.

BISH, R. L. (1976) "Fiscal equalization through court decisions: policy-making without evidence," pp. 75-102 in E. Ostrom (ed.), The Delivery of Urban Services. Beverly Hills, CA: Sage.

――― (1975) "Commentary." Journal of the American Institute of Planners 41 (March): 67-82.

――― and R. WARREN (1972) "Scale and monopoly problems in urban government services." Urban Affiars Quarterly 8: 97-122.

BLAIR, L. H. and A. I. SCHWARTZ (1972) How Clean Is Our City? Washington, DC: Urban Institute.

BLOCH, P. B. (1974) Equality of Distribution of Police Services. Washington, DC: Urban Institute.

BONJEAN, C. M. (1974) "A symposium: measuring urban agency output and performance." Social Science Quarterly 54: 691-764.

BOOTS, A. et al. (1972) Inequality in Local Government Services. Washington, DC: Urban Institute.

BRAZER, H. E. (1964) "Some fiscal implications of metropolitanism," pp. 136-139 in B. Chinitz (ed.), City and Suburb. Englewood Cliffs, NJ: Prentice-Hall.

CAPUTO, D. A. and R. L. COLE (1974) Revenue Sharing. Washington, DC: Office of Revenue Sharing.

COULTER, P. B., L. MacGILLIVRAY, and W. E. VICKERY (1976) "Municipal fire protection performance in urban areas: environmental and organizational influences on effectiveness and productivity measures," pp. 231-260 in E. Ostrom (ed.), The Delivery of Urban Services. Beverly Hills, CA: Sage.

COX, K. (1973) Conflict, Power, and Politics in the City. New York: McGraw-Hill.

DANIELSON, M. N. (1976) "The politics of exclusionary zoning in suburbia." Political Science Quarterly 91(spring): 1-18.

DIAMOND, P. R., C. CHAMBERLAIN, and W. HILLYARD (1978) A Dilemma of Local Government. Lexington, MA: D.C. Heath.

DOWNS, A. (1973) Opening Up the Suburbs. New Haven, CT: Yale University Press.

DYE, T. R. (1970) "City-suburban social distance and public policy," pp. 363-373 in J. S. Goodman (ed.), Perspectives on Urban Politics. Boston: Allyn and Bacon.

EULAU, H. and R. EYESTONE (1968) "Policy maps of city councils and policy outcomes: a developmental analysis." American Political Science Review 62: 124-143.

FISK, D. M. and C. LAUVER (1974) Equality of the Distribution of Recreation Services. Washington, DC: Urban Institute.

FISK, D. M. and R. E. WINNIE (1974) "Output measures in urban government: current status and likely prospects." Social Science Quarterly 54: 725-740.

FOWLER, F. J. (1974) Citizen Attitudes Toward Local Government, Services and Taxes. Cambridge, MA: Ballinger.

FURNESS, N. and T. TILDON (1977) The Case for the Welfare State. Bloomington: Indiana Univeristy Press.

GOLD, S. D. (1973) "Distribution of urban government services in theory and practice: the case of recreation in Detroit." Public Finance Quarterly 2: 107-130.

GOTTDIENER, M. (1977) Planned Sprawl. Beverly Hills, CA: Sage.

GRAHAM, R. L. and J. H. KRAVITT (1972) "The evolution of equal protection-education, municipal services, and wealth." Harvard Civil Rights-Civil Liberties Law Review 7(June): 103-213.

GUEST, A. M. and G. H. NELSON (1978) "Central city/suburban states differences: fifty years of change." Sociological Quarterly 19(winter): 7-23.

HARVEY, D. (1973) Social Justice and the City. Baltimore: Johns Hopkins University Press.

HATRY, H. P. (1977) How Effective Are Your Community Services? Washington, DC: Urban Institue.

HAWLEY, W. D. and D. Rogers [eds.] (1974) Improving the Quality of Urban Management. Beverly Hills, CA: Sage.

HIRSCH, W. (1971) "The fiscal plight: causes and remedies," pp. 3-40 in W. Hirsch et al. (eds.), Fiscal Pressures on the Central City. New York: Praeger.

JONES, B. D. (1977) "Distributional considerations in models of government service provision." Urban Affairs Quarterly 12: 291-312.

––– and C. KAUFMAN (1974) "The distribution of urban public services." Administration and Society 6: 337-360.

KASSARDA, J. D. (1972) "The impact of suburban population growth on central city service functions." American Journal of Sociology 77: 1111-1124.

KATZMAN, M. T. (1968) "Distribution and production in a big city school system." Yale Economic Essays 8: 201-259.

KATZNELSON, I. (1976) "The crisis of the capitalist city: urban politics and social control, pp. 214-229 in W. D. Hawley and M. Lipsky (eds.), Theoretical Perspectives of Urban Politics. Englewood Cliffs, NJ: Prentice-Hall.

KAUFMAN, C. (1974) "Political urbanism: urban spatial organization, policy and politics." Urban Affairs Quarterly 9: 421-436.

KEE, W. S. (1965) "Central city expenditures and metropolitan areas." National Tax Journal 18: 337-353.

LEVY, F. S., A. J. MELTSNER, and A. WILDAVSKY (1974) Urban Outcomes. Berkeley: University of California Press.

LINEBERRY, R. L. (1977) Equality and Urban Policy. Beverly Hills, CA: Sage.

––– (1975) "Equality, public policy and public services: the underclass hypothesis and the limits to equality." Politics and Policy 4(December): 67-84.

——— (1974) "Mandating urban equality: the distribution of municipal public services." Texas Law Review 53(December): 26-59.

——— and E. P. FOWLER (1967) "Reformism and public policies in American cities." American Political Science Review 61: 701-716.

LINEBERRY, R. L. and R. E. WELCH, Jr. (1974) "Who gets what: measuring the distribution of urban public services." Social Science Quarterly 54: 700-712.

LIPSKY, M. (1976) "Toward a theory of street level bureaucracy," pp. 196-213 in W. D. Hawley and M. Lipsky (eds.), Theoretical Perspectives on Urban Politics. Englewood Cliffs, NJ: Prentice-Hall.

LONG, N. (1972) The Unwalled City. New York: Basic Books.

LOVRICH, N. P., Jr. and T. G. TAYLOR, Jr. (1976) "Neighborhood evaluation of local government services." Urban Affairs Quarterly 12: 197-222.

LYON, D. (1970) "Capital spending and the neighborhoods of philadelphia." Business Review (May): 16-27.

MARTIN, L. (1969) Library Response to Urban Change. Chicago: American Library Association.

MASOTTI, L. and D. R. BOWEN (1965) "Communities and budgets: the sociology of municipal expenditures." Urban Affairs Quarterly 1: 39-58.

MERGET, A. E. and W. M. WOLFF, Jr. (1976) "The law and municipal services: implementing equity." Public Management 58(August): 2-8.

MILLER' S. M. and P. ROBY (1970) The Future of Inequality. New York: Basic Books.

MLADENKA, K. R. (1977) "Citizen demand and bureaucratic response: direct dialing democracy in a major American city." Urban Affairs Quarterly 12: 273-290.

NATHAN, R. P., P. R. DOMMEL, S. F. LIESCHUTZ, and M. D. MORRIS (1977) "Monitoring the block grant program for community development." Political Science Quarterly 92(summer): 219-244.

National Advisory Commission on Civil Disorders (1968) Report. Washington, DC: Government Printing Office.

National Commission on Urban Problems (1969) Building the American City. Washington, DC: Government Printing Office.

NEENAN, W. B. (1972) Political Economy of Urban Areas. Chicago: Markham.

NEIMAN, M. (1975) Metropology. Beverly Hills, CA: Sage.

NEWTON, K. (1975) "Social class, political structure, and public goods in American urban politics." Urban Affairs Quarterly 11: 241-264.

OLDMAN, O. and H. AARON (1969) "Assessment-sales ratios under the boston property tax." Assessor's Journal 4: 13-29.

OSTROM, E. (1973) "On the meaning and measurement of output and efficiency in the production of urban police services." Journal of Criminal Justice 1(June): 96-110.

PERRY, D. C. (1973) "The suburb as a model for neighborhood control," pp. 85-100 in G. Frederickson (ed.), Neighborhood Control in the 1970's. New York: Chandler.

RATNER, G. (1968) "Inter-neighborhood denials of equal protection in the provision of municipal services." Harvard Civil Rights-Civil Liberties Law Review 4(fall): 1-64.

RICH, R. C. (forthcoming) "The roles of neighborhood organizations in urban serviced delivery." NASPAA Urban Affairs Papers.

––– (1979a) "Neglected issues in the study of urban service distributions: a research agenda." Urban Studies 16(June): 143-156.

––– (1979b) "Urban neighborhoods as public service delivery units." South Atlantic Urban Studies 4(August): 121-136.

––– (1978) The Political Economy of Neighborhood Organization. (unpublished)

––– (1977) "Equity and institutional design in urban service delivery." Urban Affairs Quarterly 12: 383-410.

ROSSI, P. H., R. A. BERK, and B. K. EDISON (1974) The Roots of Urban Discontent. New York: John Wiley.

SCHAENAN, P. S. (1977) Procedures for Improving the Measurement of Local Fire Protection Effectiveness. Washington, DC: Urban Institute.

SCHUMAN, H. and B. GRUENBERG (1972) "Dissatisfaction with city services: is race an important factor?" pp. 369-392 in H. Hahn (ed.), People and Politics in Urban Society. Beverly Hills, CA: Sage.

SCHWARTZ, Barry, ed. (1976) The Changing Face of the Suburbs. Chicago: University of Chicago Press.

SMITH, D. M. (1974) "Who what where and how: a welfare focus for human geography." Geography 59: 289-297.

SNYDER, J. (1977) Fiscal Management and Planning in Local Government. Lexington, MA: D. C. Heath.

Social Science Panel on the Significance of Community in the Metropolitan Environment (1974) Toward Understanding Metropolitan America. San Francisco: Canfield.

STEGGERT, F. X. (1975) Community Action Groups and City Governments. Cambridge, MA: Ballinger.

STIPAK, B. (1979) "Citizen satisfaction with urban services: potential misuse as a performance indicator." Public Administration Review 39(January/February): 46-52.

THUROW, L. C. (1970) "Equity versus efficiency in law enforcement." Public Policy 18(summer): 451-462.

WASHNIS, G. J. (1976) Citizen Involvement in Crime Prevention. Lexington, MA: D.C. Heath.

WEICHER, J. C. (1971) "The allocation of police protection by income class." Urban Studies 8: 207-220.

WHITE, M. J. (1978a) "Job suburbanization and the welfare of urban minority groups." Journal of Urban Economics 5: 219-203.

––– (1978b) "Self-interest in the suburbs: the trend toward no-growth zoning." Policy Analysis 4(spring): 185-203.

WILLIAMS, O. P. (1971) Metropolitan Political Analysis. New York: Macmillan.

YIN, R. K. (1974) "On the equality of municipal service outcomes: street cleanliness." Presented at the meeting of the Operations Research Society of America, April.

––– and D. YATES (1974) Street-Level Governments. Santa Monica, CA: Rand Corp.

9

COLLECTIVE BARGAINING AND THE
DISTRIBUTION OF BENEFITS:
Education in New York City

SARA L. SILBIGER

Rutgers University
Newark College of Arts and Science

Drawing upon observations of escalating municipal expenditure patterns of the 1960s, Piven came to a number of provocative conclusions about the group struggle in urban politics. According to Piven, government spending was used to gain political support in a constituency in which group balance had become unstable. The instability was brought about by minority demands on government, but Piven argued that the distribution of the new benefits overwhelmingly favored not the minority claimants, but the "provider groups," in and around the government itself. With specific reference to education, Piven (1975b) asserted that not only financial benefits but also the organized teachers' successful quest for improved job security, pensions, and education policies which required hiring of additional teachers was "often prompted by new black demands. . . . In this process, blacks may have triggered the flood of new demands on the schools, but organized whites turned out to be the main beneficiaries" (Piven, 1975b).

In this and other writings of the same period, Piven and her colleague, Cloward, developed two important positions to which this article reacts. First is the assertion that organized bureaucratic providers constitute a

261

distinctive and successful addition to the cast of competing groups which contest for advantageous allocative decisions by urban governments. The present article builds on this assertion, discussing generally, and with specific reference to New York City education, the impact of unions on allocative decisions and the quality of service which accrues to the client public. However, while Piven has considered public employee unions as one among a variety of claimant groups, the present article seeks to distinguish public unions from other pressure groups because of the additional and unique tools of access to government which they enjoy. In particular, we both emphasize collective bargaining with government and its products as novel tools which set public unions off from traditional pressure groups.

The second position in the Cloward and Piven literature to which the present article reacts is their assertion that the success of the middle-class and largely white provider unions accrues to the almost exclusive benefit of white middle-class interests as part of a politics characterized by class and race conflict (Piven, 1975a, 1975b; Cloward and Piven, 1975). Looking at selected provisions of the New York City teachers' contract negotiated in 1975 and successfully defended by the union against proposals for change in 1978, this article seeks to document the group impacts of contractually determined allocations.

The first substantive section of this article distinguishes public employee unions from other urban interest groups by focusing on the unique tools of the public unions and the specific decisions for which these tools are relevant. In the second section the decisional subsystem for public education in New York City is described as it bears on our concern with contractually negotiated policy.[1] Scrutiny of this institutional subsystem facilitates understanding of the novel negotiating advantages enjoyed by the teachers' union in the New York setting. In the third section the contract outcome of this bargaining structure is appraised with reference to its distributive consequences and the Piven-Cloward propositions.

THE COMPETITIVE ADVANTAGE OF
ORGANIZED PUBLIC WORKERS

Modern public employee unions, in most of their features, are incorporable into existing theories and descriptions of interest group politics (e.g., Truman, 1951; Ziegler and Peak, 1972; Greenwald, 1977). Public unions are claimants on government for favorable allocations in competition with other possible beneficiaries of government decisions and use the full range of group techniques elaborated in the literature. Beyond the range of access points and tools available to other groups, however, public unions in municipal settings enjoy distinctive opportunities which provide them with a competitive advantage over other groups for the determination of selected issues.

One such opportunity which has analogues but no equals among other interests is the capacity to draw upon the threat or actuality of a public service strike. Although in most localities public strikes constitute illegal pressure activity, they are employed with sufficient frequency to be considered a real point of leverage (Stanley, 1971). A range of sensitive public services such as education, transportation, sanitation, and fire and police protection have, when disrupted by strikes or other work stoppages, an immediate impact on the life of a city discernible by large groups of its public. For this large inconvenienced or endangered public the salience of government is temporarily raised. Elected public officials can become the focal point of this awareness and the possible voting retribution it may engender if labor peace and needed service are not quickly restored. At least in the case city used here, New York, successive mayors have conducted labor relations with sensitivity to both the possibility (1) of arousing negative latent public opinion and (2) of antagonizing the unions themselves which are a large force in voting and campaign finance (Horton, 1973; Silbiger, 1975).

A second unique advantage to the public union is the collective bargaining process of decision making. Most points of pressure group access are theoretically available to many competitive claimants for favorable decisions. Inequality of access to an elected official, legislature, regulatory agency, or bureaucratic office is viewed as an imperfection in the political process. Collective bargaining, however, follows a closed access pattern which is inherent in the process borrowed from the private sector and supported by statute as well as practice.[2] In bilateral bargaining only representatives of the union and of the employer are acceptable participants. So-called third parties are excluded from either observation of or participation in negotiations. While the interests of such parties may be affected by the outcomes of bilateral negotiations, nonparticipants can neither represent their interests nor observe how they have been handled by public negotiators.

Bilateral collective bargaining, in addition to its closed nature, is characterized by stylistic behavior which sanctions and encourages the distribution of information to the public which is exaggerated and misleading (Spero and Capozzola, 1973). In the position-taking preceding bargaining, the news briefings during bargaining, and the claimed successes thereafter, the primary intent of the two participants is bargaining advantage. Since the information process is viewed as part of collective bargaining, it has been blanketed into the protections that bargaining enjoys. Although the trend in other arenas of access is toward "sunshine" and freedom of information, the doors of access to decision making by labor contract open to the unions only.

Beyond the contract writing period, public unions continue to have a novel and noncompetitive institutional basis for monitoring and redefining their agreement with the government, the machinery of grievance. The grievance process, predefined by the contract itself, provides the union with a standardized channel for continued bargaining and shared decision making with government. Although theoretically concerned with simple enforcement of particular contractual items, the use of grievance and threats of grievance often inhibit the employer from innovation in programs and managerial policies. The scope of grievable issues is theoretically quite wide since contracts usually stipulate or assume that any item not covered in them remains the same as in past practice. Thus any changes from practice require union consultation.

The range of issues over which public unions have the special protected access of collective bargaining is not as broad as the full range of issues of union concern. At present, most unions limit their use of collective bargaining to issues which either relate to wages and benefits or to aspects of the work situation which they believe themselves professionally most competent to determine. While they may take stands on many other issues, unions most frequently employ noncontractual techniques of pressure to achieve them.[3]

The contractual determination of wages and fringe benefits as well as many working conditions requires a bilateral allocation of a large part of the municipal budget. Strike threat, closed access, and poor information make it unlikely that the traditional role of pressure group competition or of deliberation by financial officials will determine budget allocations. Many writers have argued that the unionized work force raises personnel costs to the city (Horton, 1973; Piven, 1975b). As Spero and Capozzola note, however,

No authoritative studies show whether the ratio of personnel costs to total expenditures is higher in jurisdictions with "strong" public employee organizations or whether the proportion of funds allocated to personnel is accelerating at a greater rate than other categories of expenditures. Individual cities differ in their governmental

structures, taxing powers, political leadership, and the almost infi-
nite number of variables, which diminishes the usefulness of existing
figures for purposes of comparison. Valid, reliable mathematical
models are needed before definitive judgments can be made [1973].

Whether or not one can ascribe to the unionized work force the responsibility for a city's total personnel costs, one can assert that the distribution of that total among various employees and services will be decided in
large measure through the bargaining process.[4]

In addition to their financial impacts, the "terms and conditions of
employment" negotiated in the bilateral setting affect content and style of
urban service delivery. The range of bargainable issues (scope of bargaining) expands in response to the demands and political strength of a
particular union. Unions of public professionals have been most active in
obtaining control over policy in their service through bargaining (Prasow et
al., 1972). Such policies as class size limits, special programs for slow
learners, methods of mainstreaming handicapped children, and treatment
of disruptive pupils have all been bargaining issues in New York City
public education.

Beyond direct policy bargaining, contractual determination of many
"job security" protections can have indirect policy consequences. Seeking
to protect workers from arbitrary or discriminatory practices, unions have
contractually determined procedures for discipline, firing, layoffs and
transfers, job assignments, and tenure. All these procedures limit management's capacity to distribute a workforce according to its own perceptions
of favorable utilization, particularly if these perceptions involve changing
past practice.

Job security clauses can also pose severe constraints on the public
employer who seeks to use public jobs as tools for social or economic
policy. Job protections are usually based on seniority which is often held
disproportionately by already privileged social groups. Efforts to employ
minorities or other underemployed groups in the city often founder on the
seniority protections of the existing workforce.

Though already widely understood, the impact of these job security
items is emphasized here because it so effectively embodies the main point
of this section. The contractual determination of what appear to be simple
items of personnel administration can bilaterally bind a city to policies
whose impact bears heavily on persons or groups excluded from the
bargain.

CONTRACTS IN NEW YORK CITY EDUCATION:
THE INSTITUTIONAL SETTING

To survey the range of contractually determined policies and their distributional effects, this article examines specific terms of a specific contract—that between the United Federation of Teachers (UFT) and the Board of Education of New York City. Not all teacher or public unions obtain comparable control over their workplace even with the special protections afforded in collective bargaining. These contractual outcomes are a product of both the political setting and the skills, perspectives, and resources which are brought to bear directly on the contract decision making. In New York City these skills, perspectives, and resources are housed within a complex decisional subsystem of institutions which are rather idiosyncratic to the New York setting. If, as Cloward and Piven have argued, distributional benefits accrue to the advantage of the organized workers, we must at least consider the possibility that this outcome is a function of institutional inadequacy rather than inherent to the group struggle.

Two linked and distinctive traits of the New York City education system which impinge on labor relations are the absence of either an elected Board of Education or a separate tax structure for public schools. The seven-member central board, which presides over a system of 1,000 schools and over a million pupils, is appointed by the presidents of each of the five boroughs which compose New York City, along with the mayor. It is this appointed board which enters into agreements with the various employee unions.

The board can draw upon the services of the school system's full-time Office of Labor Relations. It can also rely on the data collection and analysis capacity available in the Office of the Deputy Chancellor.[5] The board's bargaining positions do not reflect the staff's potential and actual efforts.[6] Communication gaps between the board and the educational bureaucracy as well as within the bureaucracy itself are limits on staff impact. Further limits are posed by the political judgments of the board members.

Weakened as a negotiator by its inability to draw on an electoral constituency or on staff expertise, the board is undercut further by its financial dependence. Since there is no separate school tax in New York City, education funding comes from the city's budget (as well as from outside supplements). The board's bargaining stance is therefore regulated by the political and financial outlook of the mayor and his staff. While the board could be expected to concern itself with the contractual details that alter educational service, the mayor and his staff do not.

An almost unique feature of educational bargaining in New York City is contributed by the decentralized governance structure of the public school system. Since 1969, elementary and junior high schools in New York have been clustered within 32 school districts (high schools are managed centrally).[7] Each decentralized district elects its own school board which exercises a modest amount of policy-making and supervisory power under the guidance of the central board. Local school boards are bound by the contracts which the central board negotiates, but because of this they have been granted an unusual status in the collective bargaining process.

Each decentralized board is entitled to designate two members to serve as member and alternate to a Community School Board negotiating Council. The council is to sit in a consultative capacity to the central board during all negotiations. It is also empowered to seat three of its number as advisory participants in the bargaining room itself.

The decentralized school boards might serve, given their electoral foundation, as a political resource to the board. In fact, this potential has not been realized. Most of the decentralized boards have not viewed collective bargaining as a major concern; and many of the local board members, having run on union-endorsed slates, are not strongly management oriented. Even the most interested local board members report frustration serving on the council because of inadequate information, staff assistance, or reaction time (Stookey, 1977).

In 1978 the council attempted to rectify this situation by contracting for staff assistance with the Joint Task Force on Collective Bargaining.[8] The task force and the council developed a full set of contract positions and independent cost analyses which they hoped to bring to the board and the bargaining table. However, their efforts were frustrated by a change in the labor relations setting. A coalition of some of the most powerful of the public employee unions including the UFT agreed to join forces and bargain for a shared financial package. The city accepted this idea. Because the teachers became a part of the city-wide coalition, their interests were presented in direct negotiations with the mayor's labor relations staff, thus bypassing both the central board and its consultants on the Community School Board Negotiating Council.

Coalition bargaining was intended to apply only to the purely financial facets of contract settlement. A basic package was to be negotiated setting percentage wage increases, cost-of-living adjustments, general productivity guidelines, and any dollar-related fringe benefits or givebacks. A second tier of bargaining was to be conducted at the level of each separate service to determine the exact terms by which the financial package would be distributed within the service and the work rules which were particular to that service.

In fact, without the financial leverage which had been exhausted in the first, coalition phase of bargaining, the second tier negotiations did not actually alter work rules at all. The basic contract, which had been negotiated years ago in a period of greater financial prosperity and union militance was defended from change. Ironically, New York City had come, by virtue of its protracted budget crises, to a point where unions appeared vulnerable to city initiatives to improve the management components of contracts. Yet, the introduction of coalition bargaining left contracts looking much as they had in the precrisis days of labor power.

Complicating the institutional setting of collective bargaining even further is the novel oversight agency created by the state of New York to supervise the city's finances. Called the Emergency Financial Control Board (EFCB), this creature of the fiscal emergency has veto power over all the contracts which the city and its agencies negotiate with their employee unions. The EFCB assesses contracts for their concordance with the city's overall financial plan and with their own productivity guidelines, and usually does not evaluate work rules or other contractual terms unless such terms encumber large amounts of money or require striking cuts in service. The EFCB, then, has perhaps the strongest potential power in the collective bargaining arena, but like almost all the other actors described, leaves the service quality implications of contracts unattended.

The setting of collective bargaining for teachers in New York is one which seems to facilitate union capacity to protect gains won during the preemergency era. The actors closest to education and presumably most concerned with its priorities, the central and local boards and staff, have not been effective competitors with the union. Those more distant from education, the mayor and his staff and the EFCB, are more concerned with city-wide finance than the service implications of contracts. All these actors work across the table from a union, the UFT, which is extremely well endowed with leadership, staff, and money. Long a militant leader in the national development of educational unionism, the UFT has recently been fortified by the acquisition, internally, of the agency shop and externally by the advent of coalition bargaining. In the next section I examine some major components of the contract which followed from this situation.

THE TEACHERS' CONTRACT:
CONTROL OVER WHAT AND BENEFITS FOR WHOM

In developing an analysis of the contract between the UFT and the New York City Board of Education, I seek the fulfillment of the research goals defined earlier—a documentation of areas of service policy which are bilaterally determined and judgment as to the beneficiaries of these determinations. To achieve the first goal requires simple perusal of the contract. To accomplish the second is far more elusive. In education, particularly, measures of service quality to pupils are endlessly debated. One cannot make an objective measure of whether a particular contract provision helps or hinders educational quality though one can more easily observe whether the same provision helps or hinders teachers—in terms of such objective standards as wages, hours, job security, and so on. Teachers often argue, however, that contract practices which favor them by these criteria also favor educational quality by making the teacher more effective.

In the absence of objective measures of pupil losses and gains in educational quality, I have relied on the subjective testimony of nonteacher educational interests. The yardstick used is a comparison between the contract positions taken by the Community School Board Negotiating Council and the contractual outcomes of 1975 and 1978 negotiations. Ordinarily it is unwise to measure group success in bargaining by comparing demands with outcomes, because the demands are vastly inflated as a bargaining strategy. In the case of the demands used here, I was consultant in the process by which they were formulated and can attest to their authenticity. These demands are also a useful proxy for interest group positions because they were formulated through a process which drew upon opinions of school principals, parent groups, other civic groups interested in education, and ultimately, the council. In each of the contractual items to be discussed below, an existing practice is viewed by nonteacher educational interests as adversely affecting educational service and its recipients.

NONTEACHING TIME

The council contract proposals sought change in a number of related practices relevant to the amount and use of nonteaching time in the teacher's work week. The UFT contract provides for several types of nonteaching time. According to the contract, teachers are entitled to a stated number of preparation periods each school week. The contract distinguishes between school levels and between Title I (schools eligible for federal funds by virtue of the low reading scores of their students) and non-Title I schools. Title I schools are considered a hardship for teachers according to the contract and teachers in such schools are granted more preparation periods than those in non-Title I schools. In 1978 the council sought to equalize the number of preparation periods for teachers in all elementary and junior high schools. The council estimated that by reducing all teachers to the level of non-Title I schools, it could save $31 million in teacher time. Apparently impressed by the council position, the central board added this item to their own set of demands for second tier bargaining.[9] As will be discussed below, this proposal would have had unanticipated side effects on the distribution of educational dollars among the local school districts, but the proposal did not survive the 1978 bargaining.

A second major concern regarding the service and cost implications of preparation periods is their actual use. Preparation periods, as defined by contract and arbitration, are free periods during which there may be no "regularly programmed responsibility" (UFT Contract, Art. 7A). A teacher may not be assigned to use a preparation period to take a staff development course, to attend a faculty meeting, to hold office hours with students, to develop course materials, or other similar activities. The 1978 council contract plan contained a request that "at least one preparation period every two weeks at the elementary school level and every week at the other levels should be available for regular or ad hoc non-classroom assignments contributing to such goals as improved intra and interschool communication, staff development or experimentation." The board itself, however, never incorporated this item in its own set of demands.

A third type of nonteaching time is the "administrative period." Defined in the contract as "those periods during which the teacher is programmed for a regular activity other than teaching," administrative periods exist only in schools above the elementary level (UFT Contract, Art. 7A). In these schools the contract calls for a teacher program to include five administrative periods. The contract also provides, however, that "no more than 35% of home room teachers ... shall be given administrative assignments. In schools where the percentage is lower than 35, the status quo will be maintained" (UFT Contract, Art. 7A).

In effect, since every secondary school teacher must be assigned the five administrative periods, but no more than 35% of home room teachers may actually be given a task to perform during these periods, 65% of the home room teachers in each school receive five more free periods. The rest of the teacher's program would contain (in the high school) 25 teaching periods,

5 lunch periods, and 5 preparation periods with the effect that the teacher is contractually precluded from regular assignment for more than a third of the work week.

The service loss in this situation is compounded by another contractually based provision for nonteaching called "compensatory time." Because the contract limits the percentage of teachers who may be assigned administrative tasks during their administrative periods, some teachers must be relieved of teaching responsibilities in order to get the necessary administrative tasks completed. The administrative tasks for which teachers are relieved of classroom assignments are referred to as comp time jobs. A study by the city Comptroller's office concluded that the average academic high school teacher spends 8% of his time on comp time assignments (Office of Comptroller, 1978). The Comptroller's study estimated that 44,000 teaching periods a week were lost to the schools through this practice. The same report concluded that if all high school teachers were and could contractually be assigned to administrative tasks during the regular five administrative periods a week, 39,000 of these lost periods could be regained.

The contractual limitation on the assignment of "administrative periods" was one of the few issues on which the central board, its labor relations staff, and the council were in close agreement. Even the mayor's labor relations staff seemed aware of this item and interested in pursuing it. The speedy second-tier deliberations, however, did not provide a favorable forum for any resurgence of management prerogatives and the rule has survived in the new contract.

TEACHING ASSIGNMENTS

On the basis of an interview study of principals conducted for the Joint Task Force on Collective Bargaining, the contract proposals developed by the council contained as a major goal the elimination or reduction of the existing contractual constraints on teacher assignment. The contract provides detailed guidelines for placing teachers in grade level assignments, special classes, gifted classes, "more difficult and less difficult" classes, administrative assignments, and compensatory time assignments (UFT Contract, Art. 8). Seniority and/or rotation are the binding principles applicable here as part of the union's desire to protect its members against arbitrary or discriminatory management. The council, on the basis of the interviews with principals, viewed these practices as potentially detrimental to educational quality in which teachers who proved effective in

one assignment were arbitrarily reassigned because of contract requirements (Kossoff, 1977). The provisions remain in the contract.

SALARIES AND BENEFITS

Whether or not educationally justified, parent and civic groups regis-
tered their belief through the council that more teachers, smaller classes,
and full-length school days contribute to their version of child-centered
education. In 1975, as a result of the fiscal crisis, improvements in
teachers' salaries and fringe benefits were, to all intents and purposes,
either denied or deferred. Teachers who had not reached the top of the
increment and differential scales could continue up these schedules
although the pace of increments was temporarily reduced to one rather
than the usual two per year. In addition, a cost-of-living adjustment was to
be paid and, for those eligible, an additional annual sum for longevity pay
was to be introduced. At the peak of the financial crisis then, it was
estimated that the average surviving teacher would receive approximately
$3,000 more as a result of the new contract. Educational pressure groups
claimed that if teachers' remuneration had not been improved, 10,000
teaching positions cut by the crisis could have been retained (Seeley and
Heller, forthcoming).

In a related issue, the 1975 settlement shortened the school week by
two class periods. The contract had provided for a stipulated number of
preparation periods requiring additional teaching staff. In order to retain
the free periods without such staff, the board and union agreed to close
the schools so no teacher coverage would be required. While this decision
was a compromise in which the union gave up some preparation periods
and kept others through the shortened school day, education pressure
groups viewed the decision as a benefit for teachers at pupil and parent
expense.

The council contract proposals called for a permanent alteration in the
increment schedule to one step a year, a delay in the onset of longevity
pay, and tightened eligibility for differentials. None of these items was
adopted in 1978.

WHO BENEFITS?

In each of the contract issues discussed there is an implied tension
between the interests of teachers and those of clients—children and
parents. Though teachers contend that their best interests are coincident
with those of children, other groups claiming legitimate standing to assess

and countervail these claims disagree. The ability of the union, through collective bargaining to retain and/or augment its challenged advantages vis-à-vis competitive claimant groups may thus be viewed as a provider gain at the clients' expense as Cloward and Piven might have anticipated.

These are, however, other possible vantage points from which to assess the contract issues and their contribution to a model of benefit distribution in the city. The second approach undertaken here brings the contract to bear on the sociospatial distribution of educational resources.

SPATIAL DISTRIBUTION OF EDUCATION RESOURCES

The distribution of educational services among the "sociospatial" communities of New York City was, during the 1960s, a matter of heated controversy (Rogers, 1969; Fantini, et al., 1970; Gittell and Magat, 1970; Fainstein and Fainstein, 1974). Critics of the school system argued that it was dominated from central headquarters by a white and often Jewish middle-class power structure and outlook. The problems of ghetto schools were seen as natural outgrowths of the dominance of unsympathetic, culturally incapacitated teachers and administrators using materials irrelevant to the ghetto experience. Education, these critics alleged, was inequitably distributed so that white and middle-class neighborhoods received the most favored treatment.

School decentralization, instituted in 1969, was intended to overcome these educational inequities (in addition to relieving high racial and political tensions). The teachers' union was adamantly opposed to decentralization. Its fears, exacerbated by experiences with experimental decentralized schools, focused on desires of local communities to control hiring and firing of staff. Extremely effective at the state legislative level, the UFT was able to achieve a modified decentralization law which allowed continued central control or oversight over licensing, hiring and firing, collective bargaining, and just about all personnel policy at the teacher level.

Ironically, while the UFT has been viewed as a middle-class saboteur of decentralization, its contracts have contributed to a distribution of school resources which is favorable to the schools and districts with the largest concentrations of poor and minority children. This resource distribution pattern emerges from a combination of the Board of Education's "allocation formula" and the personnel practices mandated by the contract.

The allocation formula is the equation by which the central board determines how much money (and staff) will be spent in each decentralized school district. While it is quite complex, containing seven modules, by far the most costly is the instructional module (New York City, Board of Education, Office of Deputy Chancellor, 1975). Funds in this module are distributed on the basis of calculations which consider the number of classes in a district, the number of teachers required for that many classes given requirements for preparation and administrative periods, and the average salary in the district. It is interesting that the Board of Education booklet explaining the allocation formula never mentions the UFT contract. In fact, each one of these three major items is controlled by contractual terms.

The average salary in the district is a function of the UFT salary and differential scale combined with any effects of transfer policy which might place more costly teachers differentially. The number of classes in each district is a function of the number of children and the maximum class size limits stipulated in the UFT contract (Art. 7B). The number of teachers required is a function of the number of classes plus the number of nonteaching periods the contract provides for each teacher. Since the contract specifically requires more preparation periods for teachers in Title I schools, the effect is to direct extra resources to those districts with the heaviest concentration of pupils in such schools. The districts with the heaviest concentration of Title I schools are also those with the heaviest concentration of Title I schools are also those with the heaviest concentration of poor and minority children (see Table 1).

On top of the base allocation for teacher costs, a number of additional sums are pegged to the formula just described. Workload-weighted teacher requirements and costs serve as the basis for computing three further allocations to the districts which provide for a wide range of supporting services and personnel. This means that not only the distribution of regular

Table 1   Percentage of Title I Schools in School Districts of
Predominantly White, Black and Hispanic Children*
(60% or more)

White District Number	Percent Title I	Black District Number	Percent Title I	Hispanic District Number	Percent Title I
20	21	5	96	1	100
21	23	13	100	4	100
22	4	16	94	6	86
24	8	17	94	7	93
25	0	23	100	14	100
26	0	29	54	32	94
31	7				

*SOURCES: N.Y.C. Board of Education, Office of Funded Programs and Office of Zoning and Integration.

teachers but also of specialists, guidance counselors, librarians, lab personnel, supervisors, and other instructional as well as noninstructional staff will be most favorable to the minority school districts.

The effect of building the allocation formula this way is a marked difference among school districts in the amounts spent on staff per pupil as can be seen in Table 2. In the seven school districts which have school populations composed of 60% or more white pupils, the average staff cost per pupil is $935.[10] In the six districts where black pupils comprise majority of 60% or more, the staff cost per pupil is over $100 higher ($1,054). Where Hispanic students constitute a similar majority (six schools), staff expenditures are almost $200 higher than white schools ($1,114 per pupil).

Staff costs in districts which are mixed in ethnic composition (no group comprises a 60% majority) fall between the predominantly white ones and those dominated by a single nonwhite racial or ethnic group. The average

Table 2 Per Pupil Staff Cost and Pupil/Teacher Ratios in School Districts of Predominantly White, Black and Hispanic Children* (60% or more)

| | | 1975-1976 | |
	School District Number	Staff Cost Per Pupil	Pupil/Teacher Ratio
White	20	$ 920	22.9
	21	1,005	22.2
	22	901	24.8
	24	846	25.2
	25	950	23.3
	26	1,022	22.2
	31	899	23.4
Black	5	1,190	19.6
	13	1,056	21.5
	16	1,054	21.5
	17	999	22.0
	23	1,123	21.2
	29	904	24.5
Hispanic	1	1,155	19.8
	4	1,179	19.3
	6	978	22.9
	7	1,183	19.7
	14	1,132	19.9
	32	1,056	21.3

*SOURCES: N.Y.C. Board of Education, Office of Zoning and Integration, and School Profiles, 1975-76.

is $1,04? per pupil. When I introduce a distinction between those mixed districts where the mix contains less than 20% of white children and those where whites are a more sizable minority, the staff cost per pupil in the nonwhite mixed setting is somewhat higher ($1,075) than where white children are at least a 20% portion of the school population ($1,009).

It would be foolish to argue that per-pupil staff cost alone is a sign of educational quality differences. However, it is a measure which tells us about the allocation of scarce resources. It clearly helps to document the point that the teacher contract distinction regarding the number of preparation periods for Title I and non-Title I schools engenders a differential pattern of resource distribution.

CONCLUDING OBSERVATIONS

Unions of public employees are becoming a unique and important participant in the formulation of allocative decisions by urban governments. Their role in the New York City situation, analyzed here, is seen to affect educational finance and productivity, management opportunities to improve quality of service, and sociospatial patterns of resource distribution.

This article has undertaken the documentation of this union role for one service in one city. At this stage the report and analysis accomplish the task of making concrete what has long seemed an intuitively sensible hypothesis—that public unions, through collective bargaining, are a force whose reach extends beyond the usual arena of pressure politics.[11] This extensio. is derived from the bilateral decision making in which unions participat. with government and from the unique power of strike and grievance.

Beyond this first level of documentation, the article is concerned with the biases, intended or unintended, introduced or fortified in an urban polity by the presence of strong public unionism. The education case presented here suggests that while the patterns of power distribution have fundamentally altered to make place for decision making by collective bargaining, the distributive consequences of this reallocation are not simple. Some new advantages accrue to the employee and some, to other groups.

At the outset I noted the Cloward and Piven view that the middle-class bias of the "provider" bureaucrat and his unions gives rise to service decisions which protect the middle class at the expense of the poor and/or minority client. Focusing more specifically on allocative decisions and on socially distinct communities in the city, Lineberry (1977) suggests that a variety of bureaucratic (rather than class) motives may determine patterns of service distribution. He suggests five forms of allocative rule development founded on "demand, professional norms, on some conception of need, or equality, or rules which simply react to 'pressure.' " While these rules all stress the urban bureaucracy in decision making, they do not necessarily result in "service advantages" to any predictable communities.

More like the Lineberry than the Piven framework, the distribution of New York City educational benefits by contract indicates an inadvertent interaction of motives by various actors which contributes to the allocative pattern. Some elements of the situation described appear to rest on group pressure foundations, some on professional norms, and some (the allocation formula) on themes of equality.

Just as the motives are mixed, so are the beneficiaries depending on how one measures them. Interest groups view many of the specific contract clauses as benefiting the teachers at the students' expense. This would fit a Cloward and Piven model. However, if we look at the distribution pattern not as a tension between teachers and students (providers and clients) but between advantaged and disadvantaged students, then the impact seems to favor the disadvantaged—the contrary of the Piven expectation. This conclusion does not exclude or invalidate a client-provider distributional struggle, but rather demonstrates that impacts cut several ways and should not be oversimplified.

One final element which should be considered in the distributional equation is the impact of institutions. The New York City decisional system for educational bargaining is particularly ill-equipped to protect or regain control over contractual issues with service implications. Although it is possible to argue that the institutional setting reflects rather than creates political bias, it is also possible that the outcomes we observe in New York are simply a product of inadequate institutions. Further, comparative studies will help cast light on this question.

Many other research questions follow from the desire to understand the biases introduced into public policy by public worker unions. For example, what power and service biases follow from unionization of blue collar public employees? Do unions of such workers balance the power of middle-class unions? Is the class bias of a union such as the UFT itself tempered because the union also represents paraprofessional employees? Is the competition of groups previously played out on the public stage now being simply moved to the more closed arena of collective bargaining? How does this competition contribute to the complexity of allocative patterns we are beginning to discover?

Finally, acknowledgment of the unique access available to public employee unions suggests the need to reevaluate the role of nonunion actors. What does the novel access of the union do to the relative impact of bureaucratic managers, elected public officials, and traditional pressure groups? To what degree to the closed doors of collective bargaining alter the opportunities of these groups for power? To what degree do these same closed doors affect the opportunity of legislatures and interested publics from understanding and overseeing critical areas of urban policy?

NOTES

1. Public unions, as pressure groups, seek voice in a range of issues which transcends those determined by contract. The purpose of focusing on contract issues and institutions is to single out that part of the unions' access which is not shared by competing interests.

2. There are a few situations which differ from this description. For example, a sunshine law in Florida allows public scrutiny of negotiations.

3. For example, this was seen in the New York Fire Fighter's opposition to the passage of a homosexual rights law and the police opposition to women in patrol cars.

4. The fact that many New York bus drivers earn more than the city's university professors is a distribution through bargaining.

5. For the 1975 negotiations this office developed an excellent set of preparatory notes. See, Board of Education of the City of New York, Office of the Deputy Chancellor, Negotiating Notes, #1-7, August 1975.

6. An observer to one of the board negotiations reported in a confidential interview that the board member at the bargaining table had his position handwritten in pencil on the back of an envelope.

7. Actually, only 31 districts were created initially. The 32nd was carved out of two existing districts in the 1972-1973 school year.

8. The joint task force was created by the United Parents Association and the Public Education Association and staffed by a nonprofit staff organization called Interface. The task force was funded by private foundations and provided its service to the council at no charge.

9. Reference to contract positions for 1978 negotiations are from an initial and expanded list by the Board of Education dated March 17, 1978 and June 19, 1978, respectively, and from a list submitted by the Community School Board Negotiating Council to the Special Deputy Mayor for Labor Relations on March 8, 1978.

10. Computations are based on Board of Education figures for 1975-1976. Figures are rounded to the nearest dollar (*School Profiles,* 1975-1976).

11. Another novel arena of power for unions developing in New York City is in the management of the fiscal crisis, with unions able to bargain about their willingness to invest pension fund money in municipal bonds.

REFERENCES

Agreement between the Board of Education of the City School District of the City of New York and the United Federation of Teachers, Sept. 9, 1975 to Sept. 9, 1977 (referred to as UFT Contract).

CLOWARD, R. and PIVEN, F. F. (1975) "The professional bureaucracies: benefit systems as influence systems," pp. 7-27 in R. Cloward and F. Piven, The politics of turmoil. New York: Vintage.

FAINSTEIN, N. and S. FAINSTEIN (1974) Urban Political Movements. Englewood Cliffs, NJ: Prentice-Hall.

FANTINI, M. et al. (1970) Community Control and the Urban School. New York: Praeger.

GREENWALD, C. (1977) Group Power. New York: Praeger.

HORTON, R. (1973) Municipal Labor Relations in New York City. New York: Praeger.

KOSSOFF, A. (1977) "From the perspective of the principal: How the Board of Education/UFT Contract affects the operation of the school." (unpublished)

LINEBERRY, R. L. (1977) Equality and Urban Policy. Beverly Hills, CA: Sage.

New York City, Board of Education, Office of Deputy Chancellor (1975) 1975-1976 Allocation Formulae (June 25).

Office of the Comptroller, Division of Human Services, Bureau of Performance Analysis (1978) "The use of in-school teacher time by the New York City Board of Education." (unpublished)

ROGERS, D. (1969) 110 Livingston Street. New York: Vintage.

SEELEY, D. and H. HELLER (forthcoming) "New York moves toward more balanced teacher bargaining." Cambridge, MA: Institute for Responsive Education.

SILBIGER, S. (1975) "The missing public–collective bargaining in public employment." Public Personnel Management 4(5): 290-299.

SPERO, S. and J. M. CAPOZZOLA (1973) The Urban Community and Its Unionized Bureaucracies. New York: Dunellen.

STANELY, D. T. (1971) Managing Local Government Under Union Pressure. Washington, DC: Brookings Institution.

STOOKEY, L. (1977) "Community school board participation in education collective bargaining in New York City." (unpublished)

U.S. Department of Labor, Office of Labor Management Relations Services, Division of Public Employee Labor Relations. Scope of Bargaining in the Public Sector. Washington, DC: Paul Prasow et al.

ABOUT THE CONTRIBUTORS

DEMETRIOS CARALEY is Professor of Political Science at Barnard College and Columbia University, Chairman of the Barnard Program in Urban Studies, and Director of the Columbia Graduate Program in Public Affairs and Administration. He has published books and articles on urban government, Congress, and public policy. His latest book is *City Governments and Urban Problems.*

STEPHEN M. DAVID is Professor of Political Science and Chairman of the Department at Fordham University. He co-edited *Urban Politics & Public Policy* (1976, 1973) and *Race & Politics in New York City* (1970) and has written on the politics in urban policy arenas such as drug addiction, community action, public health, manpower and public assistance. His current research interest is examining and reformulating theoretical approaches to the study of urban politics.

PETER K. EISINGER is Professor of Political Science at the University of Wisconsin-Madison. He is also a member of the Senior Research Staff, Institute for Research on Poverty, at the University of Wisconsin-Madison. He is the author of *Patterns of Interracial Politics* (1976) and *The Politics of Displacement: Transition and Accommodation in Three Cities* (1979) and co-author of *American Politics: The People and the Polity* (1978) as well as various articles on urban and ethnic politics.

PAUL KANTOR is Associate Professor of Political Science at Fordham University, Bronx, New York. He has authored articles on urban politics and public policy in *Polity, Comparative Politics, The British Journal of Political Science* and elsewhere. His current research includes a forthcoming book on the decline of the inner city in Britain and a work on political theory and American urban politics.

ALBERT K. KARNIG is Associate Professor at the Center for Public Affairs, Arizona State University. After receiving his Ph.D. from Illinois, he taught at Texas Tech University. He has published widely on the subjects of urban and minority politics in such journals as *Urban Affairs Quarterly*, *American Journal of Politics*, and *Social Science Quarterly*. With Welch he has just completed a book manuscript on *Black Elected Officials and Urban Politics* and is currently working on research related to black and Hispanic office holders and public employment of Hispanics in the Southwest.

DALE ROGERS MARSHALL is Professor of Political Science, University of California, Davis. She is the author of *The Politics of Participation in Poverty* (University of California Press, 1971) and co-author with John C. Bollens of *Guide to Participation: Field Work, Role Playing Cases and Other Forms* (Prentice Hall, 1973). She is currently a principal investigator in the Policy Implementation Project's study of minorities and urban political change.

LOUIS H. MASOTTI is Professor of Political Science and Urban Affairs and Director of the Center for Urban Affairs at Northwestern University. He is currently serving as policy advisor to Chicago Mayor Jane Byrne and was Executive Director of her Transition Committee. He is the editor of *Urban Affairs Quarterly* and the author or editor of 13 books dealing with urban issues and policies, the latest of which is *Toward a New Urban Politics* (with Robert L. Lineberry). He is currently working on two book manuscripts: *Condominiums and the City: Housing Options and Urban Policy* and *The New Politics of Chicago: Jane Byrne and the Daley Legacy*.

PAUL E. PETERSON is Professor of Political Science and Education, University of Chicago. He is the author of *School Politics Chicago Style* (University of Chicago Press, 1976) and co-author with J. David Greenstone of *Race and Authority in Urban Politics* (University of Chicago Press, 1976). He is presently preparing for publication a book-length manuscript entitled *City Limits*, which will include material from the article published here.

RICHARD C. RICH is Assistant Professor of Political Science at Virginia Polytechnic Institute and State University and an Affiliated Scholar with the Center for Responsive Government in Washington, DC. He is author of *The Political Economy of Neighborhood Organization* and is currently working on both a multi-city study of neighborhood governance programs and a Ford Foundation grant for advancing the study of urban service distributions.

SARA L. SILBIGER is Visiting Assistant Professor in the Department of Political Science and Public Administration at Rutgers University—Newark. Her recent research interest is in public sector collective bargaining. A recently published article in *Public Personnel Management* is entitled "Collective bargaining and public employment: the missing public."

SUSAN WELCH is Professor and Chair of the Department of Political Science, University of Nebraska, Lincoln. Since receiving her degree from Illinois in 1970, she has published on state and urban politics in such journals as *American Political Science Review, Journal of Politics, Urban Affairs Quarterly, American Journal of Political Science, Western Political Quarterly* and others. She and Al Karnig have recently completed a book manuscript on *Black Elected Officials and Urban Politics*. Her current research interests include the impact of black and Hispanic elected officials, Hispanic public employment in the Southwest, political corruption, and women's political participation.

DOUGLAS YATES is Associate Professor of Political Science at Yale and the Associate Dean of the School of Organization and Management. He is the author of several books on urban politics, and, most recently, *The Ungovernable City* (MIT Press 1977).